FARM BOY LIFE STORY
Surviving WW-II
Inspiring on a true story

By

Dom De Palma
Author

Dedication

This book is dedicated to my lovely family, my beloved grandmother and dad, my mom, and all my brilliant sisters. Or so, to all those who encouraged me to write this book, thanks in advance to all my friends and all those who may be able to read the book.

Dom code

The fear for life helps us to walk safely and live longer.

Love to be loved, regardless of diversity.

It's better to be born and live a minute than never born.

Remember

Above clouds, the sky is always blue.

Acknowledgment

My deepest gratitude to all who have supported and guided this work: Maura Rocci, Anna di Giuseppe, Amanda Chiesa, Catena Ciriaco, Antonio Di Musciano, Iolanda De Palma, Netta De Palma, the Town of Francavilla al Mare, and Chieti. A special thank you to my exceptionally competent publicist, Amy White, at Amazon Publishers, and heartfelt thanks to a special person, Rosa Contardo, my beautiful wife.

I would like to express my thanks to all those who have participated, enduring my presence in every way, verbally and physically. With your support, my dream has been realized. I thank God, as none of this would have been possible without you. Likewise, I extend my gratitude a thousand times over to all those who have stood by me and encouraged me throughout this journey to bring this incredible family story to life.

I will always be grateful to all the people who shared information, photos, and their time with me, helping to reconstruct this remarkable story about the Spaccanocci families, including nicknames, old sayings, and the various locations, including the beautiful place where it all began.

The Author

In my life, among many accomplished works, I have always wanted to write something about my father. As I reflect on my personal achievements, this book reminds me of the value of understanding someone else's life and experiencing it as a boy. It brings back memories of my dad and his family, recounting their youthful adventures and the forbidden things they did together. It also delves into their experiences of surviving World War II, with what struck me the most was hearing about his adolescence.

I have long desired to be the author of his life story, but since my dad passed away in 1995, for one reason or another, I never found the time or courage to reconstruct his story. It wasn't easy, as I recall from the early 1950s, but I learned so much from him, his siblings, and other family members. One of the most impactful lessons came from my grandmother, Nicoletta, whom I lived with for over fifteen years before she passed away in 1965. Her life story, from childhood to her final days, left a lasting impression on me. She survived two wars, enduring unimaginable suffering from the loss of her parents, husband, and son during World War II. Both Grandma and Dad were, indeed, the pillars of our family, and now they live on in our memories.

Dom De Palma

The Author

Preface

In the early nineteenth century, a farm boy named Toto Nocci, along with his family, worked on other people's land. Unexpectedly, World War II began in the early 1940s, and two of his brothers went off to war. Shortly after, the boy's father passed away, and six weeks later, one of his brothers returned from the war severely ill, dying a few days later. Losing his father and a brother in such a short time devastated the Nocci family. Despite these misfortunes, they needed to endure and survive the war.

When WWII finally ended six years later, the Nocci family was reunited, but they faced the challenges of post-war life. All the siblings worked together in farming, and slowly life began to improve. However, by the early 1950s, the large family needed to separate as they grew, with more children born and everyone needing their own space. The farm boy himself got married and had to navigate the challenges of the post-war economy.

In the early 1970s, the farm boy moved to Canada, where life became even more difficult. Toto, a man of many experiences, lived the life of a poor man. By the middle of the 1990s, an illness shortened his life, and he passed away at the age of sixty-eight, leaving behind his wife Eva, six children, and seventeen grandchildren.

Many of us wonder about the extent of suffering endured by those who lived through World War I and World War II—cold, hunger, abuse, trauma—only God knows. This boy experienced a great deal of that suffering.

For my beloved dad and Grandma Nicoletta

Blank page intentionally

Table of Contents

Chapter 1
My Youthful Life.

My name is Toto Nocci, and this is the late 1930s; I am a farm boy. Together with my family, we farm other people's land. We live close to Francavilla al Mare, a small town in Abruzzo Central, Italy. Located about three km west of the Adriatic Sea, suburban to the town of Francavilla southwest of Pescara. We have an amazing property, which we can enjoy il nostro mare blue from where we are. On a daily basis, we see the sunrise to sunset without going to the shore. It is so enjoyable that many people would envy our location. In the morning, we look at the sea where the sun comes out; it seems like we can touch it with our own hand, and it will disappear at the end of the day, slowly through the mountains of Maiella. It is an incredible view. At sunrise, the sun seems like a big fireball that we can touch or grab with our own hands.

Foreigners will say,

"It is a lovely treasure in the hills without the price tag."

Many people envy our location. Unfortunately, this beautiful property where we live and work belongs to others. We are only Tenants, Contadini (peasants) working as farmers for other people. Our masters live in the city of Pescara; lucky them, or so lucky us, because we can use the farmhouse all for ourselves, taking advantage of utilizing the existing house as our principal residence. Of course, nothing is free, costing us to share everything we produce at the farm with the owner. Mom and Dad have been with them since I was a small boy; we do need a place like this; we are a big family. We named the place Spaccanocci place, like our last name, Nocci, which means Nut Crackers.

Today has been a sad day for me. My parents told me this was my last year of school. They need help at the farm, so they can use some extra help. I was eight when I started school, and now I am eleven; taking me out of school is heartbreaking. I am upset about it. There is nothing I can do, though; this will be the end of my school time. Having another chance will almost be impossible. We are a poor family. We do not own anything; we work to live, and we live to work. My family now needs me to help out at the farm, so I will; I have no choice. Quitting school to work at the farm with my family will make me a proud boy. We farm other people's land; my parents call it Mezzatriglia; it's like saying half pot.

My mom prays to God every day that everything will go well at the farm, starting from the season's harvest to the relationships with the owners and the family's health. Since we've been here, our landlord has given us the opportunity to work their land and, at the same time, occupy the farmhouse for our family; living in the same place where we are farming is an advantage; we don't need to travel as many people do, it's easier for us. Farming this beautiful piece of property, we have everything we need right at the doorstep: land, house, barn, stables, and storage house, including an area where to store straw and hay for animals. Our large family needs a big place. We live all together with my siblings, Mom, and Dad.

We always thank God for giving us this place. We are five brothers and two sisters, Leonora, Pietro, Joe, Mimi, Federico, Marianna, and then me, Salvatore, but they call me Toto; I am the last born of the family. Two of my brothers and one sister are married, while everyone else is not. My older sister Leonora is married to Franz, Pietro is married to Nuccia, and Joe is married to Lena. Joe and Lena live here with us at the farmhouse and never move out; Pietro and Leonora live on their own.

Farming other people's land does not make my parents' lives, Mezzatriglia; I never knew the difference between Mezzatriglia, tenant, or loaner; to me, they are all the same, whatever they call it. Having a property under certain conditions does not make any sense, possibly because I am too young to understand the farming system. We are loaded with responsibilities, and for one reason or another, my parents call it Mezzatriglia; I believe that means sharecropping, 50/50. Dad always talks about our landlord. I am not happy with the way they treat my parents. They are always pretending to think the way they like, asking for more results every day.

To me, they are not reasonable overall. When we talk about our landlord, Dad keeps saying they are good people. With them, we have nothing to worry about. The only thing I know about our proprietors is when they do come to the farm, for two reasons: seasonal harvesting or when they need something from us like fresh veggies or seasonal fruit. Sometimes, they ask Mom and Dad about the farm, always with a scope, no more, no less. I have a small book for writing stuff about my family, including when our landlord comes to visit us, only a few notes. In our large family, there are always weighty decisions made, so I keep a record of them. Sometimes, my brothers and my parents ask cosa scrivi su quel libro. They ask what I write in the book; I say just a little note about us to pass my time; this small book was given to me by Pietro when I started school. I kept it as my diary instead of using it for school. Being a country boy, life is hard, from morning to evening in the countryside. Unfortunately, we grow up the way we can, we live a poor life, and we suffer a lot; in simple words, you grow up as life permits.

I started working around the farm when I was six or seven; I know as a young child, the minute you learn to walk, you follow your parents to learn anything they do. Then, the minute you are capable of helping with anything, you are there to do so. At a younger age, you have nothing to worry about; you are only curious to learn and enjoy what life is all about. Helping Mom or Dad around the house makes you proud or happy. Then you grow up slowly, discovering there is no other way or opportunity to gain in life except farming. Helping them makes me proud of myself because they give everything to their children. Many times, I look to my parents, and I say to myself all they know is farming; other than that, they do not have another life. They never go anywhere. They are home or at the field, they don't know what fun is all about, entertainment for them does not exist, nor do they visit a new country or a cinema, there is no other life, sometimes they attend a local festivity, the only thing they care about on a daily basis is to worry about the family and the farmland.

My parents have been farmers all their lives; they have been peasants. We live our lives day to day without ambitions; even my grandparents were peasants. I do not remember them. I was a little boy when they passed away; we are easy people. Surviving today, not worrying about tomorrow. I have been the last born of the family, and I consider myself a little lucky boy; normally, I can get away with unreasonable things without sacrificing myself like the way my siblings do. Like they do, heavy work, be on the field all day long, rain or shine, regardless of the yearly season. Especially in the wintertime, getting wet, freezing days, they are out there performing their duty; I am at home helping Mom most of the time. I do work around the house, mostly in stalls where our occupant is, doing a lot of shit work; I consider myself lucky compared to my siblings.

In my family, I am the only one who went to school for a couple of years, and I think no one has ever gone before me, from my grandparents to my parents, including my siblings; we all are illiterate without having the chance of going to school. School helped me to learn some basics, write, and read a little. I will never forget my first day of school; when my Mom brought me there for the first time, she was so far away from home, like we walked for so long. I asked her if she would wait for me outside or would come back to pick me up. She said I am going to the town after I finish; I will pick you up; I was lost there; I hardly knew anyone. I need to thank my older brother, Pietro. If it wasn't for him today, I would not have schooling at all.

I remember repeatedly insisting on my Mom and Dad to send me to school. I was one of the late arrivals; other kids my age were already at second or third-year level; when I started, I was almost eight years old. Being with a group of kids from grade one to grade three was not easy. I will never forget my first day of school. We had a recreation time, and one of the kids came to me, calling me a big boy, presenting himself as Remo from Villanesi village, telling me it was near my house. I told him that this was my first year of school, and he was calling me a big boy. After he got my name and age, he said he knew my family, his parents share help with mine, so if I wanted we could walk together back home, that was the best thing that could happen to me, meeting Remo from our village.

In the beginning, I was worried that I couldn't handle school. Not everyone likes to study, so I was worried about failing and not learning anything; starting school at eight years old was not easy; possibly I didn't like school or the environment, but for the first time, I experienced something different. I could not give up; I was afraid of not making it to the next day or weeks to come. I would not succeed; school is something you have to like; otherwise, you waste your time. After that day, I made it without outcome. I stayed there. I will never forget that it was the first week of January 1935; in the beginning, it was difficult, but then everything went well. After days/weeks went by, I made some friends, and I then started to like going to school. Remo and I became good friends, and two and half years went so smoothly; I repeated the first-year class, and I did well until this spring of 1938. I will never forget when my Dad gave me the sad news. Telling me this was my last year of school; I was done going to school, with his heavy voice telling me that it was time for me to help my brothers. After my Dad gave me that sad news, saying school is over for me, I said to myself, my birthday is coming up soon, and I am going back to farming with my brothers and my parents to help LA BARACCA, the SHACK; it's like saying help carry the family load. La dolce vita e finita…

All my siblings were working at the farm, including my sister and sister-law, so quitting school, I was worried about one thing: I would never get a chance again to go back; before school was over, I needed to talk with my older brother Pietro, maybe he will convince Mom and Dad about it. There will not be another chance for me to go back. At the same time, I am thinking of my family. No one went to school before me, and going to school, I felt like the king of the house. Now, the family needs my help, and I need to be there and help out; I always thank God that, for the first time, a Nocci family member went to school. We are farmers, and the most important thing is that children like us need to help their families when they need it. I believe getting an education is important, so school is for people who can afford it. I am not sure, but I believe many farmer kids went to school late or never went. I am so sure for us it means a lot, boy or girl, it all depends on our family if they can afford it. I am referring to people in my position; of course, there are also country kids who can afford it. I strongly believe without school, life will be hard; we are what we are; for years, my family has suffered poverty, and all that I know I learned at school and from others is that poor people's lives have always been difficult, surviving day-to-day, no more, no less.

My birthday went by; I can't believe my whole family has forgotten about it. Working at the farm overtime these days, it is possible they might've forgotten all about it. Being an open field, we are exposed to the sun a lot and easily get sunstruck, get wet, or freeze ourselves to death. There are many risks to worry about. This is not the first time it has happened; they never remember, regardless of whose birthday is tomorrow. There are seven of us overall, so it is easy to forget a birthday. While farming, I learned one thing: you eat when you are not hungry and drink when you are not thirsty. Golden farmer's rules: you are in the field from sunrise to sunset, like it or not. Like my forgotten birthday, also other things happen when you are young. I remember one that happened in the past; I am so sure everyone sometimes has good and bad memories. As a boy, I would not want to remember bad things; unfortunately, we witness things we remember forever. As a child, I remember many family episodes; some things should not happen, like when Mom and Dad bickered because of us children. I don't agree that parents should fight because children suffer. Many times, I defended Mom, fighting because of us; it bothered me so much, even more if it was not our fault. Many times, a quarrel started because of us kids or because of a lack of money in the house. Skirmishes between wife and husband should never happen; I hated watching my parents fight. I do remember one in particular; it was a Sunday afternoon, and my Dad asked Mom for some money; possibly she had the money, but she said no. I am so sure she had her own reasons to say no, and because of that, he became like an animal, a beast.

Many times, I heard vulgar words from my brothers and Dad, scolding her like a nonhuman; it was wrong, without thinking, without respect. My family needed to be more united; communication leads to a solution to many things, and it will eliminate internal arguments; regardless of who's fault is, Mom or Dad, love for each other is sometimes not enough.

Many times, people make big issues out of anything. I remember one of our landlords saying to do your laundry at home and not show others your dirty clothes; he meant to keep discussions and arguments away from children, especially between parents and children. Many times, my parents bickered, and children absorbed it, so it was not possible to forget personal vices or things that were not necessary. A quarrel arose between my mother and my father. Mom possibly spent too much money on other necessities; I see with my own eyes that Mom was always short of money all the time. She worried about clothes, shoes, food supplies, or other needs for the house. I remember so well that when I was six or seven years old, Dad forced me to do things I didn't like, farming children grow up inside the shit, stupid rules by your parents or big brothers, I can name many things; wash yourself in the stream, walk around without shoes, risking to get bit by a snake, denied to touch certain foods, it is a failure by the parents toward their children, it happened to me many times when I was a small boy. Like other memories in their life, a farm boy doesn't forget, like the work I do, cleaning animal shit, taking all to the pit, where flies will eat you alive, washing the entire stable inside out, carrying water from the well to the stables over two hundred meters, the beauty of everything was, if you said something, you earned a couple strikes in the face, or your head.

Growing up as a farm boy, there is a mixture of things a child does not forget, good or bad. My siblings love me so much, but they command me like a little boy. Of all of them, the one who loves me the most is Pietro; he never told me anything. I do not remember my brothers telling me what to do. Normally, only Mom and Dad told me what to do, but sometimes my brothers forced me to do things I did not like, so all this created discord in the family.

I remember one incident very well in particular; my parents were arguing over something that was no one's fault, and it was miserable, reflecting the kind of life we lived daily. So many times, my brothers almost ended up in a fight with our Dad because of minor quarrels within our family. One time, my brother Federico, who was just fifteen, had a quarrel with Dad because of Mom, fighting over a trivial matter. I intervened sometimes to ensure they stopped arguing; many times, it resulted in a kick to my butt from Dad. I vowed to myself, "Never again." The next day, after Dad's argument, he gathered my older brothers, including Federico. Mom was there and admitted to us that he had been wrong many times. He said, "The quarrel with your Mom and you guys, what I had done in the past was completely wrong. I am ashamed of myself, and I hope this will not happen anymore in the future."

Nicoletta is the best thing I have in my life, the most important thing in the family. Unfortunately, sometimes I am uncontrollable, so please forgive me for what I did or do. I will pray to God for it not to happen anymore. But I am the head of the family, and I expect to be respected in all matters. Whether you like it or not, everyone must follow my orders as long as I live." After that speech by Dad, I felt compelled to say something, adding my two cents. I suggested to him about quitting going to the bar or disappearing sometimes for the whole night. He looked at me, possibly wanting to spank me or, worse, beat me up because of the conversation we were having. Fortunately, I was spared a slap on the face. After giving me an ugly look, he said, "I do not promise that, but I will do what I can to minimize my habits." I know my father; he would never apologize. By making that statement, he was sacrificing himself. It wasn't easy, but his speech was good for the family, putting an end to some unnecessary quarrels with Mom and us.

One Sunday morning, after Dad's lengthy meeting, everyone dispersed, leaving me alone with Mom. She shared a little story about Dad and his family, saying, "Toto, no more skirmishes or lies between your Dad and me." She initiated a conversation, saying, "When I met your father, we made a pact: no lies between us. We never deceived each other." I have known your Dad since I was fourteen. I grew up in a family full of lies and quarrels. They weren't my parents. When I was a young girl, they found me a job at the cemetery, working three days a week, cleaning up tombs and other rubbish. It wasn't a pleasant place for a young girl to work. Eventually, I started working full-time on a farm with other women. One day, I met your Dad, a good-looking boy, and I fell in love with him from the first day I saw him. Since then, I promised myself there would be no one else. Loving your Dad was like finding everything I wanted: a new life and a new family. God blessed me to find your Dad." She had tears in her eyes, trying to convey that, for some reason, she had hidden something from him. Continuing, she said, "Toto, I did lie once! Perhaps it was a bad one. It happened after we got married, causing a quarrel between him and his brother, where we used to live before moving here, in an area near the cemetery, just west of Francavilla. We were young at the time, farming a small parcel of land near Ponte Zelis. After many years, I got to know your Dad better. He was a man with no fear, somewhat cruel. His whole family was like that. The Nocci family was a little bossy. I got to know his family well, meeting all his siblings and relatives. Luigi was merciless, always keeping the whole family under his control. He was heartless, always a step ahead of everyone, without fear. He wasn't a god, but he acted like one." After that, she stopped, saying, "Maybe I shouldn't tell you anything, but you need to know that your Dad isn't a little angel. Let me tell you that back when we were at Ponte Zelis, one day, we received a visit from someone asking who the head of the family was."

She went on, recalling the incident, "I never saw those people before; it was a Sunday morning, and normally, no one came around on Sundays. I'll never forget it. I had Leonora on my arm; she was about a year old. I was expecting Pietro, a big guy. So, he asked for your Dad, who was in the field. He said he would wait for him and sat outside on a stone we had in front of the house. Soon, Luigi came from the field. The guy went to meet him, and they talked away from me. I didn't hear what they talked about; the only thing I heard was that they represented a crop wholesale company. They filled our heads with talk about paying well and recruiting all crops for their organization in the territory. They tried convincing us that we were in good hands and that it would be in our interest to join them, as most of our neighbors and vicinity were using them. Luigi didn't comment on it; he simply said we'd never heard that before around here. The guy insisted, saying they would guarantee the best price and provide us with peace of mind by taking all we didn't need. They were buying farmers' products in bulk for distribution across Italy. Luigi, without further comment, said we were not interested in their offer, and the guy became insistent. At that point, Luigi became firm, telling him to leave before he threw him out of our property. He was a mean guy; he didn't scare your father. Luigi told him to stay away from us; we weren't interested in selling our veggies in bulk to anyone."

After that day, your Dad inquired about these people buying farmers' vegetables. One day, together with his brothers and one of his first cousins, who was normally involved with people in commerce, he asked if he knew anything about those people. In the following days, he found out the truth from his cousin Antonio, nicknamed "Nicky," Duni, a dangerous guy. He said to your Dad, "Luigi, stay away from these people; they are strozzini, dangerous people." Your Dad never forgot that Sunday visit; he wanted to know where they were from and who they were working for until he found them. After he learned a little more about that group, he discovered they were a cooperative group, a large syndicate, living off the sweat of others. They were preying on small landowners and farmers, buying their products for less and making a profit above market value. Your Dad called them strozzini, loan sharks, senza un cuore, without a heart. While it was okay for certain farmers, your Dad never wanted to collaborate with them or pay them a percentage of anything for other small vegetables we produced on the farm. He didn't want to share with anyone; all he wanted was to sell what we had on a normal basis without committing ourselves to quantity production.

Later, he finds out who they are. One day, shortly after, he found out where those people kept the warehouse, so he ventured to where they were located. He had a meeting with the owner and a couple of others, a wholesaler company recruiting farmer products. Luigi was not interested in their offer, but he was curious to see where and how they operated, asking them to stay away from us. "We don't want any troubles. We are small farming producers and don't need a cooperative to buy our product." Time went by, and they returned one day, this time two of them. Your Dad was not home; he was helping a family near Torrevecchia, a small village near Chieti. So, I asked in a good manner what they wanted from us. One of them was a little rude, not the same guy who came before. He got close to me, awfully close; I could smell the wine he had been drinking. He said, "Listen, lady, you better talk to your husband. You guys produce the best veggies in this neighborhood. We pay well, and we do want your product. You guys produce the best in this neighborhood." He was leaving; he turned around, looking at me. I was scared; I didn't know what to do or what to say. I was afraid they would hurt my children or us. Luckily, your Dad was not here; otherwise, God knows what could have happened that day.

After they left, later that day, your uncle Vince stopped by, looking for your father. So, I asked Mom if that was the guy who died in the war. She said no; he left for South America in the early thirties and never came back. She went on, saying, "I talked to Vince about what happened. I was worried." He said not to tell your Dad anything. He would deal with it. That was the first time I hid something from your Dad. I wish I never did. Later, Luigi found out what happened. I don't know how possibly from Uncle Vince. He was very upset with me and with his brother, saying, "Never hide things like that from me, never again. I will never hide anything from him, regardless of what." Mom told me that. I said to Mom, "I will be the same way." She continues saying, "One night, he came home late with a few scratches on his arms and hands; he was still bleeding. So, I asked what happened. He said there was nothing to worry about; he had a fight at the bar and needed to settle some scores with someone. Later, I knew what happened. Your Dad, his brothers, and cousins paid a visit to those people. I was not happy about it; they ventured themselves into their place, which was a significant risk. Since then, I thought I knew your Dad, not really Toto. Then, they stayed away from the Nocci family until, one day, they came back with a political excuse. They wanted to know how we were going to support the Democrats or the Fascist party. Your Dad washed his hands, saying none of them. He knew they wouldn't get close to us or our family. Luigi made it clear to them to stay away from us; we are not interested in any of their business, regardless of political or selling vegetables. They gave us a tough time until your Dad went to war. They came around a couple of times but never in the house. Your Dad's cousin Antonio was telling me not to worry about them; they were only barking."

Time went by; in the early 1920s, they gave us a rough time again. One day, your Dad came home very worried, saying they were trying to get back into our farm business. They possibly lost a lot during the war; now, they were hungry for business, grabbing as much as possible. Luigi knew we were wasting our time with those people. Mostly, he was afraid for us, making sure nothing would happen to any of us. So, your Dad made a deal with them. It was a big decision, selling them a portion of our best veggies. After that, they left us alone for a period of time without worries about them. They disappeared for a few years, happy with what we were selling to them, until we had a choice: move from there or sell them all our crops. We had one choice: sell all to them or move out from Zelis. We are bent for a few more years. In the early thirties, we moved to a couple of separate places. Until the later thirties, we got this place; after that, all was good. Since then, we have never moved again. I have always been living in fear; possibly, they never forgot all about it. I might be wrong, Toto; do not forget they are people with no heart, exploiting others without looking people in the face. I see you sour with everyone, never happy. Mom, why all this? She says, "There are many good things in life or bad things. For many years, your father needed to watch his back; people remember only bad things in life, forgetting the good things. Do not forget one little thing in life; it is just an old saying. 'Man forgives, but he does not forget.'"

Working with my family in the countryside gives me the opportunity to gain some experience in farming and learn many beautiful things, such as wine and olive harvests, without forgetting the other small harvests we have. Personally, I believe working in the countryside is an art. Yes, it takes years to learn all the processes; not everyone can do it. Learning the system and treatments for the individual harvests is not an easy job. All are made up of different harvests; we have a great piece of property, rolling and flat land, small hills overall, planting corn, wheat, veggies, vineyards, olive groves, and soap beans. Also, a few fruit plants, such as apples, cherries, and walnuts. In addition to that, we have another partially open land for clover leaves for the animals. Our farm spans over twenty-five hectares of land with one owner and a few more actors with another owner. A mixture of soil, overall excellent quality. The farm we work on consists of two separate properties: the first one, where we live with a good portion of land, and the second portion, which is only land, no barn or place to store anything, owned by two separate owners. Mom and Dad use a good system to cultivate farmland, including keeping us all under control. Dad is a great leader, applying rules and responsibilities for each of us. All our seasonal harvests are great; we take loving care of them, starting from winter veggies, wheat grain, granola, corn, winery, always to olive, later in the year, the most important part, at the end of the year, we need to make sure we have enough to feed our family, or saving for rainy days. Soon, it will be New Year; I hope we are all together here to celebrate our New Year's Eve as one big family, as usual.

On New Year's Day, we are all together here at the Nocci family; normally, it's the best time to see each other, as are the Christmas and New Year holidays, giving us the opportunity to see our siblings and children together. At the same time, it will give my parents the chance to spend time with their grandchildren. This morning, I asked Mom if we would be together on New Year's Eve; she said, "I hope so, Toto. Do not forget that three of your brothers are married; they are obligated to the partners' families. Having wives and children, each of them may have different plans for the family in the new year." Unfortunately, I was curious to know ahead of time if we were all together with my brothers and sisters. Mom was right; each of them had their own program. Mom was right; I was the only one home celebrating New Year's Eve with Mom and Dad. Mimi, Federico, and Marianna went out to see the fireworks; everyone else, I do not know. One thing I know: we have an old saying. As a child, you stay home; when you're teenagers, be home before nightfall; after you get married, someone will guide you forever. It's been a few days since we celebrated New Year's Day. Mom had a great lunch for everyone; my brother Pietro and his family didn't come; everyone else was here, celebrating 1939.

This year, my twelfth birthday is coming up. I hope to get an accordion box for my birthday. My brother Mimi has one; Pietro has one when he's not around. I always take advantage of learning how to play, only secretly. Mom is the only one who knows about it. I like to practice with it. I am good at it; mostly, my favorite pieces are the Passion of Christ; we play only during Easter time, on Thursday of Holy Week. Mimi calls the accordion play box a four-button; I wonder why. I am in love with it. Mimi doesn't want me to touch it; sometimes I do, only when he's not around. I can play better than him. So, my older brother Pietro can play very well. Pietro loves me so much more than anyone else; sometimes, he always asks me if I want to take his box. He has a two-button box; he calls it the Two Voices. I learned how to play by myself, with no help. My family, for one reason or another, never gives me a chance to say something in their family conversations. When we do have one, because I am so young, sometimes I say, "I know more than my siblings," or "I have much clearer ideas than them." To have a chance to express my wish or my concern is impossible with them. The only thing I hear my Dad saying is, "When you finish with Mom, come down to the field to help us out." Or, after a couple of steps, he turns around and looks at me, saying, "Toto, bring fresh water with you when you come." All that bothers me so much is that he's like our donkey, Pippo, treating me like a little boy or animal. I don't know why; just because I am the last one in the family doesn't mean I should be treated like the last of the school class. Lately, they have worked hard at the veggie field, doubling the work due to the soil being wet these days. Dad likes to be ahead of the game; that's one of the reasons he's working on wet soil. Most of our veggie fields need a lot of hand work and big attention. The main work is keeping the weeds away from it. Dad always shows us what needs to be done, telling all of us, "One day, you will thank me for it."

   This winter seems to be longer than we thought; the small seedlings are already in the soil, where all the planting of vegetables goes. It is a big process; they are transplanted from the boxes and then replanted carefully into the soil, all by handwork. Dad will prepare furrows, then we will plant small seedlings, many types: tomatoes, zucchini, escarole, radish, pepper, onion, and many other crops. Our Dad is an expert at veggie planting; our fields have rich soil. We are using a portion for veggies and a portion of land for other needs. This strip of land sits next to the creek, un ruscello, a pillow like a river; there's water running all year long. We do use it to water our plants all year long. It's great; many farmers along this creek will benefit from it. Less than two months until my birthday. So, this morning, I asked my Mom what she would give me for my twelfth birthday. She looked at me, saying nothing, smiling. I said, "I would be happy with an eight-button accordion! Model Venezia, reddish color or black." She looked at me again, saying, "What's in your mind, young man? Do not plan things that will never happen; otherwise, there will be trouble, Toto." "No problem, Mom," I walk away, talking to myself, saying, "Mimi's old box soon needs a new one; possibly he will give it to me when he buys a new one." My twelfth birthday comes up on May 3rd; it's in the middle of the week, on Wednesday. Waiting for my family's greetings or having something special for my birthday; being the youngest of the family, a special treat will be nice. No one remembered as usual, so I went to sleep with a sad face. I wrote down another birthday without a gift. Early in the morning, Mom wakes me up while it's still dark. I asked Mom why it was so early; she said, "I need help at the stall; your Dad doesn't feel well." Later, I said to Mom, "I did not expect gifts, but a happy birthday from everyone last night would have made me happy." She remained ill; to console me, she said, "Come with me to Mass next Sunday; after that, I will buy you something special in the village." Mom felt bad about it; I said not to worry, "Next year, you double the gift." She goes with the ladies to the church; I said to her, "You know I do not like to go to church." After that, everybody apologized to me; well, the damage was done. Later in the spring, helping Mom with our occupants on a daily basis at the stall, I said, "Mom, soon the grain harvest will be ready; we will have people to help us out." She said, "So." I said to her, "I am in love with this typical harvest; I really like it; it's unique." Our full family is here in the open field, men cutting in front, and the women will be collecting the loose bundles behind. After that, we are going back to tie the bundles together, forming a small group of these bundles like a gazebo style. Later, days after that, they will be transported to a square yard near the house, ready to be threshed. At this point, our landlord shows up, collecting their share. After completing all the threshing, my father needs to deliver all the grain to a nearby mill for the landlord's share to be ground. It's a prolonged process; Dad keeps our share in one special small tower inside the warehouse for the grain only, protected from mice or other animals or insects. Later, he goes to the mill as needed. Dad saves mostly at home; then, when we need it, he goes to the mill and grinds the necessary. Sometimes, if he needs money, he sells to the miller what we have in reserve.

Selling our shares completely to them, Dad never does that; all our associates buy our products, like wheat, grapes, or the olive beans they purchase from us. I remember once with my father, we brought three quintals of wheat to the mill; after it was ground, he said, "Luigi, it's about two and a half quintals, more or less. For me, that is stealing." The mill people always take a percentage of it; as we needed a bag of flour, my brothers would go and pick up a sack of fifty kg at a time. Normally, we go every couple of months. Mom has many uses for it; she makes homemade pasta, bread, and much more.

A sizzling summer, so little rain, our land suffers from dryness. Dad tries to water it down and keep the moisture going; without rain, our land suffers. Keeping the ground very moist requires a lot of work; my father and I come at nighttime to water the field. The most important are vegetables; certainly, it's not an easy job taking the water from a little pond. We do have a motor pump that can push the water through the field. Thanks to God, we built a small pond inside the running creek. This stream separates our land from the Falco family's land, and we both benefit from it. We are lucky; the water runs all year long in the creek. Dad and I spend a lot of time together cleaning up the tub; this way, when we drain water, it will last hours before drying up.

Dad is a good teacher for all of us; he always tells my siblings and me what to do on the farm or what is right or wrong in life. Tonight, Dad and I are watering a section of tomato plants, so he stops for a few minutes to have a glass of wine. He says to me, "Come, son, sit next to me. I need to warn you about a few things in life." It's not a little story or a fairy tale; in our village, there is a rumor that people talk about. A normal person like us believes he is a werewolf. So, he said, "I've never seen it; however, I know very well what that is. More than one guy saw it or was chased. Luckily, as far as I know, no one got hurt. So, listen to me. I am sure all of this is true; a werewolf has existed since my ancestors." For a minute, I looked at him, saying to Dad, "Are you sure about what you're talking about, Dad? I've never heard of that before, a werewolf." I say, "Pa, what are you talking about?" He explained to me all about how someone, a normal person like us, can become a werewolf. They come out at nighttime. "Werewolf" was the first time I heard such a thing in my life. I know a wolf; we have them around in wintertime, but a werewolf? I know my brothers always talk about ghosts and vampires to scare me off, never werewolves. Papa says to me, "Remember, Toto, anytime you go out at nighttime by yourself, first of all, stay away from ponds and water creeks." That story by Dad gives me a chill. I asked if my brothers knew about this; he said yes, many people are aware of it. "So, your brothers know," I ask. "Where does he live?" He said no matter where, what's important is you stay away from those places. "Remember, Toto, son, there are other terrible things in this world, so that's why I want you to be safe and stay away from troubles. In life, Toto never plays the hero or macho man, regardless of whether it's a fight, a quarrel with others, or any dangerous situation. You walk away from it; it's better to be safe than sorry, son."

After that long chat with my Dad, I said to myself, "Can this be possible? Why don't they go after this guy or see if anything can be done to cure him, the wolfman?" I never heard that before. Soon, our winery harvest is coming up; everybody needs to help out, including my brothers, my sister Marianna, and my sister-in-law Lena. My Dad always says, "Unity makes power and strength. A strong group will get things done faster." Dad is the type of guy who wants things done without questions to be asked, regardless of what others or everyone else says; he's the one who decides everything. There are no complaints from anyone; he's the boss of bosses, and without anyone complaining, everyone needs to follow the way he wants to run the farm work. Our family, we are all good with it, without questioning him. There are other farmer leaders like him, but for some reason or another, they are not the same; people envy my Dad for the way he gets satisfactory results or runs our farming system. He always says, "A good harvest gives us satisfaction, fills our warehouse, and keeps our family happy. The most important thing overall is that our landlord will be happy." Normally, with a good year-end, everyone will be happy. It is important to have a good result from the harvest; we consider ourselves a little lucky because of the variety of products we produce, which makes it easy to survive throughout the year.

Landlords are happy and will not complain. Then, that is another big problem. Regardless of the return, they always expect more from us. All year long, like a broken record, they come by and make comments about the farm production and results. We do want to get more from the farm; we need to survive for the full year with it. Our share is minimized for one reason or another. It's not an easy life for my parents. Being a large family, sometimes there are disputes among us. It's not an easy job for Mom and Dad; it's difficult to keep up with it. Regardless of what happens in the house, Dad keeps everyone happy. My brothers Joe and Mimi occasionally help other farmers; they are paid good money for their services. Mom can use the extra money for the family, which helps the system to fill the pot and survive through the year. Dad believes a family should never struggle or be short of food or personal needs.

Mom and Dad always used to say to us, "If my family is suffering, everyone else suffers."

Landlords are never happy. My brother Pietro got married noticeably young because he did not want to stay at the farm, serving and hearing people complain every day about farm results. I do not know if I would do the same; possibly, one day, I will need to make that decision or something similar. Getting married so young, for some reason or another, makes your life harder. Our parents got married young in the old days; they used another method. Today, people are no longer in a hurry; they want to enjoy youth life longer if possible. As far as I know, even today, all marriages are arranged ahead of time, fixed by parents. I don't like that. Having your life decided by other people is not right. Mom always says, "You are too intelligent for them." I ask why, and she says quite simply, "Because you ask too many questions, and you want to know too much in life."

Talking about landlords, each harvest, they want more from us, an increase in production, regardless of how well or badly we have done for the year. I may be seen as a bad boy because I call them leeches; to me, they are bad because they are never satisfied no matter what we do. Proprietors act like gods, always pretending to want more from farmers like us; they are like weeds or bad grass, hard to destroy. Each harvest time, they are here at the farm to ensure that we do not steal anything from them. Then, as the old saying goes, everyone pulls the water to his mill... they are here to look after their share. With all respect for our landlords, I can also understand that they are the owners; however, they should consider that we have been here for years, so we are hardworking people, honest to all levels. Overall, our country hosts are free to ask or dictate anything they want. I can see them now, like a dream. Without hesitation, they show up on time and sit on a chair at our warehouse, our winter storage, nearby, with their book, writing down the number of incoming products. The most followed harvest is wheat, grapes, and olives.

Our landlords, on a harvest basis, normally supervise everything we do, making sure we do not steal anything. Mom and Dad have nothing to hide, so to me, all this does not sit well. I am learning about landlords; they come to the house, take a walk in our warehouse, and see what we have stored; possibly, he wants to legalize part of our retained product. In the end, regardless of how good or bad the year went, he will complain! They are like vampires, sucking your blood up to the last drop; they always want more from their property. Working the land, we always need our masters, who endure us in many ways. Sometimes, we are short or run out of money, lacking the necessities for the family, and sometimes, because we have a bad year on the farm. Then, when you need help from them, like support or money, you must sign a document, like a promissory note, for a year. Dad always says, "Sign a blank promissory note." At the end of the year, you will pay them out. My parents always contribute in many ways: fresh vegetables, chicken eggs, and sometimes a lamb at Easter, among many other things, based on their request. Otherwise, you need to pay interest on it, so contributing to old-fashioned ways helps to eliminate the interesting part. Sometimes, extras like olive oil or wheat, the best, we need to deliver to them at their house. As I said before, I do believe they are vampires that suck blood to the last drop until it dries out. These are some of the reasons why if you work on other people's land, you will never achieve a better position in your life.

Our landlord lives in the city of Pescara, in a big house that looks like a castle, a beautiful home in a big town, over three hundred square meters. God bless them; they have nothing to worry about. I've been to their house once; I'll never forget it. My mom and I delivered some fresh fruits and veggies when I was about nine at the time. My eyes caught right away the beautiful features of that palace. They have radiators for the heating system, electrical lights throughout the house, and a washroom with a large tub, sink, and more. During harvest time, they come to collect their share. At the end of the day, before leaving the farm, as usual, they talk to my parents like a broken record, "Mr. Nocci, we need better results." It's the same story every year. I asked Mom, "Before the end of summer, I want to spend a little time at the beach." She said, "In your dreams." I said, "That would be a nice change. I hope you, Marianna, and Lena will come or something. This way, they have a chance to see (il mare) and meet some new friends. It will be nice." Mom's friend always goes during summer weekends; it will be good for them to relax for a day. I will ask Dad for it to give us a break next Sunday. If we go, I will arrange with Francesco, the fisherman, to take us for a ride in the small boat.

I am twelve, living so close to the sea, going to the beach is just impossible. I never go; my parents and my brothers always tell me the sea is for foreigners and fishermen. I do not know how to swim; it's a shame. Most of my friends can swim like a fish. As children, there is no freedom, always work and home, no recreation in life. I hardly have any friends; before you know it, you become an old man with no teeth left, ready to disappear from this world.

After that weekend at the beach, a beautiful day (al mare), everyone had fun. I thanked Dad for letting us go. We had a tour trip in the water; even if it did not last long, we had fun. Mom and Lena never saw something like it. They will remember it for a long time.

I am a farm boy with so much on my mind. I certainly cannot become a doctor or a lawyer, but I can learn a trade. My passion is to become a builder. Possibly, I will learn how to build homes or barns for farmers. When I was ten, I needed to do something special. We had a crazy spot for a toilet that needed to be cleaned on a daily basis. I said if I built a great box on the ground with cement, with a little shed above it, I would create a great restroom for everyone to use. When I built our exterior toilet box, Mom complimented me on it. It's only a dream for now; I hope one day I will build a house or stalls for animals. There are many things I can do, like my big brothers out there; they do a lot for other farmers.

This summer went by so fast. After that weekend al mare, Joe complained to my parents, referring to the beach day. We had an enjoyable time with Mom and others. I don't know why he complained; he is the one never home, always taking off. God knows where he goes. For him, working at the farm seems to be allergic to the medication. Federico and Mimi are the ones more at home and in the field. I am helping Mom at home, or I help them in the field, cleaning up rubbish. Normally, I take Pippo, our donkey, with me; he likes me. Sometimes, if I leave the house without him, he starts clamoring like a dog.

My Dad is a family leader, organizing farm work and family affairs like a professional organizer. We have meetings with the full family a minimum of four to six times a year. Being the child of the family, I have little to say and no decision to make. Joe and Mimi have more power overall. Federico, Marianna and I need to keep quiet without saying anything. Mom normally will have her say for us. They are the oldest at home after my parents when it comes to family decisions or experiences. Only Joe has things his own way. I do not know anything about running a family affair or farming.

Learning or leading a farm activity requires experience and responsibility, needing big leadership. The only thing I know is helping everyone, regardless of cleaning the stall, barn, or other work. The best is when I take our cow to the field, helping Dad plow the land. Unfortunately, Dad is always worried about that. He just teaches me what it's all about. He's afraid I might get hurt with the landplow.

Since I was five, I call my Dad Luigi. I never forget when I was playing with Federico and Marianna to play Moscow hide and seek. I was hiding behind the wall, and the two of them had to find me. Dad was not too far, so after I counted to ten, I looked around, and Pa was whistling. He taught me a direction where Federico was. I went to touch him, and he got angry with Pa, calling him by name, saying, "What a Luigi, you are a spy." So I began to call him Ligi as much as I call Mom Nicoletta. Calling my parents by their first name, sometimes people think they are not my parents. I remember once the Marshall Santoro came by. I said to Mom, "Hey, Nicoletta," and he said, "This is your son, Nicoletta." She said, "Yes, Mr. Santoro." She doesn't like to be called by name. She keeps telling me, "I am your Mom, not Nicoletta."

I do believe farmers care about parents. Possibly, we respect them a little more than anyone else. We are not figli di Papa. I am referring to more educated people, in other words, people who are more easygoing. Parents only do their duty. I am talking about rich people, of course. T, this is my opinion. I am just guessing about how high-hand people educate their children. Possibly, it is the same love. We peasant kids, it is an obligation on our behalf.

So many times, I heard that there are quarrels and personal interests between parents and children. Most of the time, big quarrels happen because of money or property. Sometimes, kids want to take over the inheritance. All that starts or influences an uneasy relationship between brothers, sisters, in-laws, parents, etc. Surpluses are major problems in families. We do not have that problem. Our farm is loaned to us. If they want it back with a year's note, they can kick us out. I do not know if the landowner will do such a thing. We've been here so long; I hope to stay as long as possible.

This morning, I asked my brother Mimi about my going back to school for a couple more years. He told me to talk to Dad. I said, "Out of the question, I know the answer." So he suggested having our next family meeting later in the summer. That might work before school opens again, hoping Dad will say yes. I'd love to go back to school and help out more. The family needs help when it comes to reading some documents, seeing notes from our landlord issues, and keeping better records in the books. My parents always get cheated when it comes to splitting the harvest collection.

Summer is going by so fast. After our family meeting, Mimi asked Dad about Toto going back to school, telling everyone it would be good for our family, only for a couple more years. Then, as I said before, everyone said no at that meeting. Mom patted me on the back of my head, saying it's impossible, son. You know how much work is around the farm. With the new harvest at the door, it's just impossible for me to go back to school. Soon, it will be grape time, and we will start the winery harvest. After that, only the olive harvest remains. The harvest takes about two weeks, depending on whether we get help for it. Otherwise, it will be a longer process to get all the work done by hand. We need to bring all the baskets and boxes to the outside of the furrows to be loaded onto a wagon, and from there, they go to the warehouse. It's a big job for everyone. Normally, we always get some help, but this time, no one came. Not Leonora's family, Pietro, or our neighbor. No one. Then we managed on our own.

We are lucky to have two strong cows to pull the wagon home on a regular basis. I'll never forget when the other cow we had was getting too old for farm work, so Dad sent it to the slaughterhouse. After that, he picked up these two young cows and named them Magna and Violet, which were strange names. This is my Dad. He has spent all his life looking after our occupants in the stables, making sure they're treated like humans, like people. Being a slave of humans, animals don't like that. They do major work on the farm, such as plowing dirt and towing our wagon. They are lifesavers for us. Our cows listen only to Dad and my brother Mimi. Yes, they are special, younger cows. The reason we gave them names, Violet and Magna, is because Violet has beauty mark on her right shoulder, a mix of brownish violet and blue color, and Magna because she eats so much, twice as much as the others. Despite that, she never gets fat.

Dad talks to them all the time like he talks to anybody in our family. Sometimes jokingly, I say to Pa, "Hey, Luigi, you love our cows more than us." He laughs, saying they bring food to our table. My major job is looking after our animals in the stable. I like it because they don't talk back or scream at you like my brothers do. I clean them every day. I worked with Violet and Magna a lot. Every day, I need to be nice to them and look after them. So, once or twice a week, I prepare a special food, cooked fodder, and cabbage, including mixed wheat Caniglia or maize bran. Violet and Magna love it. They always want more. They moo at me all the time. Then we have Pippo, our donkey. He doesn't eat much. There must be a reason. I never know why. Pippo doesn't like what I cook for Magna and Violet. He only likes hay and green four-leaf clover. So, we call him Pippo. My family always treats Pippo as a donkey, so I gave him a guy's name. They gave that bad name to this poor animal who works more than anyone else. A donkey in Italian means someone with no brains. Erroll.

Since I've been working on the farm, I get exhausted easily. Mom says I am weak and need to eat more. Can you imagine my parents are both over fifty? So, they get exhausted sometimes, too. Soon, the winery harvest will be over, and everyone will need some rest. We have a small festivity coming up, St. Mary of Grace, in our village. The winery harvest will take two weeks of challenging work. I say it's easy jobs for women and heavy jobs for men, the most important work left for this year. We do have another big one coming up: the olive harvest. It's a difficult one. All the olive plants are on small hills, and it is uncomfortable to pick olive beans from the trees. Someone needs to do it.

This particular parcel of land retains an excellent quality of soil, mud, and light stone. It's a mixed ground, brownish soil, easy to work with. Not many weeds grow on it, making it easy to keep clean. This parcel of land gives us satisfactory results. It takes years to grow these plants. For some reason, we call this parcel of land "Le Colline Delle Civette," The Hills of the Owls. Next to the olive groves, there is a mini forest, possibly fifty hectares, with many types of trees. They call it the vampire forest. One of these days, I will walk through it. Perhaps there are good things in there: mushrooms, asparagus, and possibly fresh oak glands for our piglets. Thank God we have this hill, giving us excellent products, mostly olives and vineyards. It has such good soil; unfortunately, it's on a ravine, making it hard to work on. Perhaps that's why they call it The Hills of Owls.

For a period of time, there have been rumors about WW2 at the door. I don't know anything about it, just people talking, as I said, rumors, nothing else for now. Dad sometimes comments on it and what can happen. Dad lived and survived WW1 for almost three years. Since then, he's been a man without a heart. For him and around him, nothing existed. He doesn't want to see another war in his lifetime. Since WWI, he has become bitter all his life. Mom says since then, he has been sour. He has been rough with us. Believe me, for as long as I can remember, he has always been like that. In addition to that, he has had some health issues, problems he won't talk about. Keeping all to himself. Memories: he does have a couple of junk in the warehouse, old pieces of WW-I Rifle with a bayonet. I noted once while searching for something I saw the sword and the rifle from the old war. I don't know why he keeps such old tools, perhaps as souvenirs.

Later in the summer, in a few days, we are celebrating Santa Maria Delle Grazie (St. Mary of Grace), a big festivity for our village. It's a big time; all the people in the vicinity participate, and I am sure our parish priest will be happy to see many people at church contributing to the enormous collection for the Roman church. These festivities last a full day, and our family has always helped to ensure the success of this beautiful holiday. I am very much involved, participating in all activities and lending a hand to our priest. It makes me proud to be involved and contribute to our parish. After the second morning mass, there is a procession. Four people will carry the statue on a wooden plate, so everyone in the street will be blessed and will give money to our saint.

This festivity is good for everyone, kids and adults alike, providing a relaxing day without worries. Living in the same village, many people who have never met each other will have the opportunity to get to know their neighbors. This party usually includes many rides and stalls selling gifts and souvenirs. Additionally, there are other stalls selling items such as peanuts, ice cream, lupins, and apples, among many others that are harder to describe. The St. Mary festivity is loved by everyone and provides an annual opportunity for all neighborhoods to come together. There is even a pub bar where people can enjoy a sandwich, beer, or glass of wine. The party will continue until late at night, with people dancing on the stage and enjoying meeting other local residents. Farmer people will discuss the future and other activities for the village. It's a big day at the St. Mary festivity.

Chapter 2
Sibbing's Gone to War

As the saying goes, "After the storm, the pleasant weather," but this time, it's quite the opposite. Earlier this morning, we had an unexpected visit from local authorities; two of them paid us a visit, and my dad knew what it was all about. They came for Mimi and Joe. Federico is too young to be called to the military, and I was right: Joe and Mimi need to join the army group. It's not a suitable time for us as we're in the middle of harvesting, both in the winery and soon with the olive harvest. We rely heavily on Mimi and Joe, and if both go, it will be a disaster for our farm. Our family depends a lot on them, and it will be harder to manage our commitments without my brothers. The olive harvest is approaching, a very demanding job that requires many hands, and we need all the help we can get.

Dad talks to the brigadiers, pretending that Mimi and Joe are not around, claiming they went to help other farmers for a few days. My brothers occasionally do help other farmers, away from here. This time, Dad exaggerated, saying they might not come back until later in October. We were lucky; these guys never catch on to the meaning behind Dad's words. Dad normally doesn't lie, but because he needs Joe and Mimi to finish the work they're involved in, he resorted to it. Joe is always helping others, fixing barns, vineyard skeletons, and other structures for farmers, so he uses those excuses. My brothers are experts in that type of work, including building barns, barracks, and sheds.

Losing Mimi and Joe would be a disaster for our farm at this time of the year. We desperately need help, and it will be extremely hard to replace them. All farmers are in the same situation, busy during this time of the year. Finding anyone to help us out on the farm will be impossible. We work from dawn until dusk, hoping the brigadiers will let my brothers go for a little while. My father knows one of them very well and didn't hesitate to ask him to come back, Mr. Nocci. I told Dad I guarantee they will be back here soon. They left saying, "Mr. Nocci, we understand. See you soon."

After the brigadiers left, Mama Nicoletta started crying uncontrollably, muttering to herself, "Do not take my sons away." I had no words to comfort her. I believe they let them go for a few days or a couple of weeks because they knew our family well, but we don't know when they will be back. Mom continued crying for a long time, screaming to God. I thought to myself, "What does God have to do with it?" The only thing we can do is pray.

One day, I went near my mom. She stopped crying, but I could see the pain in her heart and the worry in her eyes about her sons. She already experienced war with her father, and she wouldn't want to see another one. War brings pain and sorrow to families and mothers.

As she said, "May God help us out," two of my brothers need to join the army. We know this isn't just a military journey; it's wartime. We hope to see them come back one day. Soon, Mimi and Joe will be gone. God protect them. We will pray every day for God to bring them home healthy and safe.

I spent a little time with Mom and then sat next to Dad. He shook his head, saying he lied to the brigadiers for many reasons. He didn't want them to take the boys now, and he wasn't sure they were ready for this. After the marshal left, Dad said, "Let's not forget that we have a lot of work in the countryside. Let's not stay here and cry; these are wasted tears." There is so much work to do on the farm. Dad continued shaking his head, telling me, "War is a gamble, Toto. You never know when you're coming back if you come back." After that, Dad kept talking, hoping I wouldn't experience any of this. He said, "Pray to God this won't go too far."

Mom turned pale, her face full of worry about her sons leaving soon for war. Soon, my brothers will be gone, and we need to move forward. We have a big responsibility on the farm. With Dad's experience, we hope to manage our farm work. He's been farming all his life, surviving three years in WWI. Sometimes I wonder why he never talks about it or shares anything with us. We know he lost family members; one of his brothers never made it back home. Dad keeps a few pieces of junk from WWI saved in the warehouse: an old firearm that probably doesn't work anymore and a folding sword, most likely a century old or so, a pocketknife he always keeps with him.

Sometimes, I joke with him about the hunting knife, asking which pig he killed with it. He jokingly tells me, "Anyone who bothers me." My father doesn't talk much, and sometimes I wonder why. We're family; we should share everything, the good and the bad, including bad memories. We know what Dad went through during WWI, so he needs to talk about it sometime. I'd like to know more. God knows how much he suffered in those days.

Then, Mimi left right after the brigadier visited, but Joe never left. Dad wants them to go at different times for some reason. It's been a few weeks since the brigadier came, and I'm surprised they haven't returned for Joe. Thanking God, we hope our brother remains home as long as possible. After we complete our winery harvest, Joe and Federico will be a great help for our olive harvest. I don't want to say anything to my parents about this. We hope Joe stays without being called again.

Sunday afternoon, I joked with my brother Joe, saying he was lucky the brigadier never came back for him. He didn't seem to like that, but I continued, asking why Mimi left and he stayed. He said I was talking too much, and I replied, "Age before beauty." We always pick on each other; we're twelve years apart. He said he's my older brother and not to talk to him like that. I teased him, saying he ran like a snail and couldn't catch me, repeating it until I ran to Dad for safety. Dad was at the stables, and when he asked what was going on, I told him about Joe not being called for the army again and how he wanted to beat me up. Joe explained, and Dad scolded him for it. Then, I said to him, "Why don't you go to Celano? Maybe you'll be safe there." He didn't understand, saying our country needs us and we have obligations. "One day, you'll understand, Toto," he said.

This year has been full of surprises: a scorching summer, a new war, my brothers leaving, and my father being unwell for years. Poor Mama, she's suffering so much. After the olive harvest was completed in late fall, we had another big job left for this year before the Christmas holidays. We need to complete our seeding before winter

and clean up all the land before the dangerous weather sets in.

I've taken on many responsibilities since I quit school. I help Mom with housekeeping and tend to the animals at the stables. Mom and I have a routine every day, and she's so good with the animals. Dad and Federico leave the house around six in the morning, and Mom and I wake up at five. We're committed to our work, and it's like taking a walk in our garden every morning for the two of us.

Since my two brothers left, our workload has doubled, and I miss them very much. Even though we sometimes argue, Federico and I joke around more. We also get help from other people on the farm, like Pietro and Leonora. They always lend a hand when they can. Dad sometimes tells us to drop some olive grains for the birds during the harvest. I was too young at the time to understand why he said that or what he meant by it.

"I never thought dad would say, Feed the birds."

For years, he used this phrase, and finally, I caught onto its meaning. I decided to demonstrate it myself by throwing a few beans on the floor, saying, "Here, birdy, come and eat." My dad got upset with me, saying, "One day, you'll have kids to feed, and I'll see if you do that." Overall, I learned a valuable lesson from my father. Sometimes, parents do things to help the family survive. Dad did it without malice, without hurting anyone. Perhaps it was the right solution to hide something from others. He said, "If we drop some on the floor, we won't have to share with the landowner. After all is done, we can come back later to pick it up." It's like a second collection. We can do a lot with it, gaining extra olive oil, which isn't easy these days. I realized how fortunate we are because the owners don't come to the countryside to watch what we do. Holy God, all of this makes sense.

"Feed the bird."

Soon it will be Christmas, and my mom has a tradition of making special treats for the occasion that we call "Xmas sweets." She does an excellent job with them, whether they're fried, oven-cooked, or made over fire embers. These special cookies, made with flour, eggs, sugar, and jam, are absolutely delicious. They're all homemade, with just a bit of baking powder or yeast. After letting the dough rise, she cuts it into small portions and shapes them by hand into round, thin, leaf-sized pieces. She creates a full basket of them, usually weighing anywhere from eight to ten kilograms. Mom usually makes enough to last us throughout the holidays, sometimes even making extras to give away to others, like doctors or property owners, which always brings them joy. She truly is a great cook, and I wonder how she manages to do it all. People trust her cooking because they know that to eat well, you have to use natural resources like she does. Eating country-style food gives it a different flavor, and everything, from chickens and rabbits to lambs and other wild animals, is homemade. And let's not forget about almonds and chickpeas, caramelized with sugar, all made at home.

Mom is an extraordinary woman in every aspect: her personality, her beauty, and her talents. God bless her. She is everything one could desire, a person with a heart of gold. She puts a thousand percent effort into everything she does, and there is no room for hatred in her heart, only love for others. Mom, Nicoletta, is everything a woman can be; she's like the sun and the stars. She shares everything she makes, and she takes incredible care of everything, whether it's the flowers in the garden or the animals in the stalls. She is the life of our family, and I hope she lives forever. If I were to lose her one day, I don't know what I would do. Mom has been the leader of our family for as long as I can remember, with rules for us boys, my sister Marianna, and my sister-in-law Lena. Sundays are especially important to her; she calls it God's Day, and she believes in having church and family together, with lunch in the early afternoon. She feels it's important to have everyone together for the Sunday meal.

We also have other commitments on Sundays for the family; the animals in the stalls need attention. In the mornings, it's the guys, and at night, it's the women. I'll never forget one Sunday morning when, after we finished cleaning the stalls and were returning to the house, I noticed a bee's nest outside the toilet shed near the corner of the small shed. I called my dad over because I don't like bees; I've been stung by them many times in the countryside. He came to look at it and said not to worry; they would leave soon as they couldn't stay there long, or they would freeze to death. For some reason, he left it there, but I said to him, "Why leave them here? They're a danger to everyone." I clean that toilet every day because of Mom; otherwise, I would leave it uncleaned for a month. No one helps me with it, but they all like to use a clean toilet. I call my brothers lucky skunks because Dad always reminds me, like a broken record, to clean the toilet box every day, otherwise he would do it himself.

Since my brothers left, I've been tasked with the dirtiest work. None of them like to clean the stables or washrooms, not even Mom, my sister Marianna, or my sisters-in-law. Being the youngest, I'm treated like a little puppy, and it bothers me. For one reason or another, I've become the slave of the united Nocci family. Many times, I've talked to Mom about it, but she never agrees with me; she always tries to protect everyone, prioritizing the family's unity. Keeping a big family together isn't easy for Mom, but she always maintains peace regardless of the situation. She tells me not to worry because one day someone else will take my place, as if I'm stupid.

Lately, Federico and I have been worried about Dad's health. Our family doctor comes so often, and we're not sure why. It's possible his heart isn't doing well, or Mom isn't either. After my brothers left, Marianna, Lena, Federico, and I mostly worked in the fields together, like donkeys, to keep up with the farm work. I often joke with Mom, saying, "Mother, if I join the partisans, how will you manage without me?" She starts laughing and tells me not to worry, but I tell her she'll see. Sometimes, I've considered running away from home and becoming a monk in Chieti. But leaving everything behind and becoming someone else's slave isn't for me. There are many options, but I don't know how I'd manage without my brothers, especially without Mom. My family means everything to me, and without them, I'd be like a fish out of water. Running away from home is impossible. Since my brothers left, our workload has doubled. We're out there from sunrise to sunset, committed to our farm. Unless it's a special holiday or a rainy day, we work from dawn to dusk, with no other choice.

As far back as I can remember, Dad always finds work for us, rain or shine. There's always something to do around the house, warehouse, barn, or stables. Christmas is coming soon, and I suggested to Dad that we take a couple of days off. But he said no, and we're going down to the field instead. Federico and I requested about a week off, but Dad insisted. Early in the morning, we left, saying we had a messy job to do: cleaning up a small reedbed area to create a passage from one side of the reedbeds to the opposite side. This place is like a miniature bush down the hill, leading to the vegetable land, with a strip of reedbed before the creek. I don't like going in there during summertime because it's always full of snakes. Dad wants to create a track to go through it, making it easier to walk through the bush. He says it will be beneficial for many reasons, including saving chopsticks for tomatoes, cucumbers, cherry tomatoes, and more while also providing a faster passage to the vegetable field.

On Christmas Eve in 1939, it was getting late as Federico and I made our way back home from the field. We decided to take the fountain road, hoping to find Marianna and my sister-in-law Lena there, perhaps doing some last-minute washing before Christmas. Sure enough, they were there, but it was almost dark. We helped them bring the wet clothes home, where Mom was preparing dinner for everyone. Without my two brothers, things just weren't the same. After dinner, everyone dispersed; Lena went to the room with the baby, and Mom and Dad went to bed early. Only Marianna and I stayed up a little later, playing cards for a bit. Christmas without my two brothers felt empty, and I couldn't help but wonder how they were doing. My mom would always say, "Only God knows." I'd do anything to know if they were okay, to find out where they were and what they were doing. Most importantly, when they returned home, I hoped they'd share every detail of their experiences with me, which I would diligently record in my notebook. I longed for the day when they could celebrate Christmas like everyone else. God bless my brothers.

As a farm boy, I have ambitions and dreams swirling in my mind. One day, I'll bring them all to fruition. I don't mind hard work, but I refuse to live the same life as my parents and brothers. They work tirelessly on the farm from early morning until late at night, without much reward. One day, I'll have my own family, away from farming. I envision having my own place, living life on my own terms. I want more from life—personal possessions like an accordion, a bicycle, a big kitchen with a wood stove, and many other things my mom never had. I want to provide the best for myself and my future family, maybe even having ten children. I look forward to achieving my dreams one day. I often tell my mom that farmers are like Roman slaves; we're born slaves and die like slaves. It's a tough life, working like a donkey without much reward. I refuse to farm for the rest of my life. As soon as I have the chance, I'll seize a new job opportunity. My brother Pietro did it, and he's happy. Why shouldn't I? I'll even consider going back to school if it's possible after this war is over. I want to do something different. Right now, my family needs me, and I want to help them. I refuse to serve our landlords for the rest of my life; they only care about profit, nothing else. Peasants who work on other people's land never have a chance to secure a better future. We're all conditioned the same way, regardless of whether we occupy a landlord's house or just work the land. Property owners always impose rules on us, sometimes reasonable ones that contribute to a better lifestyle or help with purchasing new farm tools or seeds when needed. But it's just another way to push us to work harder for a better return at the end of the year. With my brothers at war, our strength is diminishing, and everything becomes more difficult. I hope that one day, all of this will have meaning in our lives. I love chatting with my parents about our landlords, and Dad needs to speak up more.

I'm confident that this spring they will come around to discuss the full-year program, which will be the best time to speak up. Regardless of what happens, I'll be there with them. As farmers, we deserve some respect, and I'm sure we have rights. Sometimes, Dad overhears me talking to myself, telling me not to worry. Our landlord for the last few years, has always complained; they just want more from us. Dad always tells me to stop paying attention to it, insisting that they're not that bad. He believes landlords always have something to say to their peasants, and in the end, we need them more than they need us. Dad might be right, but this seems to happen every year, usually between August and October, during the big harvest production—whether it's winery or olive time. Unfortunately, we always do our best, but working on the farm accumulates stress and aggravation. When the results don't come, our family struggles or suffers because of a bad harvest. It feels like our fate is in God's hands to get a good result. To me, everything seems fine, considering the amount of work we put in. Mom and Dad, at their age, can't give more than two hundred percent.

Dad's health hasn't been so good lately, and we all worry about him. His physical condition, including his heart, is unstable. Federico and I sacrifice a lot to take some work off Mom and Dad's hands. Sometimes, we ask for help from our married siblings to lend us a hand, especially during major harvests. All other work we handle by ourselves. We have two landlords: the first one owns our house and the land, and the second one only owns the land. One of them is very flexible with us and keeps his own rules, while the other, where we live, is cruel. I call him Mr. Vampire, a bloodsucker. There's no mercy for us farmers. What makes me laugh is the things they demand. They act as if they're doing us a favor. I wonder, without the peasants, who will work their land or do everything for them? When he says, "Nicoletta, potrei avere della verdure fresche?" (Nicoletta, could I have some fresh vegetables?), my mom goes and picks up what he wants, regardless of whether it's cold, raining, or hot outside. They demand a lot from us.

This Christmas holiday has brought many surprises: my brothers are gone, my parents aren't well, and the farm work is getting heavier. With so much work to be done, we know Mom will recover fast, but we're more worried about Dad. Without him, our farm is lost. Working in the fields isn't easy. Tending to the ground where the vegetables go cleaning weeds all over the farm—

whether in the vineyards, wheat fields, or olive groves—takes up so much time. Sometimes, it takes days, especially when we're working in the olive area, where we can't use a tractor or our cows will do the job for us.

We clean up olive tree branches and vineyards, not to mention the weeds that grow without invitation in the soil. Keeping the weeds down requires a lot of energy and time. Vineyards and vegetable plots require more attention, needing care all year round. Fortunately, we have many tools to cultivate our fields, such as vineyards, vegetables, and olives, as well as to sow wheat. One of these tools is a smaller hand pump used to spray special water on seedlings. We use a product to sterilize the water, which we call "water copper" in our dialect. Then we fill the small hand pump, which has a 20-liter tank carried on the shoulder like a sack. Spraying it on the seedlings is incredibly stressful work, but it's essential. It protects the fruit flowers when they bloom from natural diseases or insect bites, ensuring our products don't spoil. It's our way of safeguarding the crops from natural leaf diseases.

This morning, as I walked down to the farm pit, I wanted to talk to my dad and Federico about Mom. They were happy to see me at the field, as usual. I whispered to Dad, "Hey Luigi, what's up? What are you working on?" With his big voice, he said, "Today, we'll start preparing the land for spring veggies." I didn't see my brother Federico or Lena. I asked Dad where they were and why he was alone. Dad, who doesn't talk much, simply said, "They're helping the Falco family today." I pretended I hadn't heard him and asked again who they were helping. He looked at me and said,

"Don't worry," as he continued working the soil for our vegetables with the hoe, side by side.

Finally, I found an opportunity to open a conversation about Mom. I told Dad that Mom hasn't been well these days. He said, "Do not worry too much; she's tired and needs a little rest." I didn't want to answer him back, pretending everything was fine. He looked at me and said, "Toto, are you okay, son?" I replied, "Yes and no. We need to talk about Mom." So, he stopped for a minute and asked, "What is it, son?" He always calls Mom "Nicoletta." I said, "Nicoletta, since Joe and Mimi left, she's not well. This morning, looking into Mom's eyes, she seemed very tired. She's aged so fast lately. She's not the same anymore, and I'm very worried about it. It's not just tiredness; I also think since Joe and Mimi left, she's not accepting the idea that her kids are gone for now. We're in a tough situation here, and she's worried too much about it. Mom has been depressed for one reason or another since Dad hasn't been well, and my brothers are gone. She always seems to be morally down. I told Dad that if she continues like this, she needs to see our family doctor."

After talking with Dad about Mom's situation, we decided to keep her away from any work commitments for a little while. We'll worry about the stables where our occupants are. We'll let her rest for a few more days; possibly, she will get better.

Later in the day, on my way home, I saw one of our neighbors, a family friend, Zio Tommaso. He's an old friend of Dad's, and we call him Zio Tom sometimes. Dad and Tommaso have known each other for a long time, since childhood. They are from the same neighborhood before moving here. So, we walked together up the hills, chatting about this war. He only said two words: "God forgive us." He believes this war is unnecessary and will kill farmers' economies. He reminded me that during the previous war, we suffered so much, and we didn't need another one. Zio Tom said, "Toto, remember, this war will take away food from our mouths to support the army and this stupid war. I'm sure the next harvests will not be divided equally anymore. There is a possibility the landlords will ask for additional support. We'll need to share all farmers supporting this war. Since this new war started, there's been new gossip from our government. We'll be restricted to a limited food supply that we're allowed to keep at home. This has happened before in the twenties and thirties. We're slaves of the system, which isn't everything, son. Believe me; this war will go far away." I said to Zio, "No one has come so far," and then he said, "Lucky us. Keep your eyes open and start hiding your supplies from your warehouse. Don't keep the storage full."

After Zio Tom left, I started talking to myself as usual, thinking if we needed to give out all our harvest products, we'd be better off not working in the countryside field. I'll talk it over with my parents later. As soon as I got home, just before dinner, I stopped by the stable to check if anything needed to be done. I didn't need to look after the animals; everything had already been taken care of. As I walked up to the kitchen, I saw Mom preparing dinner. With a soft voice, I said, "Hey Nicoletta, how about a fresh coffee?" She always corrects me, saying, "I am your mom, not Nicoletta." I replied, "So what, Mom? I call you Nicoletta because that's your name, right?" She said, "Of course," giving me a dirty look, and said, "Hey, you never contradict your mom, understood?" Later, we continued that conversation. I said, "Okay, do you want to tell me more about yourself, Nicoletta?" She threw a large wooden spoon at me, but I was laughing at her, saying, "You're crazy, Mom." Playing with Mom always brings me joy. Afterward, I went outside to do some things around the house. She had already prepared the table for dinner, so I knew it would be ready soon. Normally, we eat at seven in the wintertime, sometimes later in the summertime, depending on when everyone gets back home from the farm. After I came back in, I could see she looked very tired. I said, "Okay, Mom, here's a coffee for you. It will give you some energy. Sit down for a few minutes and enjoy." She said, "No, soon we need to eat." I insisted, "Mom, I made this coffee for you! Have some before dinner." Finally, she said, "Okay," and asked me to see if everyone was ready for dinner. I went and looked for Dad, Marianna, and Lena; they were cleaning up inside the warehouse. It was almost dark, and I asked, "How long will you guys take?" Dad replied, "Not too long."

After I returned to the house, everything was ready for dinner. Mom was sitting near the fireplace in the kitchen. I told Mom that Dad would be half an hour before they were done. Since my brothers left for the war, Mom never smiled. Today, for the first time, she looked relaxed for once. So, she said, "Come and sit next to me." She sat on the wooden bench we kept around the table for lunch and dinner time. Normally, we use wooden benches or homemade chairs; Dad built all of them. So, she sat next to me and whispered to me, "I love all my children, you a little less." I replied, "Thanks, Mom. Always you need to hurt my feelings, it looks like you enjoy doing that, right, Mom?" In one way or another, she laughed. I was happy to see her laughing. Then she said, "You know why? Because you are a naughty boy. And I hope to spend the rest of my days together with you, Toto." She continued, "I do have a little secret to tell you." Looking into her eyes, almost crying tears of joy, I said to myself, "I hope it's something good, something special." I was anxious to hear Mom's secrets, so I said, "Okay, Mom, tell me." She said, "My name is not Nicoletta. My real name is Maria Nicole, two names. But don't worry, you can keep calling me Mamma Nicoletta."

After revealing her Christian name to me, she said that's the name she was baptized with by her mom and dad. I asked Mom the reason for the two names. She said, "I was born in Brooklyn, New York, in America. We came back home when I was two, and since then, everyone started calling me Nicoletta. So, here I am, Nicoletta." I continued asking Mom a bunch of questions about her childhood life. She said, "I don't remember anything from my childhood, nothing. I just wanted you to know a little about Mom. I hope one day you remember that you had an American mom." We had an enjoyable conversation, and she mentioned having an older sister, though she didn't talk much about her. She said she was happy to be married to Dad, as her life before meeting Dad wasn't great. I asked her why her name was Nicoletta and not Maria Nicole. She explained to me that Nicoletta was more traditional for an Italian name, and everyone started calling her Nicoletta. They said Maria Nicole was more for a boy. We stopped talking about our family as everyone came back in for dinner, but our conversation was never finished. I'll ask another time.

I said to myself, "She was born in America. We can go there anytime. New life, big city, a lot of money." Then I said, "Reality is different." In the following days, we continued our conversation for hours. One day, I asked Mom if I could go to America. She said, "Possible." After that, she looked at me and said, "My parents didn't do so well there." Continuing our American conversation, she said, "I married your dad when I was twenty. Your father was a new life for me. I was twenty-two when I had Leonora and after that, Pietro. After that, I was expecting Joe, and your dad left for the war, leaving me with two small children and one on the way. Being alone with two small kids wasn't easy, and I was afraid. Life was miserable, and there wasn't much help. The only people who were there to help me out were your dad's family. I was expecting Joe, and with all the work at the farm to be done, it wasn't easy. Thanking God, he came back home after over three years. Joe was almost three years old, and we enjoyed his return. We were so happy to hug him, even though he was unrecognizable from the war. He was destroyed, and many times, I asked about his life during the war and how difficult it was for him. He never talked about it with me or us, but I hope one day he will tell us a little about his years in the war." I said to Mom, "Sometimes people don't like to remember tough times in life. So let it be, Mom. I'm sure one day he will say something to us, a little more communication or about the life he's been through, other concerns in life, and how he dealt with them, day-to-day life, what it's all about." We know he's suffering not to tell his life story. I said to Mom, "I'd love to hear many things about you guys, and your life together. We're here talking about him today. We'd love to know what he did all his life since he was a child. I'd like to know more about our family. I never met my grandfather Antonio or my grandmother Anna Domenica. I don't remember anything about them. They say he was a hard man to deal with, a cruel guy, like Dad, so they say."

Sometimes, Dad seems like a mute or a reticent person to me. We make a big mistake not talking about it. My feeling is people should talk to someone about it, not keep everything inside. Talking to others helps unload the anger inside you. In the end, it's better to say what you are thinking. Holding everything for yourself is not a clever idea. I slept in; I've been so tired lately, rushing to my daily commitments. I saw Mamma Nicoletta feeding the chickens. She was leaning down. I ran to her, and she went down on her knees. I got scared and asked Mom what the problem was. She said, "Nothing, just my head turned." I helped her to the house, and she sat next to the big fireplace. I made her a coffee and said, "Hope you'll be okay, Mom." I said to myself, "New Year, without Joe and Mimi, the house feels empty."

In the middle of the week in January 1940, I heard a motorcycle driving into our house from the opposite side. We call it "La Fonte Di Pizza," a sharp road from the main provincial road connecting to Chieti, our province. Soon, he got to our house, and I was curious to know who it could be. It turned out to be a carabiniere with a motorcycle, a good-looking one. It was very strange; I had never seen him before because it had been a few months since my brothers Mimi and Joe left. I wondered what he was looking for and asked him. He said he wasn't lost. So, I asked, "Who are you looking for?" He said, "Your father." I replied straightforwardly, "He's not here." I asked the brigadier what it was all about and why he needed Dad. He looked at me and said, "We have a notification for the family." I asked, "You want to give it to me? I'll make sure he gets your notes." He looked in his pouch and started searching, saying, "Sorry, it's possible I left it at the caserma." I asked what the notes were all about, and he explained that there was a telegram saying Nocci Domenico was coming home due to a bad illness. So, he left without saying anything further. I was upset; I didn't know an officer would come here telling us about my brother coming back sick without any proof or a piece of paper.

After he left, I said to myself, "This guy must be a fool, coming here and telling us that. I hope he's wrong about my brother." Mom wanted to know who it was. I said nothing, "Mom, they got the wrong house." I didn't want to tell her anything about it; she was wondering who was sick, as she still wasn't feeling good. So, I didn't tell her anything.

On a daily basis, after I finished my morning routine around the house, I rushed down to the field where everyone was. Today, I saw my father at the pit, but my brother Federico and Lena were not there. Approaching my dad, I thought to myself, "I wonder if this is good news or sad news about Mimi coming back. He must be extremely sick if he's coming back, or if the carabinieri are wrong. Otherwise, they would not send him back."

After talking to my dad about Mimi coming back, everyone was concerned about it. A few days went by since the carabinieri officer came to the house, and we were on edge about Mimi. Sometimes I asked myself if there was no better way to inform a family of such important things. I do understand that sometimes things happen, especially during wartime, but there's no respect for families. The carabinieri sometimes act like they have no proper education. Here, we have a saying: "Carabinieri walk in pairs to correct each other's actions." Unfortunately, there was little said about this guy. Sometimes all sayings must have a reason. In the meantime, there was still no sign of Mimi.

Soon, spring was coming up, and for farmers, it was most important for my parents to focus on planting vegetables, with no time for anything else. My mind always kept going to my brothers who were away. I would love to know where they are these days. We were busy working on the farm. Dad's health had been on and off, and he had been coming to the field less lately due to his condition. For the last few months, we understood that his health was not incredibly good, so we should not depend on him too much these days. We also looked forward to seeing Mimi home soon. Federico and I were focusing on farm work, preparing the soil for spring seeding. At the same time, Mom was informed by Dad about Mimi coming back home. Mom worried about him, asking every day when he would be back. She was already very worried about our father's health, and now with Mimi too, she would surely suffer more. Many times, she cried because of Dad's condition. Lately, we hardly saw him in the countryside, only occasionally, as his heart would not permit farm work. Mom did not like to talk about it, but we knew he was not well. Unless there was a mistake by the caserma, I did not believe so. The officer pronounced the name correctly. Unfortunately, we could only wait for further notice. If he was not coming home, either he had gotten worse, or he was getting better.

Federico and I worked hard these days without anyone's help. There was no news about Mimi. I wanted to go into town to talk about it with the marshal, as we knew him well at the carabinieri office, and he would help us out. This way, we would know what was happening with our brother. Going to town was about a forty-five-minute to one-hour walk from our farm. Provided my parents agreed, tomorrow I would take a walk to see if there was any news. I did not sleep all night. Mimi, Federico, and I shared the room together, and Mimi's spot had been empty. Federico sometimes came and slept next to me since Mimi was gone. We always joked about how he liked our bed because it was double-sized, built in a box with wooden flat sticks and a large mattress stuffed with sheep's wool. His mattress sat on the ground, stuffed with corn leaves. I did not like it when someone came and slept in Mimi's place. Sometimes my cousin came over, and we all slept together in a small bed. I was a little jealous, so Federico came and slept in Mimi's place. He joked that he would beat me up someday. I told him to give it his best shot. We always fought, and he kept saying he would beat me up, and I would remember it forever. Federico was older than me and stronger. He was the strongest of all my brothers. Federico took after Dad, a big boy with a strong build. All my brothers were big boys except Pietro. We were all tall, at least 1.75 meters and up. Even my two sisters were quite tall. Sometimes I wondered where Pietro came from. I should ask Mom if Pietro was her son or if they found him in the river. He was the shortest of all of us. His face was three hundred percent like Joe's. If he were the same age, they would be twins. But he was not afraid of anyone or anything. For some reason, he was like a wild animal. No fly would go near his nose. On top of everything, Pietro would beat anyone alive. He was the kind of guy you didn't want to mess with. Federico was a typical Dad, with a strong personality. He did not let anything slide, regardless of who you were.

This morning, I told Mom I would go to town to the military camp. There was an Italian camp just before the town. After that, I would go to the Carabinieri office to see if there was any news about Mimi.

Going down to the main road, I came across Josie, Mimi's girlfriend. I was surprised to see her going somewhere, so I chatted with her for a little while. Then I asked where she was going. She said, "I am going to see your mom." Walking away, I met a family friend, and we started a little conversation about my brother coming back anytime. He was surprised about it. Normally, they do not give any notice to the families unless he's dead. This guy was in the military, so possibly he knew about it. I asked him more questions. Giovanni, who lives near the military camp, was part of the finance military. Then he returned, not in good health, possibly like my dad. After chatting with Giovanni about the Red Cross, he said if someone gets hurt or sick in the army, they are not sent home that easily, especially when you are in the war. He said to go home and stop looking for him. Mom is depressed these days. I do have a main concern about her. Possibly she's tired these days because Dad's health is getting worse. Normally, she never complains.

It's the seeding time at the farm. Mom, Marianna, and Lena are helping with it. Unfortunately, the weather is not helping so far. We need to take advantage of any good day from now on as they come. I asked Federico to go for a short walk with an excuse, without the lady can ear me. I asked Federico about Mimi coming back home. Giovanni, our neighbor, told me they do not notify anyone unless it's his death. Federico said to me, "I told you it was a wasted trip going to the town, so let it be. We will wait for it."

Since Mom is not well, Federico and I do extra hours. We hope she soon regains her strength for housework and helping us in the field, including with the animals in the barn. Normally, Dad always helps out, but now he's not well. Only Mom has everything on her shoulders. I had coffee with Mom this morning. She was happy. She never talks much. She looked at me and said, "All good, son." I said, "Yes, Mom." I wanted to see Luigi before I left for the field. I asked if everything was good. He said, "I do not know. I have a feeling this time I will not make it." I comforted him, saying, "You are a strong man. As usual, you will come out, Dad." After chatting with my father, I realized that he was sick. I walked out with tears in my eyes. I am worried about him, a big concern about both Mom and Dad. "Lord, why all this? Dad has been suffering for so long. I hope God helps us out..." I just left Mom little to do, giving her a few more days to catch up with her physical condition. I asked my brother Federico to help me out sometime at the stall until Mom was ready. He always ruffles with me, saying, "You do extra time at the house, we do extra time at the field."

The farm needs more manpower. We'll see where we can get more help. Arguing with my brother is a waste of time. Today was another exhausting day. I am on my way back home without helping Federico pick up tools or anything in the field. I saw Josie never left from our house, spending time with Mom. She is a good woman. She stayed around helping Mom at the house, sharing the load with my sister Marianna. She has been here for almost a week now. Josie gets along with Mom. She comes only because Mimi is not here; otherwise, she would not be here. I am sure her sister would never permit her to come or stay here if my brother was home. We have different mentalities in central Italy. People are a little different from northern Italy. We have a smudged mentality here, no freedom to marry who you like. Sometimes weddings get fixed without meeting each other. So, what will you pretend later? Not all the time works! Life will become a nightmare, with marriages prepared by others. In Abruzzo, we have a saying, "Donne e buoi, dei villaggi tuoi." Women and oxen of your own villages.

Lately, Dad's health has become increasingly critical. He's not well. His doctor came to see him two times in the last month. The last time was on Sunday, later in the day, when Doctor Cicca came to see him. I like this guy. He comes with a horsey bike to our house, which takes a good half hour to get here from his studio. Visiting Dad so often makes us happy, and we appreciate his services. His fee is reasonable. Since Dad's not doing well, he's been coming for years, at least two times a year, since I remember. He talks to Mom about his condition. This morning, our landlord came by to visit him. It has been a few days since he's been to the farm.

He's up and down from the bed. He is very weak. We can see Dad's life slipping away day by day. Dad is only fifty-five. He's a young man. I hope he will pull through this time. Dad hasn't been well for years. His heart is very weak. Our mother always says that since he came back from the war, he has never recovered. Since we got Mimi's news a few days later, my brother and I talked about it, or so our father's condition. He has been critical the last couple of weeks. What will happen if we lose him at the field? It will be a big problem. All the land we loaned, too much to worry about. Working hard at the farm, the two of us, then it will be impossible to keep up with it. Federico is always positive. We can manage the farm without Dad or other help. He's like a bull. He does work for three men. For him, farming is eating a piece of cake. I wonder sometimes where he gets so much energy. I am weak compared to Federico. Everyone says I need to eat more. Sometimes they make me laugh. The only meat we have is chicken and sometimes a rabbit, only on special days if we are lucky or major holidays.

Franz stopped by this morning after hearing about Dad being sick. He sat with me and Federico, saying, "Your dad's not doing well these days. We know it's been a few years since he's been like this. I want you guys to know, possibly this time he will not pull out from this." We looked at him, squaring. "What you think we're not aware of it? If Dad's dying, we need to be strong and manage this farm until Joe and Mimi are back."

Walking back home with Franz, we chatted about Dad's health. He said to be ready for the worst. I do not know how we will get by without Dad in the field. If something happens to our father, then it is a problem. Federico and I, we are still young boys. We do have little experience on the farm. Certainly, we will have problems. There is one person we can count on: Uncle Tommaso.

Winter 1940s. Lena and Marianna prepared dinner for everyone. Mom asked about Mimi again if there was any news. Since my brothers left, we have no news. So, Federico went and hugged her, saying, "We all want to know where they are. We need to be strong and wait, Mom. As soon as we know anything, you will know about it." It has been days since we heard the first time from our deputy about Mimi coming back home. Then, seems he has disappeared into thin air, into the void. Sometimes, I speak to myself, saying it cannot be someone who will disappear from nothingness. Seems my brother vanished.

The next day, we received a visit from our family doctor to see Dad's condition. We asked if he could look at Mom since she was not feeling well. The doctor reassured us that she was okay, only tired, and everything else was okay. Lately, Mom always stayed near Dad, lying in bed next to him. So, we kept her away from the stables, from any heavy work, only staying in the house. Soon, she will be back to her normal routine. I am sure Mom never gives up on anything. We know housework, stables, washing clothes, and everything else is on her.

Since the last time the doctor came to see Dad, no change, the same conditions in the last few weeks. Hope he will get better soon. We are missing him in the field or around the house. Has been a little time since we thought Mimi would come home. Today, no news. Hope for the best. I don't like waiting so long without a telegram or a note from local authorities. Who knows when he will arrive. Mom is desperate, asking every day for him or Dad to die. Only God can tell us what is happening. I am not sure what is happening to our family. The world falls on us lately, a load of stone on our shoulders. These days no anyone can take it out. With Joe and Mimi gone, we do not know if they are alive or dead. Possibly, our older brother Pietro will need to go back to the army. Federico will soon be going for sure. God, we are desperate. I have been wondering, Lord, how all this is possible with so many people in the world always coming to bump into us. Since this war started, our family has come apart. God, forgive us for our sins. Mom prays to God every day, but it has served no purpose. Today, like yesterday, nothing changed. We do have faith in God. Federico and I are working in the field twelve hours a day to keep up with our farm work. With our cow, we are plowing land and seeding, including scratching the crust of the earth where weeds are.

February 4th, Carnival Day. Our village today celebrates the carnival. We do contribute to this FESTA on an annual basis. Every year, we participate in the big parade. We need to be cautious this day. There is an old story about the carnival, a giant man who scares people and children away. I do not believe in fairy tales. Unfortunately, sometimes, there is some truth about these old sayings. For me, it's another invention by man. Everything can be true. I say we are skipping if you do not experience something like that. It will be hard to believe this old story. I assume it's only a legend.

Celebrating carnival in our village, everyone enjoys it. This time of the year, we are extremely busy on the farm. With Dad in his condition, no celebration. Carnival Day, there is a saying, "Every joke counts," only a saying, but there are people who take advantage of this party. The way I see it, on Carnival Day, they do build an opportunity to steal or damage other people's properties or beat up someone. There are many reasons this carnival is dangerous to others. Most be careful on Carnival Day, especially nighttime. I remember not too long ago, I was in the second year of school, not too far from our farm. Someone blew out an old shack where people were working to build fireworks for New Year's Eve, or unique events, and other festivities. I say they were lucky. No one died, only a few people got injured. I did stop to pick up a couple of masks for me and my brother Federico. Soon I got home, I put one on, like Pulicinella, a famous phantom from Napoli. The fantasy of a man like Pulicinella can be something that becomes reality. I need to show my sister there is an enjoyable life out there. Almost I got beat by Marianna with a broomstick. Mom was laughing for the first time since my brothers left for war. I was glad I did that for her. Hope her heart stops bleeding for a minute. I strongly believe our heart is like a vessel or a tank bigger than the universe. It never fills up, only sometimes makes tantrums.

Chapter 3
Deaths in the family

After my jokes, I asked Mom what the family doctor said about Dad, whether he's getting better or worse. After that smile, she seemed revived again but remained silent, as if to say something without saying it explicitly, as if she wanted to convey that he wouldn't live long. She didn't say that, but I could read it in her eyes; he's not well.

Uncle Tom came by to see Dad. Many people have been stopping by lately to say hello to him, as if he would live longer. I'll never forget when Zio Tom said something good to me one day: "Being a peasant, you never get anywhere. If you want to get rich, you need to get involved with politics, people." I'm curious to know more about it. My first question will be how they will solve this mess of war. The only person I know who can advise me is Father Rocco, our parish priest. Possibly, he will be well informed. Our church priest, as far as I know, is part of the Catholic Party, a Catholic man who will certainly talk about his party. I need to ask my father after dinner; I will have a little conversation with him.

Getting into politics is good; we get to know a lot of people. It's good to know someone there. Possibly, they will send me back to school or get me involved in the world of politics. The more people I know, the better it will be. Considering what I learned from school, we have three major governing parties. The most well-known is the Catholic Party. The Catholics are the strongest political party. Then there is the Communist Party, very well known as the Communist Party of Italy, which was founded in 1921. They have been gaining strength lately. And then there is the National Fascist Party, which I will never be a part of. Talking about politics, for me, is an organized group of people who all plan their intentions to eat over poor people.

TUTTI MANGIONI, DA PALERMO A COMO.

An old Italian saying, "From Palermo to Como," refers to two cities, starting from Sicily and ending at the border of Switzerland. Palermo is in Sicily, and Como is at the border of Switzerland, so we say, "da Palermo a Como."

I hope one day I will join and be part of a political party. Possibly, I will do my part to serve farmers like us. People in politics are "MANGIONI," it's like a game. Because in the end, it's all political talk. They only worry about themselves, of course, that's in my opinion. I hope one day I can be part of these groups. If I do, I have my own ideas for it. As much as I care about other people, I will make sure everyone does it. All I know is in politics, you need to be smart. Convincing people is not easy; being a politician isn't easy.

I strongly believe my sister Marianna will do well in politics. The only problem is I've never heard of a woman in politics before.

In March 1940, I forgot all about politics. Dad needs a lot of attention lately, and we're all worried about him. Mom is very worried these days; it seems to be a major concern. After the last visit of the doctor, it's possible he will be back at the field soon. Federico and I don't believe it. We understood that it was bad, but we thought Mom was exaggerating. For a moment, everyone has been offering words of comfort to her, saying he will be okay and soon he will be back in the field. I do believe Dad is done working. We're happy just to see him around the house without pretending to come back to the field. Give him time, and you will see that he will recover.

I'll never forget a terrible dream; it was a haunted night. A long, exceptionally long nightmare. I thank God it's morning. I wonder what it was all about; I beat myself up with these stupid dreams. I want to be a normal person, like everyone else, without warnings, without knowing what is happening tomorrow. Having dreams like this drives me crazy. I'd be better off not knowing anything about what lies ahead. God, please stop crucifying me; give me an easy life, like everyone else.

Walking down the field together with Federico, I said to him, "What do you think about Dad's health? Are you as worried about his condition as I am? The last time he came to the field, or we were together, has been over a month now." Federico says, "I have a feeling Dad will not get well enough to come back and help us on the farm site." I never answered back; possibly he knows Dad more than I do. I'm full-time at the field, plowing dirt. Sometimes, by the end of the day, I look at us and laugh. We look like frightening sparrows with the dust we have on us. We become the color of the earth.

On a chilly, freezing day, we work until late at night. I'm wearing a heavy military jacket, given to me by my older brother Pietro when he was in the military. Lena, Federico, and I are finishing seedings, or I should say sowing lettuce, tomatoes, and chicory. That way, by the end of March, it will be ready. We transplant them and get them ready for the second schedule until they are ready for planting in the ground. We have a small greenhouse where we sow everything before transplanting. Possibly, we need a larger area to give them time to grow more. Then, we transfer them to the ground four to six weeks from now. We got home, death tired, without dinner, and I went straight to bed.

Overnight, a new dream. This time, I remember it. I don't know what this dream was all about. I just hope it does not affect my family. I've had other dreams before, but never like this one. Such a bad one. Federico wakes me up, calling my name. I didn't even hear him talking; my mind was so far away from everything. After I wake up, I ask Federico, "I will be late going to the farm; I need to talk to Mom about this dream."

Later in the morning, March 12, I tell Mom all about my dreams. She asks me to explain it to her in a better way. I tell her, "I'm climbing a mountain with Dad. I'm ahead of him, and he's losing ground following behind, away from me, remaining at a distance to the fairway. I asked if he needed help; we were on a steep mount, not easy to climb, with a big escarpment below us, like a big cliff. At that point, I stopped; I wanted him to catch up with me. It was difficult to go back. Suddenly, I slipped into the void, clinging to my rope. I regained control, so I wanted to help him. For some reason, I cannot reach him. I start to turn around, going back to help him out. He keeps going further down. I was screaming, 'Dad, stop! Please let me help you out!' There was no way I could get to him. He was looking at me, saying, 'Don't worry about me; you go on. Make sure you get to the top.' Dad was greeting me, saying, 'Make it to the top, okay?' A big cloud passed through, covering the view of his face. After that, no sign of Dad. I was screaming my lungs out, 'Dad, where are you?' He disappeared into the void, and thin air cleaned up the clouds slowly." Federico woke me up; I was crying. Federico asked me if I was okay. I said it was nothing, just a bad dream. I didn't know what to do. Mom asks me to be careful. She doesn't know. Mom pats my head, saying, "It's just a dream. Don't worry about Dad. The last couple of days, he walks around the house a little. Or so he went to the stable to see our occupant. You better get going to the countryside and help your brother."

After chatting with Mom, I need to move on; today we have so much to do. I wanted to tell Mom all about my dream, but she repeatedly said not to worry and not to pay attention to dreams. Then she said a sentence that stuck in my head: "Dreams are like ideas; they come and go for no reason." Before I left, I went to see Dad. After chatting with Mom for a while, she says, "I do not believe in dreams, son, but just be careful today out there, OKAY."

On March 12, 1940, the dream I had didn't make sense. I don't know what to think about it. I do believe in my dreams, but unfortunately, this one doesn't sit well with me. Something might happen, I hope not to my family. My first thought was Mimi or Dad. I remember other dreams, all of which came true. Sometimes knowing what can happen in the future is not good. Life needs to be normal without knowing ahead of time.

Federico and I were working at the farm when Tommaso came and called us up. Jokingly, we said, "Hey, uncle, what brings you here today? No land to be plowed?" He had a dull face, as if someone died. A bad expression on his face made me think of last night's dream. With a faint voice, almost crying, he said, "You guys need to go home now." Federico asked him what happened, but Zio didn't say anything. "Your dad's not well," he said. Federico wanted to call the doctor, but he said, "No, just go home, boys." With so many bad dreams I've been having these days, I knew something would happen.

I ran like a crazy person. I knew something had happened to Dad. Running down the field without stopping, possibly for a kilometer or two, someone stopped me. I had never seen her before. A lady dressed in black asked, "Where are you going with all that haste?" I looked at her, but she never answered me. The only thing she said was, "Crying doesn't take away the pain," before slowly walking away. I needed to go, so I walked slowly home, knowing something had happened to Dad.

Soon I got there, and I heard Mom, Lena, and Marianna crying. Franz and Federico were there too, saying, "We knew he had been sick for a long time." I, the youngest of the children, had no words. Mom hugged me, saying, "Papa is gone." I asked Mom what happened; he was much better yesterday. He wanted to go to Ponte Zelis this morning, so we walked a little. He started collapsing; hardly we made it back. I called for help, but no one was around. Franz happened to come here; he helped me lay him down on his bed. After a few minutes, he stopped breathing. Mom felt so guilty; she had no words to say. I looked at everyone's faces;

Franz was the only person talking, encouraging us like nothing happened here. Dad was gone, now lying in the room. How he died, possibly a heart attack or a collapse, to die like this is impossible. What I didn't realize was that yesterday he was better. Now he's gone. No one said anything; the only thing I could see was everyone crying.

I walked outside; it was late at night. Without saying anything, I screamed again and again, like a crazy person, talking to God. He's crucifying us in many ways. I walked to the stables, remaining there for a while. When I heard someone calling me, "Toto, where are you?" It was Zio Tommaso looking for me. He sat next to me; I said, "Go home, it's late." He said, "It's almost midnight; you need to get some sleep. Tomorrow will be a big day; you need to be strong. Tomorrow, we will do your dad's funeral. I know how close you were to your dad; he was my best friend. Unfortunately, he's gone; no one can bring him back."

After the funeral, the whole family supported Mom. Franz was close to Mom; he was close to the family. He organized the funeral for my father, including cemetery arrangements. For some reason or another, he never said anything about why Dad always went to their house that morning. It was very strange that Dad, in his condition, walked all the way to Ponte Zelis. Why did he need to go to Leonora so far away? Thank God he made it back here. He had done it many times before, but lately, he was not in the condition to walk so long.

Nocci Luigi,, Death certificate

March 12, 1940's

After Dad's funeral, the whole family came back home, with so much silence in the house, everyone around Mom. Lena prepared something to eat for everyone. There were also Pietro, Nuccia, and children, including Franz, Leonora, and children. The oldest among them was Leonora's firstborn; she was ten years old, a little younger than me. All the others were younger kids. Dad's funeral was without Joe and Mimi. Unfortunately, no one knows where they are. They were the only ones missing at the funeral. After the funeral, we took a couple of days off, spending time with Mom, as is customary after someone in the family dies.

In the meantime, we never got any news about Mimi. Mom kept asking every day when Mimi would come home. Federico and I were close to her, a big comfort, saying, "Do not worry, Mom, soon he will be home." A couple of weeks went by since Dad died. While working at the farm, we wondered what happened to Mimi, who never came home. Mom kept asking about him, hoping he would be back soon. We did not know what to say to Mom anymore. Federico and I lied to Mom, saying he would be back soon. Since Dad passed away, we were all desperate about it. We needed to know what happened to him.

Early one morning, I visited the police station, talking to the marshal about Mimi, who never made it home since we received that verbal note. I asked, "Please, can someone help us find my brother?" The marshal had no words for me except to say, "I will let your mom know as soon as we find out where he is." The last time I looked for him, I lost hope. It had been too long since we thought Mimi would be back home. A few days later, I went back to the Carabinieri Office. There was no news about Mimi. The marshal told me he would personally come to see Mom if any news appeared. Mr. Santoro told me to go home; they would let us know if they heard anything. I would let Mom and Josie know, but there was no news as of today. Since we got news about Mimi, Josie kept coming to the house, asking about him and spending time with Mom. It was nice of her to come by and spend time with Mom.

Two weeks went by since the last time I was at the Carabinieri office. Federico and I were planting tomatoes in the ground when we spotted a Jeep car. We rushed home; it was Marshal Santoro. We hoped he had good news about Mimi. The marshal was having coffee with Mom. Federico said hello to him, and the marshal responded, "Hey, trouble." We knew there were some hard feelings between the two of them. Once Federico was taken to the Caserma for a quarrel in one of the local bars, just boys' skirmishes in town, nothing serious. The marshal never charged him. Federico said, "So nice to see you, boss." The marshal looked at both of us, whispering, "Boys, your brother, we don't have anything since the last telegram. We only know he was in Yugoslavia." After telling us he was coming home, there could be many reasons why he's not here. What happened to him, no one knows. We can only pray to God that one day he will be back. Federico and I continued pretending that Mimi was alive and would soon be home. At the same time, we worried about the farm. Federico was teaching me important things; I had no idea why he kept telling me what to do so urgently. I didn't know the reasons or why he wanted me to learn so quickly. I asked a few times, saying, "I am here; I will follow in your footsteps, brother. I don't need to learn so fast."

After the death of our father, Federico and I had a lot of pressure on us. Mom never recovered from the loss of Dad. Since he died and Mimi went missing, who knows what will happen next.

April is a rainy month, but so far, we have been lucky; the weather has been good. It gave us the chance to catch up with farm work. Normally, we need to make up for rainy days sometimes. After Dad passed away, we lost some valuable time, so we needed to work extra to catch up. Usually, the weather is bad around Easter time, but this time it has been okay. The most important thing is seeding, and that's been done. We have a festa coming up this weekend. I will ask Mom to go to the church with me in town. Next Sunday will be St. Liberata's day, and it would be nice if we go. Normally, St. Liberata is celebrated on May 1st, like Labor Day in Italy. St. Liberata's festivity is done on the Sunday closest to May 1st. If we go, I can ask the priest to say a mass for Mimi and Dad. The Lord will help us out. During dinner, I asked Mom if she wanted to go to mass on Sunday for St. Liberata's occasion. I am sure everyone agrees with me. Mom said no, she didn't want to go anywhere these days. I said to Federico, "Since Dad died, she has not left the house. Today is only Monday; we have a full week ahead of us to convince her. I am sure she will come." I will convince Mom one way or another. Going to mass with me will be good for her. I am the only one who jokes with everyone these days. No one says anything to bring the mood up in the house or to make Mom smile.

I said to my brother Federico, joking as always, "Mom loves me more than all of you put together. I'm so sure about that; it's natural for moms to favor the youngest. For one reason or another, I have that feeling." Federico just looked at me without saying anything. I figured he was not in the mood for a joke. "I wish I were older so I could contribute more to help the family," I continued chatting with him. "Do not forget, brother, I will be thirteen soon," I reminded him. "Who knows, maybe this time everyone will remember my birthday." "This time I will ask if they buy me the accordion," I added. "I was looking for it last year. Maybe this year they can afford one. Sooner or later, I will get one."

"We are halfway through the week, and Mom never said she would come to Mass on Sunday," I said to Federico. "I will remind her tonight. I am sure she will go. She loves going to church when she can." Federico looked at me and said, "You finished talking to yourself?" "You are breaking, do you know what?" I retorted. "I was talking to you, prick," he replied. "I am not talking to myself. You must smoke some weed, brother. You are worse than Dad sometimes."

"Telling me I talk to myself, we are continuing our work without saying anything," I continued. "For a little while after that, he says to me, 'Hey Toto, you are a stone heart, or so unscrupulous person. You think only for yourself.' I said, 'Just because I speak to myself alone?' Then I said, 'You are a deaf and dumb mole.'" My brother could read my mind, and then he said, "You are a little devil. Joe was right." I pretended I didn't hear him and continued talking, "Do you think Mom will go to church on Sunday?" Federico continued to ignore my conversation; something was bothering him.

It was late in the day, almost dark. I said to Federico, "We should go home; it's getting late. I'm tired, bro." He stopped, sat on the ground, and said, "Come close to me, brother. I need to talk to you about something." I was tired and wanted to go home, but I was also worried about my brother. I sat next to him and asked, "What is it, Federico?" He looked at me with a pensive expression, then said, "Toto, last time I walked Josie home, I was worried about her." I realized why he had been so annoying lately. He continued, "I hugged her and told her not to worry about Mimi; he will be okay and will soon be home." Then he added, "I joked that if Mimi doesn't marry you, I will." I told Federico that wasn't nice, but he explained, "I wanted to make her feel comfortable, saying he will be back soon and not to lose hope." Our family is going through a tough time. Dad is gone, Mimi's fate is uncertain, there's no news of Joe, and the farm requires a lot of attention. We're doing the impossible to keep up with the work in the fields.

After seeing Josie that day, I started worrying about her. If Mimi doesn't come back, she might do something stupid. I looked into my brother's eyes; he seemed worried about her too. I said to Federico, "I will ask her if she wants to go with me and Mom to church on Sunday. Maybe we can tell if she's okay. What do you say?" He replied, "Yes, I don't know what to say." It was a polite conversation. We walked back home, and Mom was waiting with dinner ready at the table. She seemed to be catching up a little overall.

On Friday morning, Mom and I were working in the stalls, looking after our occupants, when Marshal Santoro showed up. Without saying good morning, he said to my mom, "Nicoletta, come with me please." I asked if I could go with them, but he said no. They needed to go to the hospital in the province. After they left without saying anything more, I ran to the field where Federico, Lena, and Marianna were. I yelled to them, "Federico, Lena!" Federico asked, "What? Why are you yelling?" I replied, "We need to come home. The marshal picked up Mom to go somewhere." He asked, "Where?" I said, "I'm not sure, possibly to the hospital in Chieti. Don't worry about the marshal; he's a good guy. Maybe they went to see someone." But I was worried. It might be about Mimi. We sat back and waited all day for Mom. It felt like waiting for a year. In the late afternoon, Mom came home with tears in her eyes. We asked what happened, but Mom had no words for us. After a few minutes sitting on a chair, she whispered, "Mimi's come home. He's in the hospital." We asked how he was, but Mom said, "I do not know. They didn't want to say anything. Can we see him in the morning?" "No," she replied, "not yet. Maybe soon." We were all anxious to know how Mimi was doing, curious about his condition and when we could see him. Mom said they needed to assess his condition, possibly by Monday. They needed a couple of days before they could tell us anything.

I was relieved he was home. I was sure he would be okay. The night was long. Federico and I talked until later. After losing Dad, we were much closer. Our family had been suffering a lot lately. The weekend passed, and on Monday morning, while having a little bite and coffee, I said to myself, "God, you are so hard on us. Did we do anything wrong? Our life is so miserable. Why do you keep punishing us like this? Is it something to do with our family or with me, God? I do believe in you sometimes. I'm a simple boy;

I say things without thinking. This is me, God." Federico and Mom went to the hospital. I assumed they wanted to know more about Mimi. Lena, Marianna, and I waited all day for them to come back home. Late at night, when they finally returned, we received the shocking news: Mimi had died. My brother Mimi was gone. He was dead. I said, "Oh God, how can that be? Less than seven weeks, losing my dad and my brother in such a short time." Mom was desperate; she cried every day. Now, losing Mimi, she was beyond despair. Josie had come by a couple of times; she should have seen Mimi over the weekend. Now, with Mimi's death, everything happened so fast. We never had a chance to know what happened to Mimi.

Domenico Mimi Nocci

Died April 29th, 1940.

"Unknown illness"

After Dad and Mimi died, our family was destroyed. There was no more strength in our system. We felt useless, unable to say anything about anything. Mom had no more tears left. All of us in the family couldn't look at each other, otherwise, we'd start crying. There was nothing to say, only pain in the family. Mom just accepted life as it was. I never forgot what the marshal said before: "This is the war…" It wasn't fair. Life no longer had the purpose of moving forward. How could you lose a father and a brother in such a brief time? Lord, please let all this not be in vain. At least give us the strength to react. All these are disgraces. Protect us from any further misfortune.

Moving forward in life, in less than two months, Mom lost her husband and son. What else could happen next? The death of two family members in such a short time. Only God knows the suffering we have in our family. On Sunday, later in the afternoon, Josie came by again. Mom had talked to her so many times about Mimi. She's a good lady, a family person. I started crying myself, seeing her despair. She needs to move on. Mimi is dead; there is nothing else to say. Mom should close this conversation; it's over. BASTA. FINITO. That is the end of it.

I went out to the stables, my brother Federico explaining to Josie that we're all suffering these days; she's not the only one. Federico talked to Josie for a little while. It's wartime, the type of life we're in these days, without knowing what can or will happen tomorrow. Later in the day, Mom continued talking to Josie. After all, Josie was there with Mom. I said to her, "Move forward with your life." She started crying. Federico walked her out, talking to her for a couple more minutes. After that, we saw Federico come in, saying to Mom, "I will walk Josie home. After that, I will go and see Pietro. I might be late." Mom said, "Don't be late. I don't need to worry about you too." Since that day, Federico walks Josie home and visits her often. I just wonder why. I hope he does not fall in love with Josie. I do care about Federico falling in love with anyone, the only thing is he's much younger than her. I believe a couple of years for sure. I do not know; I will not say anything about it. It's not my business. I have the impression those two have feelings for each other. Falling in love, I just hope Federico does not do it because of Mimi.

Then, in later times, I was right. Federico is in love with Josie. He goes every weekend to see her. Mom never figured that out as of today. Since our big loss to our family, we have had no news about Joe. I hope he's okay. It's been almost a year since Joe left. We're in late summer, and we got help from Franz and Leonora at the farm since Dad died. Zio Tommaso helps out; he is here a lot of the time. Federico and I, with Mom and Lena, manage the farm work so far. Soon, we'll be done with the vineyard harvest, and we will take a couple of days off. I am writing a couple of notes. Firstly, last night, late in the evening, Federico said to Mom, "I need to talk to you." Federico had an almost red face.

He did not know where to start. He walked around the table like a crab in the kitchen. He did not say anything. Then he turned towards the door and spoke! "I am getting married." I looked at him and said, "What!!!" Federico had no words. Mom lost her voice; he completely lost his words. Federico repeated himself, saying, "I want to marry her." Mom remained there, without saying anything. I said to Mom, "Hey, Nicoletta, are you okay?" Without a word, no one said anything or imagined what was happening. I did. After Federico walked Josie home, I knew something was going around. Then I said, "I already knew." Mom shouted at me, saying, "You didn't tell me anything." Mom was upset with me, saying, "To me, you are un figlio di una mamma buona." She meant a son of a bitch to me, just a bad boy. Then she turned to Federico and said, "I am happy for you, son. Happy you, happy us." Mom did give Federico a remark, saying, "First thing you need to know about it before you commit yourself. But remember one thing, son, I am telling you that because you are a young man.

Getting married is a big step in your life. So, pay attention. Open your eyes wide and look! Because, that is not an object you can exchange tomorrow." After all that preaching from Mom to Federico, he did marry Josie. Federico's marriage was good for the family. It changed the spirit of the house, giving everyone a bit of joy. Since Federico got married, we had extra help. I was happy for him. The only thing bothering me was that Federico was so young.

Later in the fall, Federico received a military note that he needed to go to the army. We all worry about him. I was right; sooner or later, they will come for him. Federico asks for two weeks of grace, hoping to get a little time to help at the farm. Santoro, the Marshal, a family friend, managed to get a few weeks' delay. Anytime we need help, he's there. We are in the middle of the olive harvest, and we need him to help us finish this before he goes. Thanking God, we were granted two extra weeks with Federico helping at the farm. Federico is only nineteen years old, but he works for two people. Believe it or not, talking to God, I said, "Going to war at nineteen years old, what are the chances of survival out there? God, protect all of them from this nonsense war without knowing the reasons." Later that night, without saying much, I talked to him, saying, "Why don't you go to Celano, run away from here, and stay there until this war is over?" My brother was speechless for a couple of words. The answer was no, saying, "Our country needs us, so I will go. No one in our family before deserted; we need to serve our homeland. Since the family history, we never backed off; it's our obligation to serve our country, like our father did, or like our grandfather Antonio. Now it's our turn to serve and protect our land, so going to Celano is out of the question." Celano is almost at the border of Abruzzi and Lazio; a lot of refugees will go there to escape this war or other problems with the law. Dad had a little thought when Joe and Mimi were called to the army at that time. If he would have done it, today Mimi would still be alive. I feel useless with so much work to be done. Winter is coming soon, and I hope God will give us the strength to face this miserable life. Everyone was silent over the weekend, knowing that Federico was going away on Monday. Federico talked to Mom and Josie without saying anything to me. Regardless of the silence among us, it seems like someone else died.

Saturday, later in the afternoon, we were all at the farm working. It was too early to go home. I found an excuse to leave early. I said to them, "I will go home now. Mom was not great this morning; she might need help at the stables. Unless anyone else wants to go." Lena said, "You go, Toto. We'll stay a little longer at the field today until dark." Later in the evening after dinner, I sat next to Federico. I wanted him to smile. I gave him a solid punch in his stomach and said, "Hey, big brother, are you okay?" Federico and I quarrel sometimes, or we fight jokingly. He is closer to my age overall. My other brothers are older than Federico. Marianna is between the two of us. With my sister Marianna, we should joke. First of all, she doesn't take a joke. Another problem is she's rough with everyone. She's Picchia' forte; she will beat you up. Friday night, we will enjoy our brother for this weekend coming up for a couple more days. All my thoughts were about him, how he would survive at nineteen years old, going to war. God help and keep him and Joe alive.

After Federico left later in the week, I wanted to talk to Mom. For some reason, since my dad and my brother Mimi died, she never regained confidence in herself. So, I asked mom, "Can we talk?" I went right to the point. I said, "Nicoletta, you need to take a few days off without worries. Let Lena and me take care of outside work. Just worry about the house a little and cooking, nothing else. Please stop crying. Okay, mom? I will talk to Lena and Josie about this. You need to listen to me sometimes for a change." Mom did take a few days off without worrying about anything. Since our loss, she has become so much depressed and lost weight. She is aging so fast. I said, "Mom, please stop worrying. Spilled milk will not come back. Dad is gone, so is Mimi. We need to move on, Nicoletta. I am thirteen; I must grow up to become the man of the house. I have no choice; we must react to our misfortunes. No more 'if,'

LA VITA VA AVANTI, LIFE GOES ON,

After that personal outburst with Mom, I saw her crying. She knows we cannot manage the farm on our own, so she is worried just as much as everybody else. Possibly, for a little while, then we will manage, but soon we need to see which road to take. For a few days, she looked like another woman. She knows that since my brothers left, we have no resources to lean on. We are stretching day by day for food and clothing for the family. We need help at the farm. God, help us out. We can't go on like this, counting the days since Federico left. I always pull out my book to write down something, only family notes. But lately, there's not much to write or say. Not even when Mom and Lena keep me out of family responsibilities. Since Dad died, lately I have been without someone telling me what to do, except for Mom, who says if I need any help, she's there. Sometimes she pretends I know what needs to be done without telling me. I wish I knew everything, but I don't know where to start. So today, I can say I will be free to decide what to do the next day...on my own, regardless of what Mom and Lena decide about the future. Since Papa died, there's no one here to command. Sometimes Mom guides us, but from time to time, she comes at an inconvenient time. Maybe she doesn't have the strength for it. We've been going with the old dad rules without having a family head. I know we are or will be in trouble soon.

On Christmas Eve, normally, Mom prepares a good family dinner for everyone. This year, we have two of our family members gone and two in the war. Only God knows where they are these days. During dinner time, we're all around the table. I look at my sister Marianna; she's incredibly quiet. She knows something without saying it. My sister-in-law is incredibly quiet, too. Josie stops eating for a minute. I was worried about no one talking. So, I said, "Is everyone okay?" with a soft voice. Josie whispered, "Mom, I need to talk to you." Mom got up and went to her. "You okay, Josie?" Mom asked. "No, Mom," she said simply. "I've been vomiting lately. I'm not sure why. Maybe I'm sick, or maybe I'm pregnant." Mom's reaction was, "Don't worry about it. Maybe it's nothing." Then she went on to say that we will see a doctor. Josie said, "No, Mom, I'm okay, just some vomiting, nothing else." Continuing the conversation with Mom, she said, "I will see the midwife after the Christmas holidays."

With that announcement by Josie, we're all happy for her. Mom offered to go with her to see Lady Bruna, our family friend who delivered little Luigino, Lena's boy. After Mom said, "Okay, I will go with you, Josie," I said slowly, "Can I speak up, Mom?" I said, "Lena has a boy, and Josie will have a girl." She looked at me and said, "You shut up, Toto. Okay, the family is growing again if Josie is expecting." After Christmas, during very cold days, Mom went to Lady Bruna with Josie, and we found out she was pregnant, possibly a couple of months along, saying the baby was coming sometime in the summer, end of July. I said to myself, "Now we will be in trouble. We need more help." With Josie expecting, possibly we will not be able to get much help out there. From Josie, we will be another short person in the field. After Josie's situation, my first reaction was we needed more help. I wonder if Pietro and Leonora might help. Leonora, with three kids, and Pietro with two, they have their own family problems; they don't need to worry about us. Possibly, they will help out on weekends. Pietro is free only on Sunday; he works in the city, having a full-time job there. God bless him to get that job. After he came back from the military, he got that job. How? I do not know. I believe it is a respectable job. I'm not sure if he makes good money. Being free only on Sunday, he needs to rest or so. Leonora has her hands full overall, with kids to worry about. It's a struggling life for everyone. Sometimes, we always ask for miracles. We can't ask for help all the time.

Since our losses, Mom has not been well. We try to keep her out of farm work, but since Federico left, she has come to help in the field with Lena and me. Lately, she is not well enough to help at the farm. We asked her to take a few days off until she was better. We know she will recuperate fast; it's happened before. Mom will be back soon; she is a strong woman. Our family doctor will come to see her after the holidays, or so he did see Josie. Mom is a healthy woman; she never gives up on anything in life. Now, we are focusing on farming work, with Zio Tommaso helping. We need to manage the work in the field. Lena and I work most of the time in the field. In the winter, we do a lot of cleaning up, cutting off weeds around the vineyard and olive plants where the tractor cannot go. Zio Tommaso and I try to stay on top of farm work lately as much as we can. Since Dad passed away, he has been so close to me, showing me many little tricks at the farm site. Unfortunately, we should not always depend on Zio Tommaso. We need to look up and resolve everything on our own or seek more help. Hiring people these days to come and work on the farm is not possible. I remember when Joe and Mimi used to work for other farmers. They were paid in cash, giving Mom some help. So, everyone else filled the pot. We were a happy family. For some reason, life was beautiful. Now, we are all working hard, sharing all good things at home. Dad always used to say a happy family will make life easy for everyone. Now they are gone, all I can do is cry about it.

Going to see our neighbor down the hills, Mr. Falco, soon as I got there, he was happy to see me. He said, "Hey, Toto, who brings you here?" I got right to the point for a reason I went there. I am stuck with veggie seeding, and I wonder if you can help out for a couple of days. Mr. Falco is a wordless person. To catch up, we need his help. With a short word, for some reason, he's asking about Mom. As usual, never talked much, so I pretended I didn't hear him. "Mr. Falco, Mom is okay. Please tell me if you will help us out," I said. He said, "Yes, no problem, Toto." So, before the rainy season started, we did all the seeding. Lucky for us, soon we got a lot of rain at the farm. During the rainy season, not much work can be done except picking up rubbish or other things left behind from before. Normally, we accumulate deadwood branches and weeds, that need to be cleaned up sometime soon or later during the year. I hope the rain will stop soon. I will do some work around the barn and stalls. There's so much to be done. Soon as I walked in, I saw the ladies, everyone around the fireplace. Mom opened a little conversation, saying to me, "Toto, you don't eat much. You need to eat more regularly. I'm worried about you. Lately, you look like an asparagus." Without saying much to Mom, I said, "Don't worry." After that, she asked if I wanted to go down the field to pick up some veggies. After you come back, we need to talk about the farm work. On my return from the countryside, more drizzle, but I was curious to know what Mom meant about farm work.

After dinner, Mom asked us to pay attention, so she found the courage to speak up to us, starting to assign everyone responsibilities. We need extra time out there. Zio Tommaso will be there as we need him. Hope we can manage the farm work ourselves. She looks very tired. She should be laying down. I asked if she wanted another coffee. She lifted her right hand, saying no. She didn't even have the strength to speak up, telling me, "No." Then she said, "I just need to relax for a couple of days; you and Lena worry about the stables until I am a little better." Sometimes, we ask too much from our life. We follow the old proverb; you see that it works. Walk slowly, you go far. Lena is the oldest of my sisters-in-law. She speaks up sometimes, never contradicting Mom. Saying, "I know we are short in manpower since the boys left. I believe we can manage the farm on our own, provided we get organized and each of us will contribute. We need to have a direct responsibility." After Mom gave us her intentions, a verbal list, she knew inside-out farm work. No one can tell us more, only Dad. God bless where he is. She went on talking to us; we need to keep Josie out of these commitments. She will help me around the house, as long as she's okay with the pregnancy.

Easter holidays were approaching in 1941, and I wanted to do something special this Easter. I wanted to bring back a long-standing tradition – singing the passion of Christ for Good Thursday. As I walked back to the house to make sure Mom was okay, I greeted her with a soft voice, saying, "Hey, Nicoletta, how about a fresh coffee?" She corrected me, reminding me she was my mom, not just Nicoletta, but I insisted on calling her by her name. After that, I went along to do other things, spending most of the rest of the day outside. When I returned, it was almost dark, and she had prepared the table for dinner, starting to cook as on any normal day. We usually had dinner at seven during wintertime and at eight in the summer, depending on when everyone returned from the farm.

Farming meant we didn't have weekends off or week-long holidays; it was just work, work, work, regardless of the time of year. With Easter approaching, two weeks away, it was a year to remember, 1941, without my dad and my brothers. We had an ancient tradition of playing Christ's passion song to honor our God.

It had been years since I saw small groups playing the Passion of Christ in our neighborhood, from house to house. I wanted to make it special this year, considering the work we had on the farm and housekeeping for our occupants. Seeking help from others to form a group of three or four people wouldn't be easy, so I needed to contact our close friends Tommaso, Toto, and Franz. We would show up at every door in our village and play the song so people would remember who Toto Nocci was. Perhaps down the road, if I needed help, someone would be there to lend a hand.

I needed to figure out the plan. First, we had to finish most of the necessary work on the farm before Easter, no later than Easter Thursday. With the Easter holidays approaching, everyone would take a few days off from farm commitments, except for minor work at the barn.

On Thursday, we would put together our group. Since I was good with the accordion, I would use Mimi's two-bass accordion – now mine regardless of what others said. Together with Tommaso and Toto, the three of us would play the Passion of Christ, a small band.

The three of us made a great band. Zio Tommaso was a good singer, and Zio Toto played the bagpipe (la zampogna) – a big one – and could also sing. We would enjoy this serenade dedicated to our Lord. So, we needed to practice before Thursday. The sooner we started practicing, the better. Toto and Zio Tom knew the song, but we needed to refresh our memories, starting as soon as possible.

After telling Mom about it, she was happy. After this weekend, we had to start practicing and memorizing the entire song. After talking to all of them, we planned to get together on Monday night to start practicing until Wednesday. Three nights of practice – Zio Tom and Franz knew the song well, Toto less so. We worked hard on it, ready for Thursday afternoon. We would start in one of our houses, taking the motion of our chests, and after that, we would be good to go.

We started at Zio Tom's house, and then we went on a tour, house by house in our village, and then to our neighbors' farms and vicinity. We were so happy about it, and we played until the early morning of the next day. The song would reflect Christ's death story, as far as I knew.

For century, our antedate plays the passion of Christ.

Passion of Christ Song

<u>Refrain:</u> Christ does not return to the Father e andato.

Our Lady Maria cries, that her son has betrayed,

Adventuring herself to the court of Pilate,

Maria asks Pilato for forgiveness for his son.

No needs to be judged by anyone,

Praying Pilate release God son before the court has done.

Farm Boy life story

Refrain: *Christ does not return to the Father e andato.*

No one breathing's a Great silence is born,

a woman in crowed as spoken...crucify him,

the all crowed shouting crucify him, crucify him.

Pilato has No mercy, refusing to be condemned by Christ.

People's, continue shouting, crucify him, crucify him, y him.

Refrain: *Christ does not return to the Father e andato.*

So, Pilato's its claiming to Christ,

Defend yourself...from the crowd,

Before I command to crucify God son, condemning has been done. Non-Roman condoned Christ,

Pilato's washed his hand, asking God No roman to blame.

Your people wanted to be crucified Christ, so it will be done.

Refrain: Christ does not return to the Father e andato.

Clear water in the basin, Christ's face has come,

Pilate proclaims I am not the man of your condemns.

To the cross has been sent, dying's has innocent man. A silence born; teen voice has spoken to everyone, Saying...

Father forgiven them; they don't know what they done.

Happy Easter to everyone, the passion of Christ is done.

We arrived home dead tired, leaving some stuff in the village in case Marianna was willing to go and take it back home. This way, we could move on and get things done at the farm, giving us a good holiday break. We took the wagon using Mangia, and then I showed Mom what we brought home – many beautiful gifts, eggs, sausages, and even Easter cakes shaped like bunnies. I told her that they loved our song. People never stopped giving, and many gifts filled our chest baskets. After overfilling the basket, we left it with a family nearby the village. All the people we visited fell in love with our song, and we collected many more gifts overnight. The next morning, we went back to pick up the surplus from the day before. If needed, I would bring Pippo with us to carry all the gifts.

On Good Friday before Easter, without going to sleep, I called Mom, asking, "Nicoletta, should we spend the day at home, or go pick up some fresh veggies for the holiday?" She didn't answer. I approached her, asking again if everything was okay, but God knows what she was thinking. I walked away, deciding to go and pick up some veggies on my own for the weekend, as well as some fresh food for the barn occupants. My sister never volunteered to help, and sometimes my sister-in-law came, but everyone else refused to help at the stables. Without asking a second time, she did. We could enjoy the Easter holiday. Normally, we would go to our community church for Good Friday mass. Our church was in the middle of a little forest of pine trees, with a small parkette in front of the church and an old well nearby. It sat on a high point of a small hill, with views of Francavilla to the southeast and Pescara to the northeast. Annually, we celebrated the recurrence of San Mary. Every year, there was a big festa, and normally, people from all over the town would enjoy the event. However, since the war started, very few people showed up. Last year, less than half compared to previous times. I wondered if the next one would see many people, possibly only locals. Our family had nothing to celebrate these days - only tears. Mom was strong and reacted to everything, but all this hurt a lot.

Later in the spring of 1941, there were so many days when Mom didn't show a sign of happiness. For her to find a smile seemed impossible. On Good Friday evening, after the holy mass, we were walking back to the house when Mom stopped to talk to Lady Marianna, a good friend of hers. They owned a small farm near the church and were a well-off family. Mom, as usual, talked using her hands, and I could figure out they were talking about the kids. Overall, I waved to them, saying, "See you at home." Marianna had two children - one my age and a younger one. They were a small family, much younger than Mom and Dad, and occasionally they came to help us out. Mom always repaid them in a natural way, such as with olive oil or other supplies. We had the best olive oil overall, and Mrs. Colossi didn't have any olive plants on their mini farm. All the extra olive oil we collected, Mom sold to other people. Thanking God, we had enough. Many families were struggling for food in town or near the seashore, where they had no sources available.

This war has created a lot of shortages in food supply, and many people are suffering. We farmers consider ourselves a little lucky, as we still have flour and oil compared to the people in the cities and towns. As of today, no one has touched our extra supplies or food. We don't know what's happening out there with this war; our landlords haven't shown up lately. I wonder if they're hiding food that they've kept for a year or two away from home. Who knows? It could be a reserve for the future for the family. Tonight, I talked about it with Mom and Lena.

It's Saturday before Easter, and it's been a few months since my brothers left for war. We haven't received a single note from them. Anything that comes to the post office isn't being delivered, so we need to go and see if there's any news or any letters for us. I'll see if there's anything, and then I'll stop at the local bar, where all the big boys spend time after work, including weekends and festivities, playing cards.

Since my dad passed away, my life has become lost, like a boat without a compass, with no direction to follow and no one to teach me what to do or which road to take. Going to that bar is a good place to relax. It's about fifteen to twenty minutes down the hill close to our Adriatic Sea. I change my direction and decide to go to the bar first to see Mr. P. To get there, I need to pass by Marianna's house, which is the most beautiful part of the journey. It's on my way down, so I walk in front of Mrs. Colossi's property, my mom's friend. Hopefully, I'll see her daughter Diana, a beautiful young lady who's my age. She has gorgeous long reddish hair and looks twenty years old. We went to elementary school together, and I went up to grade three while she finished grade five. Being farm kids and going to school in these days isn't easy; it's a bonus unless you're from a wealthy family. We say "figli di papa" – not everyone is "figli di Papa." Passing by the country road at Marianna's house, I have no luck and see no one. I hope on my way back, I'll have better luck.

After I get to Mr. P's bar, there's a big rumor going around – not too long from now, even young people under eighteen years old will be called to military arms, including younger boys and girls. I say to Mr. P, "To do what? To shoot sparrows?" Then some guys start laughing. I say, "If that's the situation, I'll join the partisans. No way I'll go to war to help the Germans. Before you know it, you might end up in Africa or somewhere far. As far as I know, the partisans are here, fighting for our country." Then Mr. P says, "What you said is from nineteen, now they're down to eighteen. Will we be called soon?" I don't believe it. In the army, including younger people, we're just numbers. They're children, and soon they'll be calling boys like me - eighteen years old and up. It's crazy. No one knows what's happening these days. I say to myself, "No one can say anything except God." The only possible thing that can happen is that we need to go, regardless. Since my brothers left for the war, we haven't known anything about what's happening out there. We're left behind, waiting for the day to see them come back.

The people at the bar think they know everything to talk about. They know less than I do, believe me. They're here to drink and just to chatter. Since we lost my dad and Mimi's mom, Mom always prays to God that one day, Joe and Federico will come home. Only Christ knows if they're alive and if one day they'll come home. I need to get back home; it's late, and my mom is worried by now. I better get going before it gets dark. As my dad used to say, "Better safe than sorry." Honestly, I'm not afraid of anything except God. There are people who tell Mom that I'm not like my brothers - how to say, a special one? Other people say I'm not a believer because I'm not a good Catholic. That doesn't mean I'm not a God person - such a person who doesn't have respect for life. Trust me; I agree with my dad – walking safely is better.

Walking back to the house, I take the shortcut. Normally, not too many people like to use this donkey road. We have a nickname for it – "la Stradarella." There's an old story about this road, this shortcut from the main road to St. Mary's Church. Not too many people know about it. First, you go up the rapid hill, and then when you reach the park, you're on a gravel road. One hundred meters down to the main road, it's not easy to walk through. It's very narrow, with dry bushes and trees, including dead branches, stones, and a few big stones leading to near our St. Mary's Church. If two people walk together side by side, they won't fit. There's a small

road at the top that makes it a little easier to get to the park. I wonder why Dad says this road belongs to the devils - to stay away. Walking up to the main road, I ask myself, "Is it possible this war will last all this time?" What I know about, or I should say, what we know about what's happening out there? I'll never forget Dad's saying, "Being afraid helps you live longer and keeps you out of trouble."

This small mule track Leads to the parkette of the church, down to (la Stradarella).

Almost at the top, I need to catch my breath. I wonder why they call it a mule track; first, you need big lungs, and second, it's a scary road. So, people never walk alone here; with others, it's okay. Dad always tells us not to take this road alone; it belongs to the devil people. Stay away from it; it's better to be safe than sorry. Many times I've used this shortcut, and I got home safe, almost dark. Mom was waiting. I said, "Hey, Mom, there are rumors that they will call boys from eighteen and over to the army soon." I looked to Marianna, "You're only seventeen, soon to be eighteen; don't worry." She gave me a dirty look. "Okay, sister, farming is safer than going to war. This war smells like shit; we boys will all end up at the front soon." Mom didn't like hearing these conversations. She's despairing because of the war; she lost a son, and two others are out there without knowing where they are. I don't want to hear anything about this war. I make myself clear to my family. We don't have a clue where my brothers are, if they're alive or dead. No one knows. For me, life is reality; everything else doesn't matter. Using an old saying from my father, "Tomorrow is a new day." I say, "If I wake up, one thing is certain: no one gives anything for nothing; if they do, there's a reason."

Walking through the countryside, I noticed the ears of wheat were yellow. Before long, they'll be ready for the wheat harvest. My sister and sister-in-law need to help out. Josie will do soon, possibly by the end of July, so she's out of the list. Bruna, the delivery lady, has been consulting with Josie a couple of times. This morning, she needed to pick up the delivery lady again at the house. After consulting with Josie for over an hour, she said the baby wasn't ready; it was a false alarm. Possibly a few more weeks. So, she said, "Please don't keep calling me for your pain." Then she went on to say, "Possibly a month from now." Normally, she's good. Mom always says she's better than a doctor. I asked Mom when we'll know if Josie's having a baby. She's getting all these pains; she's big, like a balloon. She told me to shush again, saying, "It's not your business."

We completed the grain harvesting. I asked one of our owners to get together sometime with them later in the summer regarding the farm we occupy, by the end of August. The grain harvest went well with the help of Uncle Tom and other neighbors; we solved the harvest. After many false calls by Josie, a little time went by. It's later in July. I said to Mom if Josie's baby doesn't come out, we need to bring her to a doctor. She told me not to worry about the baby coming out; they'll come out when they're ready. At that point, I asked Mom if she had the same pains as Josie when she was expecting me. She looked at me and said, "What do you want to know?" I said, "Nothing; I just want to learn what these things are all about, no more, no less." After that, she asked me to worry more about the stables. I figured because Josie needed attention the next few days, I better let Mom stay home all the time.

August 1st, 1941—no one will forget this date. After so many false alarms, we all remember this day vividly. Mom and Lena had the baby delivered without Lady Bruna. "God, finally she is done," I said. A beautiful little baby girl! We were all happy; everyone was there. Many people came—Zio Tommaso, Mrs. Ciocco, Diana, Leonora—it was a full house. I was happy for Josie; she looked healthy, and the baby was beautiful. I looked to Mom and said, "What do you say, Nicoletta?" "A beautiful baby girl, dark hair like you, long face," Mama Nicoletta was so happy; she looked like Mom a little.

After Josie got the baby, we reorganized ourselves. We have a commitment at the farm; it's getting out of hand. Additionally, we need to meet with the landlord—possibly before winery time. Lately, the manpower we have and what we need are completely out of range. All the work to be done is beyond our strength; unless we get help from others, we won't be able to manage. We're looking for trouble soon. This time of the year, people take holidays in the middle of August, relaxing at the beach for a few days. I'm not indeed taking days off. Josie is recuperating so fast after the baby is born. Possibly a couple more weeks, and she'll be ready to give us a hand. Soon, we will baptize the baby. We named her after Mom, Nicoletta—Italian tradition. Her dad is not here to celebrate her baptism. I pray to God for her dad to enjoy his daughter's birthday.

Winery time, Sunday morning, I said to Mom, "We have a meeting with Mr. Monte to discuss mainly manpower for the farm." We have another proprietor, Mr. Capo, for another part of the land we work on. Mr. Capo can wait until later in the year— possibly before Christmas; we'll talk with them. Mom didn't want to meet with the landlord, but I did. We went to see if we were good for a couple more years without worries because of the manpower shortage. Since we lost Dad and Mimi, my brothers in the war, we are doing our best to keep up with farm work. Our house has become a cemetery; no one talks or says anything. There's so much sadness in the house.

During the meeting with Mr. Monte, one of the owners, I didn't know where to start or what to tell him. I hope he understands the position we are in these days; possibly, I'll have Mom talk to him. Later in the morning, Mr. Monte arrived. I invited him inside the house where Mom was. She had already prepared things for him to take home, then she offered coffee. At which point, he said, "Nicoletta, is there something you want to tell me?" I said to Mom, "Let me explain to Mr. Monte." She anticipated me, saying, "No, Toto, we need to talk about this." So, here's where we are. Mr. Monte anticipated Mom, saying, "Nicoletta, you don't need to explain anything to me. It's been years since the Nocci family has been working our land. Although in the past I have sometimes been rough with you guys, we have always collaborated together." It was a friendly conversation with our landlord; Mom and I were happy about it. Mr. Monte went on to say, "Today, all farmers are in depression, regardless of owners, tenants, or people like us. Every farmer is going through inconvenient times, so you guys don't worry. Do the best you can; don't forget, my share will go to support the war. I've been donating to the army for two years now. So, don't worry; no one's bothering you guys. We will talk when this war is over."

After our landlord left, he came back, saying, "Nicoletta, please don't keep too much reserve in the warehouse. You never know; we can receive control anytime since the restrictions of the war came." Without any further comments, Mr. Monte left, taking with him some of the goods Mom had prepared for him to take home, without any complaints. After that, in good faith, our landlord came back, saying to Mom, "Nicoletta, I never brought this to your attention. Since Luigi died, I have a promissory note to be signed if you want me to live here, and next time, you give it back to me. I know it's been over a year. I wouldn't know how to ask you about it. Forgive me for not telling you before." Mom was surprised; she believed there was no money owed since Dad died. Mom was caught off guard, so she asked how much. Mr. Monte said, "For seeding, he paid before he died." She said, "Okay." I said, "I wonder why he waited so long." I asked Mr. Monte if there were any other promissory notes unpaid from before. He said, "Yes, there are two, of two hundred and fifty lira each." I said to Mom, "Nicoletta, why not make one and rip the other two off?" He said, "Okay." Then he said, "I will come in the morning and bring the new one; I will make it for the total amount." Mr. Monte did come back the next day; he showed Mom the previous one. It was about three hundred liras, plus the new one of fifty lira, for a total of three hundred and fifty overall. I said to him, "Mr. Monte, the amount is right on this promissory note; no problems with it." So, I noted that the amount was right; the interest rate was left blank. I asked why. He said, "Because I never charge any interest to your parents if they pay before the year is over." I said, "Pardon if I ask; I am new. It's the first time I see these promissory notes. So, if they don't pay on time, what will be the interest you charge us?" He started laughing, saying, "Do not worry, son; Mom knows a couple of dozen eggs." He left. I said to Mom, "We need to pay off by the end of the year; a couple of dozen eggs over fifty cents is good in our pocket." She said, "If we have the money."

It's been over six months since the last good rain. Our land is suffering from dryness, and lack of water. This was another dry summer; watering our products is just impossible. We are behind; I do what I can. Possibly, we need more manpower.

Our farm needs more attention. The women and I cannot keep up with the work we have. My siblings give us a hand occasionally. Pietro works in the city, and Leonora has her own mini farm to worry about. Marianna has been helping out lately, and I'm happy about it. Soon she'll be eighteen, and she's good company in the field. With no experience, only Lena, my sister-in-law, is a bulldozer. She plows dirt like a man, better than anyone else. She's okay with it and never complains. I hope Josie will help us out soon.

Soon I need to ask for help, possibly from our neighbors. Sometimes, they come in exchange for other favors. Or we have Zio Tom; he's always available when we need help. He will do his best to help out. From spring to fall, he helps plow our land. Thanking God, the work he does with his tractor is worth more than ten men's efforts for the entire year. Our community is small, and each of them has its own problems to solve. It's not easy to ask for help from others.

Sometimes we ask our landlord to help financially because there are people who would come, but they pay for it. We cannot afford or allow this luxury of having people for a fee. Our landlord doesn't give them any excuse. He wants it done, however we do it, as long as we do it. One thing is certain: they collect their big share quickly. Any other minor plantations are ours—vegetables, fruit plants, wild fruit. We sow a variety of veggies, and they do not care about that. In the end, they are happy with the great collections. Normally, they settle for the three main harvests: wheat, winery, and olives. For them, mostly they care about the three major harvests, which they sell or donate to support communities. All politics—they never say where it all goes. The only thing we know is the delivery location; other than that, it's anonymous. I do remember my dad always contributing more than fifty percent of the harvesting. Now that he's gone, I give them nothing. I warned Mom no more giving free vegetables or other supplies.

A period of sacrifices; we certainly need to continue with what we have. Reinforcements in our manpower for land work are impossible. From time to time, Mom helps us in the field. Other than that, Lena and I do not ask for much. Mom's job is housekeeping, picking up veggies for the market. Sometimes people from the village come, or she saves the best part for the suppliers. We do have people coming to the farm and pick their own. I'm not happy about that; they do a lot of damage to our plants. So sometimes, I ask Mom to get it for them. We do have a mini-market. Mom supplies them with mixed veggies located down to the main road, close to the sea. Mom delivers any leftovers sometimes; she will clean up, selecting the best ones, and we deliver to a small store nearby, Mr. P Bar. They pay well, unfortunately, we must deliver to them at nighttime or early morning. We will be taking a risk to do that. If we get caught, it will be the end. We will be charged with smuggling, having no permit to sell or wholesale. To get a license, we need a special permit for it. Sometimes in life, you must risk a little to get something in return. Certainly not to end up in jail, as my dad used to say, "Money is never enough."

The family is in need of help. Mom always can use some extra money for household needs. She needs much more than food with two children in the house and six adults. It's not easy to move forward. Since Federico left, I've been alone at home. As a family man, I always ask for help from others when I am stuck. Besides Zio Tom, no one volunteers to help at the farm. After Dad and my brother died, we all are suffering. I am lost out there. Sometimes I do not even know where to hit my head first. I feel like crying; other times I do not know where to turn. My days are long, morning to night. Sometimes I stay late at the farm, watering veggies by myself. The only company we have is my house women and the kids. I am discouraged. Resolving issues at the farm is not an easy job. I am doing the best I can. God knows how much I would like to help my family more or give Mom a better life.

It's a critical time. Mom is too exhausted, and we are alone these days. We do not have the strength to move forward anymore. We need to react, to come up with and sell ourselves new ideas. Possibly something that helps solve all these problems at the farm. I really do not know where to start. The family is destroyed. This reminds me when Mom was desperate. I am a young man; Lena and Mom are great. They are good leaders. Unfortunately, our shortage in manpower will kill us. This is reality.

GROWING SO FAST; MY FAMILY NEEDS ME NOW.

Without my father, the load is on me, Mom, and Lena. They are good leaders, but sometimes they panic when they don't have a solution on the farm. Thank God I have them. By myself, I wouldn't know where to start. I ask Mom many things about how to deal with certain fieldwork, which I do not know how to begin. I am a young boy growing up without my dad. I need to learn fast. Unfortunately, I do not have my brothers' experience. I am jumping from one area to another without producing much. Asking for help is out of reach these days, almost impossible.

Everyone has the same issues. Young people are taken away by this war. This is the reality of life. Many children are left behind because of this war—parents, brothers like mine, or family members—possibly never to return home. Yes, we are young people. I do not know if we should consider ourselves lucky to stay home, waiting for their return, hoping one day they will be back. The luckiest ones are the ones who come home. All we can do is pray to God. Since this war started, we lost Dad and my brother Mimi. Federico left for this damned war. We have no one to support our family. With two small babies in the house, the only person giving us a little support is Zio Tom. Sometimes he comes and helps us out at the farm. Everyone else has disappeared. For some reason or another, all close friends are gone since Dad died. Pietro and Franz do help, but other than that, no one else.

Since our brothers left, we never got any news about them. Normally before the war, there was mail coming. Now, nothing. Possibly we need to go to the town and see if there is anything.

Mom doesn't like me going to the town. Even if Mom says no, I want to go. I said to her, "Nicoletta, I am going to the town Saturday. I will stop by the post office or carabinieri office to see if there is anything from your sons." Mamma Nicoletta's first word: "No! Stay home. I do not want to lose another son out there. The Adriatic coast is full of Germans; you know how dangerous it is for a younger boy going to town. Stay home." I answer Mom, "It's okay. I will be safe, and I will go, liked or not...I am fourteen, a young man. Mom, liked or not, I will go." After that skirmish with Mom, I am going down to Francavilla without saying anything to Mom. This morning, I left going to the post office. I am taking charge of myself. It's my life, without asking Mom or my in-laws every single time. I am walking down to the seashore. After that, possibly, I will stop at Mr. P bar before I come home. Walking away, she keeps talking, "Come straight home. Do not make me worry." Yes, if I do not stop other places, to the bar to see some old friends.

Going to the beach or to the town was almost the same distance from our house, just a little further, so I went straight to the town. I want to reach the local post office to see if any mail is there from my brothers. On my way down, I met some people. One of them, I knew from elementary school, Remo. We started talking about things. Remo is one or two years older than me. They own a small parcel of land just southeast of us, a great house in the village, and a small barn at the mini-farm for animals. We walked down together to the main street, talking about this war. We believe it will have a substantial impact on our economies. People who will get hurt the most are farms. Remo and I strongly believe the war will continue for a few months, possibly years. Two other guys were walking with Remo. He introduced me to his friend. I asked where they were from. Remo said from the city of Pescara. These two seem to know more about this war than us. Possibly, living in the city, they have other solutions or are pretending to know about this war. City people always have different opinions. Walking together, I asked how old they were. Remo said older than us. We all agreed that only God knows at this time what is next. We better be prepared for the worst—the only words they said. Our city is under surveillance, and Pescara is a target for the alliances to sit on it. Our Adriatic Sea connects to major ports and the Mediterranean Sea.

Sometimes I ask myself, why did Italy form these alliances? I remember in school, our teachers first taught us about these alliances with other countries. Many years ago, since 1879, with Germans, Austria, Hungary, and more—God knows who else. To me, this alliance with other countries was a bad move. We should worry about our own land, our own country. We have our own problems before others'. All this does not look good. So, the less we move around, the better it is.

We separate at the bridge dividing the small town from the open land farms area. There is no limit of city/town line. There was an old school where all the surrounding local farmer kids went, now occupied by military soldiers. God knows where these guys are from. Our school was relocated to a new neighborhood. There are soldiers around our territories for about a couple of kilometers. I hope they don't stop me before I get to the post office. Along the main road, I spot many other soldiers with jeeps and trucks, coming from the north and going south toward Ortona. There's a lot of movement in town. I wonder what is going on...

Soon, I got to the post office. Lucky me, it was open until noon. I got there just before lunch. I asked if they had any mail from the military army for the Nocci family. The guy was rude, with a loud voice. I believe it's normal for people working for the government or his position, especially when it comes to a farmer boy. He had a loud voice, saying, "Can I help you?" I repeated myself, asking about anything for the Nocci family. He said, "Yes, there is something. Just wait here. Give me a couple of minutes." I said to him, "Why are you screaming instead of talking?" He said, "This is my voice." After waiting for a little, I sat near a large window at the door's side. I was getting nervous waiting for that camel. I started walking around the large room. I went to the main door and waited there, looking through the window with a large screen. As I was waiting, a car went by. It's like you see a whitefly around— not too many. This road is the major road, connecting north to south Italy. As usual, I am talking to myself, saying, "A younger man like me dreams one day to drive a car." The first thing that comes to my mind is my mom. I can drive her to the town or to the market for the sale of her veggies. For us, owning a car one day is a dream, just impossible. Well, dreams sometimes come true, or so they say. Dreams do not cost any money. Unfortunately, that is reality. In the meantime, I have been waiting for over fifteen minutes. The postman never came back out from the back room. This sucker! I start shouting, "Hello, hello," more than once. I cannot be here all day.

There was a lady working there who said to me, "Give him a couple more minutes. Possibly, he's having a cigarette back there." So, I waited a few more minutes. I wanted to go to the back and kick his butt out. Finally, here he comes, showing up with a bad tone, "Sorry, can't find this envelope." He lied to me, saying he could not find the envelope. After waiting so long, I said, "Thank you. See you guys next time." The jerk answers me back, "Don't be a fool or a kid." I said to myself, "Better let it go if I want to sleep home tonight. The carabinieri station is next door. It won't take long for me to get arrested here." I left without another word. It was almost two in the afternoon. I had no lunch, just a boiled egg in the morning and coffee since I left home this morning. Going back, I stopped at our local bar/eatery, Mr. P's place. I had only seventy-five cents in my pocket to spend. I saw some strangers, unusual people, soldiers dressed in plain clothes possibly. It was a busy place, no room to sit down. I never saw so many people in my life. Mr. P's bar is a small place, and all this makes it look even smaller. I said to Mr. P, "Full house today. New arrivals." He looked at me without answering, no comments. I said, "I will have a small bun with a little sauce and a small bottle of soda." I asked how much. Softly, he said, "Nothing. Santa came by early this year." I gave him twenty-five cents. He was really generous to me. The only thing he said was, "Take out, Toto." I said, "No problems." I looked at him with a bad expression. He knew I didn't like it.

The Nocci family gives this bar a significant contribution over the years. I said to myself, "Having patience is the virtue of man." After the post office coincidence, now this. I picked up my lunch bag. I left in a hurry, no questions to ask. I felt sorry for Mr. Pasqualino. Unfortunately, in that neighborhood, it's the only bar open. Everyone calls him Mr. P. It's the only place around. This bar has been around for a long time. It's called "Il Torchio," the wine press. A bar and eatery in our district where all men go for a drink, play cards, have a sandwich, or play bocce. There's another bar north of our farm, a little further than this place. My dad used to go there sometimes. The only problem is that not too many people would go there. Dad used to say, "You stay away from that bar." I never went there. I guess if you build up a bad name or reputation, then it stays with you as long as you live, for the rest of your life. My old man had some concerns about us going there, especially me and Federico. We were the youngest in the family. It's not a place for us. People believe it's a nocturnal place. Many people do not like that bar. It's an underworld place, how to say, a worrying night or monstrous thing—prostitution, gambling, and more. God knows what else is going on. All bloodsuckers go to that bar. One thing is certain: Dad kept us away from that neighborhood. I remember one time as a boy, I was seven or eight years old. One evening, Franz came to the house, telling my father that he needed to go there. There was a possibility of a big fight going on that night involving Joe, Mimi, and Zio Tommaso, possibly other family members. So, Dad knew what it was all about—a possible showdown between people from different districts. There's a relation between villagers' people. I believe a big fight with different zones always happens. People always fight for some reason or another. There have been rivalries for years. That's what dad talked about. So, they left quickly. Immediately, I noted my dad always had a knife with him, a typical trench fighting knife.

The next day, I asked Federico what happened there. He told me not to worry about it and to stay away from there. It's not a place for boys. I was pissed off. Everyone used to treat me as a little boy.

After the bar, I stopped to see this beautiful young lady who owned a grocery store, including a tobacco sale, about five hundred meters from the bar. Miss Tina—she owns a mini-market. Anytime I would come to this area, I go crazy. I wanted to see her. She's a beautiful woman. I needed to pick up some coffee beans and a pack of tobacco for Zio Tommaso. Mom loves coffee. I had just enough money for about a hundred and fifty milligrams of coffee beans and a small pack of tobacco for Zio Tommaso. Tina is a big girl who likes to smoke a lot and drink or so. She's a city girl. I like smoking. The only problem is I do not have money to buy the cigarettes. Possibly, they are over twenty-five cents a pack—the ones I like. Well, here I am at the mini-store. A hundred grams of coffee will last Mom a good month. I always compliment her for the way she keeps the store clean. After that, I give her my good sense of humor before I leave, giving her a good smile, saying nice red hair. I am fourteen, so sure she is over twenty-five, God knows. It's getting late. Time to go. It's getting late. By now, Mom will worry about me. Going back home, I went by the mule track. This will save me time. I hope she forgives me. She loves coffee. Mom always uses the same pot, over and over again, saving for tomorrow. After a long walk, I am back home. Looking for Mom, she's not around—possibly in the barnhouse. I called her many times—no answer. Soon it will be dark. I was worried. I will see what she's up to. I am sure she is at the farm doing something. I will take a walk down the field. Possibly she picked up a bundle of grass for the animals. She is always worried about our occupants. I asked her why she was there. It can wait for tomorrow. She said, "I do that for you. Tomorrow, e tutti i santi non si lavora."

Chapter 4
Close-knit family (sad days)

This coming weekend, we are celebrating Ferragosto, All Saints' Day, with my family. After my brothers left, leaving behind their wives, Joe had a kid, Luigi, and Federico had a little girl, Nicoletta. We all live together at the farmhouse. I said to Mom, "Hey, Nicoletta, it's Saturday night. What are you doing so late on the farm?" She looked at me with half-words and said, "It's about time you came home." I apologized to her, saying, "Sorry, Mom." With a simple word, I opened an easy conversation with Mom. I stopped on the way to see some friends, but I got you something good." She said, "What?" I replied, "I will not tell you unless you give me a big smile. Or else, I have another surprise for you, Nicoletta." "What now, Toto? You spend all day out, possibly you spend all your savings," she said. "Mom, you know something? You worry about every penny we spend—me, Papa, and others. Look, Papa is gone, Mimi is gone." We went on with that conversation. I said, "I enjoy it when we bring you something. Just take it without complaining." She repeated herself, saying, "I do not want you to go and spend money. We do not need anything at home, especially if it's your savings money." "Oh, Mom, please do not worry about me or the rest of the family." She kept reminding me day by day, "Important is not to spend money. I am telling you for your own sake. For the last time, keep all your savings hidden in a safe place for when you need it." After that conversation with Mom, I said to her, "Money comes and goes." Walking back home, I said to Mom, "Nicoletta, let me tell you something. I do not want to be a farmer all my life. I do not want to spend my whole life digging the ground. I am a stubborn person. I do not like working on the farm for the rest of my life, okay?" "I am young. My dream is away from plowing dirt. Farming, one day in the future, will be an old story. One day to come, I will have non-farming relations. I will be working in the big city like my older brother, Pietro. So, I hope to make good money for my family. Mom, you can live with us. You will be happy and enjoy life more." After chatting with Mom about my future, we walked back home slowly. She is in her mid-fifties, considering she works at the farm, doing manly man's work. Her life was not easy for a woman working day and night—country people's life. Mom did farm work or housekeeping with a large family. It must be hard for her. Mom got married to Pa at a young age. She was twenty years old. Life was hard, especially for a young woman not used to farming life. She had my older sister, Leonora, in 1909, then Pietro in 1911. She was expecting Joe when Dad left for WWI, surviving over three years before reuniting with the family. Dad was a big guy, 1.8 meters tall, over 100 kg. An extraordinarily big man, surviving WWI. Mom always tells us his life was different for some reason or another. He never was the same. After he came back home from the war, Mom always talked about the way he was affected or destroyed by the war. As much as he lost weight, including some health problems, getting back to a normal farming life was not easy for him. A few months went by before his physical health and stress were recuperated. The most important part was he got close to his kids again. In later times after he got back to a normal life, we had Mimi, a boy with dark curly hair. Then we had Federico. Dad used to call him Blondie—almost blond. He gave him a nickname, "Bambolotto." Dad used to say he would be the new Casanova in our village. I do not know the meanings or reasons for that nickname until now. I am a younger man myself, so I figured it out. Being a good-looking boy attracted a lot of young women. I had been out all day. No excuses. I said to my family, "Sorry. I know you guys have been alone. I thought Mom was home." I got a slap on the back from Mom, saying, "Do not lie." On the table, we went along having dinner as usual. To change the atmosphere, I said, "How about a fresh pot of coffee, Mom, for everyone?" Mom looked at me, whispering, "There is none." I pretended I did not hear Mom. After a few minutes, the coffee was ready. So, here we are—fresh coffee, specially made by Toto. Everyone was surprised. After dinner, I stayed up late, keeping the leftover coffee in the pot. Normally, after dinner, everyone goes to sleep at once. The ladies finish cleaning up, and everyone goes to bed. So, I found an excuse to talk to Mom alone, saying, "This fireplace eats more than our animals in the stables. I just finished adding some wood, and it is already gone. So, the embers are dying." Teasing the glutton in the fireplace, because of a wood soot, the glutton is dying. I started, saying, "Mom, it's a little cold tonight. Can I pick up some more wood for it? I need to talk to you about something. I like to keep the fire going for a little while without my sister and sister-in-law." I asked, "Please, Mom, wait until I come back from the barn. I just need to pick up some more wood for the fire." It was a little late in the evening. I did not know where to start my conversation with Mom. At the same time, I needed to talk to her about the letter. Walking around the kitchen room, I was nervous, worried about the way Mom would react or scream at me, saying, "You're crazy. Why take that risk going to town?" I know my Mom. I should have let her know before I left. After I started talking, I was right—the reaction of Mom was crazy. Almost waking up everyone in the house, I wanted to explain myself. But she would not give me a chance to talk. After she calmed down, I said, "Can we talk now?" I went to the post office, Mom, to see if there was any mail. It's been months, and we do not get any news about my brothers." She was concerned, asking me why I took such a risk going all the way to town. I kept repeating myself, "Mom, it's not that far away. The post office is just a walk after the river bridge." Then she said, "I know where the post office is, so what did you accomplish going to town? Was there anything?" "Yes, a letter from Federico addressed to you?" She asked, "What does it say?" I didn't open it, Ma'. "Okay, please open it," I said. I opened the letter, and there was a small note with a photo on it. I was so happy to see him on a horse with a military costume. He looked like a big boss. Federico was a good horse rider, and possibly he is at a cavalry group. He looks like Dad. Mom was happy to see Federico's picture. You should have seen the expression on her face—some tears from her eyes. Mom said, "What does the letter say?"

Mom/Josie, I am okay, please do not worry about me, I will survive, you guys stay safe hope see you soon love Federico.

I said to Mom, "First, you stop crying, then I'll read the letter." She said, "Okay." She was curious, without giving me the time to read. I was the only one who could read or write a little? I had a couple of years of school, so not enough to be a good reader. This guy's writing was only chicken scratch. Hard to read.

The next morning, Mom had coffee for everyone. Smiling at me, she said, "You went to the market store yesterday to see Tina. You are a little brat. Change your habits or your head..." She meant to change my habits or mindset. "I've told you many times, do not spend your savings money. You know how hard it is to save a few lives. So please listen to me for once. From now on, no more spending, okay?" Mom cares about every little thing, especially when it comes to money. "You are the worst." I wondered why Mom worries about money. I repeated myself, "Mom, money comes and goes. Do not forget, what goes never comes back. We do have a lot." I said to Mom in a happy tone, "Nicoletta, will you talk to Lena and Josie about last night, please, Mom? I need to make sure she will let them know about Federico. Or please show Josie the letter. We never got anything from Joe. It's been so long, almost a year since they left for this ugly war. Later this summer, another harvest is coming soon. We need help."

Banging my head all over the place, I would not have a clue where to start. We need a solution before it's too late. Mom and I asked so many people for help. The young ones are gone, and the oldest ones need help themselves. So, we need a plan to move on. After arriving in the countryside, I felt like crying. I decided to go door to door to people we know for help. I would take a ride around the village. Who knows, I might see some old friends of my father. Someone could give me an idea or help us out. I would not always go to Uncle Tom for help. It's not fair. The only problem is I do not know how to go these days. Zio Tom has his own family to feed. I do not want him to worry about us.

I got back home late. Mom was sleeping. I saw Josie was up; the baby was crying. I picked her up, and she stopped. Looking at me, I said to her, "Hey, little one, why are you crying?" So I asked Josie to give her the evil eye. She said, "You think she has one?" I said, "Yes, it's the evil eye!" Asking Josie, "Who did you see today?" She said, "No one, just one of the people asking for a donation, came by. A lady and a young girl, asking for alms, 'lemosina.' I said, "What the... I am sure she gave the evil eye to Nicoletta." I felt like screaming at her not to let strangers in the house. After I calmed down, I took a few seconds to relax. I counted to three, and then I said to Josie, "Please, next time, do not let anyone in the house or open the door if you are by yourself." She said, "No, they stayed outside." She was worried for a minute, saying, "Okay, Toto."

I stayed up late. I heard a coyote, possibly around the stable. I went for a little walk around the barn. There was nothing to worry about. Normally, we keep an oil lantern lit all night in the stable area to keep our occupants alert.

In the morning, I woke up early, around five. I knocked a couple of times on Mom's room door, whispering, "Ma, Ma." No answer. Finally, I opened the door. I saw her sleeping together with Marianna. Since Dad passed away, Marianna sleeps with Mom, and Josie shares the room with Lena. I didn't want to wake her up, so I walked out slowly, closing the door quietly. I figured it's better to wait a little longer before I go. Mom came out around six, almost sunrise. It was daylight outside. I had the fireplace going, and I made a coffee pot for everyone before they got up. I said to myself, "As soon as they are up, it's ready for them."

I was ready to go. Mom came out and said, "Where are you going so early?" I replied, "I am going out this morning, Mom. I will be back later today. Please ask Lena and Marianna to help you out with the stables, taking care of the animals." She asked, "Where are you going so early?" I said, "I am going to visit Leonora this morning. After that, I'll stop to see Pietro. We have a big harvest coming up, and we need a lot of help. It's been a long time since I saw them. It will be a good reason to stop by, and at the same time, I will ask for some help." Mom said, "No, don't bother them." I said, "We need to have as many people as possible, so I will go."

Walking to Leonora's house, I could smell the aroma of coffee from afar. That told me Leonora was up, an early bird as usual. She's always up early in the morning with three kids. It's not easy overall. Everyone in the family starts from zero, with no help from parents or others. None of us can afford to give up when we get married. Secondly, these days, we get married so young. It's not a joke. I reached the door, and as usual, she kept it open. I walked right in, yelling, "Good morning, sister. Franz here." She almost had a heart attack. She said, "You fell off the bed this morning. You are here so early." I said, "I am the earliest bird of the Nocci family. Next is you and everyone else." Softly, she said, "Who brought you here, Toto?" "I needed to see my lovely sister. I love you so much, so I wanted to make sure you're okay these days." After a scorching summer, she is a typical mom. She gave me five cents. "Sure, you needed something to show up. Possibly, you need help." "Hey, now you've got me upset, sister," I retaliated. "You never need anything."

After we quarrelled a little, she said, "Have a coffee. Franz will be back soon." I asked Leonora, "Where did he go so early?" She said, "Don't worry. He went to the barn." She meant the shack. "Forgive me, sister. You have a shack and a small stall, no more, no less." She said, "Always, you are making fun of our barn." With a joke, I said, "No, Leonora. I want to say it is a small stall." Then she said, "By the way, there have been foxes around lately, attacking our chicken coop. So I suggest we all get a shotgun. We can shoot them. We need to catch them. In the meantime, Franz walked back in. "Hey, little brother, where did you come from?" Franz is a regular guy like my brother Pietro, 1.60 to 1.65 meters. I am fourteen, and I'm taller than them. I looked at him. "You call me a little brother? I am way taller than you." After that little joke, I had a coffee with them. I said, "I need to talk to you." Franz said, "Are you in trouble with some girls, brother?" Leaving, I said, "No, this is no time for girls, maybe in a couple of years. I explained that we needed some help and the situation we were in at the farm. Without letting me continue, he interrupted me. "You know how hard it is these days. We manage all by ourselves. Whatever. We will be there helping. We know the family situation. You don't need to explain."

Since Dad passed away and with Mimi's tragedies, everything has been so hard for everyone. With a deep voice, Franz said, "One day we might need help, so count on us." Without wasting more time, I hugged him and my sister, thanking Franz. I said, "We all appreciate it. Mom will be happy to see you guys soon."

On Sunday, which is the only day Pietro is home, we have a gravel road that takes us down the hill to a main asphalt road.

Pietro's house is about a fifteen-minute walk from the main road. This main road takes us anywhere you want to go, north and south Italy along the Adriatic coast. As soon as I arrived at Pietro's house, I remembered a story he told me once. Because he lives not too far from the main road, a stranger walked right into their house in the middle of the night, waking up everyone. Pietro pulls out a shotgun from under his bed, yelling at him to get out, delinquent, before he shoots him. It takes me thirty minutes to go to Pietro's place, a nice walk. As soon as he saw me, he said, "Everything okay, Toto?" I said, "Yes, nothing to worry about." We talked a little, and then I asked my brother where Nuccia was. He said she was doing a little cleanup in the garden field. They use that small parcel of land for veggies. It's good sandy soil, not too far away from the Adriatic Sea, perfect for planting veggies.

Pietro is my older brother, and I love him like a father. For him, I'm a son. He and I are sixteen years apart. I call him big brother with a smile, patting him on the back. He said, "Who brought you here? I wasn't expecting you these days." He asked about Mom and everybody else, and then slowly he asked about Mom's health. He asked if it had gotten any better since the last time he saw her. I said, "Okay." I started a conversation about how much work there is at the farm. Since Federico left, it hasn't been easy for anyone. The farm needs more than what we can manage. I've been giving it my all, twenty-four-seven, without stopping lately. I wonder if he anticipates me, saying, "You know I will come up and help when I can. I work six days a week, so I have Sunday free. Not much, but I will come up and give you guys a hand for the next few weeks. You know I've always been there." I said, "Do the best you can." Walking away, I gave him a hug, saying, "We love you and your family, brother." I said to myself, "I hope one day I will have the strength to be on my own like he did." With tears in my eyes, I said to myself, "He has two children. We hope for a miracle; otherwise, we need to see how we will manage the situation."

Walking away from Pietro's house, I figured I would stop by St. Mary's church before going home. There's always a late mass. I hoped I would get lucky and see Diana. I got there early and saw Father Rocco. He looked at me and said with a half-word, "It's a miracle Toto's here." A little sarcastic for a priest, he said, "Hey, what brings you here? Normally, I see you only on Easter and Christmas." Correcting him, I said, "No, Father. It's the recurrence day of St. Mary's festivities. I'm always here to help out." He laid a hand on my shoulder and asked how long it had been since I last confessed. I said, with a short word, "I do not remember, Father, possibly since my first communion." He didn't like that. He slapped me on the head and asked why I did that. I said, "Why did you do that, Father?" He said, "You're not ashamed of yourself." I said, "I do not remember, Father." He asked me again, so we did it now. "No, you'll be late for the mass," he insisted. "Now, we have plenty of time for it." I repeated myself, "You'll be late for the Mass." He looked at me, saying, "That's bad, son." Finally, I convinced him, promising that before St. Mary's festa day in late September, I would be there and confess myself.

After a few people showed up, my eyes were all over the small church, but there was no sign of Diana. I said to myself, with my luck, she's not coming to mass today. So, after the mass was over, some people left and others stayed back to chat with Father Rocco. Going back home, I wanted to stop in the village to see my friend Remo. It was a muggy day, so I didn't take the gravel road. I walked through side streets, finding some shade from tall trees. It saved me time. Soon, I reached the crossways and met a gentleman walking toward our small village, so close to St. Mary's church. Looking at me, he said, "Hey, young man, do you know where the church is? It looks like I am lost." In life, Dad taught us never to voluntarily give information to strangers. I didn't volunteer him any information. I stopped for a few seconds, looked at him, and said, "Who am I, the local informant?" With a solid voice, I asked, "Who are you?" He said, "Wow, don't get scared. I just need to know where St. Mary's church is." I was a little sarcastic with him and said, "Me scared of what?" So, I started walking again. Walking away from him without answering back, I said to him, "If I am scared, I'd stay home. I am a big boy; I can look after myself." I didn't turn around. I was gone, continuing my route and minding my own business. At that point, he understood that he had to cooperate if he needed help. Then, he apologized and said, "Okay, son, stop." I stopped, and after he caught up, he said, "I am from Rome. I do not know this area very well. Can you help?" Then he said, "Nothing to worry about. I will find it on my own." I said, "Okay." I didn't think twice. I went on, minding my own business. So, he called me, saying, "Stop, please." I said to myself, "He is a very educated person, just a little stubborn like me. Just a stranger in our neighborhood." So, I stopped and asked him, "I do not know who you are and what you are looking for."

Walking away, he says, "Stop, please. If you know, help me out." Possible he got lost, so I turned around. I said, "Okay, I am Toto. I know where St. Mary's church is. So, tell me who you are and what you are looking for, and I will help you out." Then he introduced himself, saying, "Sorry, I am Peter Bianco. I am from Rome." "You are telling me you are from Rome?" He insisted, coming from Rome. This guy breaks my... I walk away. I did not think twice. I left; he followed me towards the village. I said to myself, "This guy needs help." So, I stopped for a minute until he caught up to me, saying, "I walked from the bus station to here to see Father Rocco. I am part of the Catholic church. Please, can you tell me where the church is?" We were about a thousand meters away. He should see the church from here because the big pine trees cover the church building. It cannot be spotted from here. I said, "Okay, Mr. Bianco." He was very tired. So, I said to myself, "I better accompany him to the church. I am sorry for before, so we need to go back. From here, a little walk." So, he opens a little conversation with me, saying, "You are from this neighborhood?" I said, "Yes, I am. My name is Toto. I am from the Nocci family. We have a farm nearby here." Continuing to talk, I said, "Your last name tells me something. We have some landlords with that name." I kept talking to him, asking if he is Jewish. He said no. Possibly my background is...

Walking back to the church, just up the street five minutes away, I continue a light conversation with him. So, I said, "Tell me, Peter, you are here to see Father Rocco, right?" He said, "Many years." I ask, "Why, then, are you staying for St. Mary's festivity at the end of this month?" "No, not possible." When he saw the church, he looked at me, saying, "I'd never find it. It's in the middle of nowhere, hidden in bushes and trees." I said to him, "Hey, slow down. What bushes? Only trees and a beautiful lovely parkette. What did you think this was, St. Peter's church in Rome? I've never seen Rome in my life, or St. Peter's church." I said to him, "Our church can host seventy-five people or more. We can fit more with extra chairs." It was the latest mass, early afternoon past one o'clock, so I stayed to the end. I said to myself, "Two masses in one day. I beat all records of my lifetime. I will make up for another time. Unfortunately, I do not come that often to mass." I am sure Father Rocco will be happy. I want to make sure this guy is not taking me for a ride. You never know in life; anything is possible. I sat at the last row observing the rest of the mass. Most are local people, possibly all good Catholics except me. I was baptized and had my first communion in this church, but I never did my confirmation until today. I wonder why Mamma Nicoletta is very religious, vice versa my dad, who never goes to church. For him, the church is another organized business asking for money from anyone. He always used to say, "The church, they are the richest people on earth." It has been a long day, and I need to go home. At the same time, I want to make sure Mr. Bianco sees Father Rocco. He went for a walk outside. I am approaching our priest. Other people like to chat with him after mass, private conversation. I step in front of everyone, "Sorry, Father, quick questions. I will need to go. Pardon everyone."

St Maria delle Grazie,

Cont. Villanesi, Francavilla al Mare, Chieti.

The priest was surprised to see me again, saying, "Hey Toto, what is happening? Sorry, there's a gentleman looking for you. I want to make sure you know him before I go. His name is Peter Bianco." He looked at me. "Are you sure?" "Yes, Father." "Okay, you can go. Nothing to worry about." I was curious to know more about the guy. "Okay, Father. Please let me know if you need me."

Going back home, I noticed there were people working at the farm, catching up with their work. It is important. You need to work on weekends, holidays, sometimes. I wonder if all this makes sense in life. Sometimes I ask my Lord, why this dog's life? All the work we do is only partially paid back. We are peasants, always at the mercy of the Lord, who gives us a good year-end. Most of the time, what will make a big difference is mother nature, the seeds' product, and the effort we give. Not enough. There are many reasons a harvest can go sour, regardless of the attention and effort we give to it.

Today has been a long day. Since this morning on the road, I stopped at the Pera fountain to see if Mom was there. Not too far from our church, where our ladies go to do laundry. I figured Mom might be there. I can help out, bringing up washed clothes when they are wet. They are heavy.

This fountain produces so much water. God knows where it comes from. It is a source from a rocky ravine. Years ago, they managed to build a tub where water falls from a pipe that is hundreds of years old. The nature of our Lord, Crazy, has the big tub full, discharging to a small creek down the hill, running all year long. People can use that water to wet plants or keep the ground humid as needed. I saw Mom and Lena washing. No one yells. Lucky them, there is good shade above the big tub, a couple of maple trees. They must be over a hundred years old, which gives that area a fresh breeze overall.

It's late afternoon. I said to them, "Good morning, my ladies." Soon, they see me. Lena whispered, "Thanks, God, we have some help to bring back all these wet clothes." Mom said, "It's afternoon, not morning." I played a little dumb. "Ladies, you do not need help." Mom looked at me, smiling. "We knew you would come this way before going home." "I said, "Why is that, Nicoletta?" "This country road takes you to the church but also Mr. Colossi's house. You think I do not know, Toto?"

Mom, she's the worst of a wizard. "What do you know, Mom?" She said, "Every time you go out or down to the national road, always you are going by Diane's house." "Ho, Mom, same old story. It's nothing wrong. I go by there. It's easy to get to the main road. Mom, forget the road belongs to everyone." I use a different approach, saying, "The road belongs to me, too. Tell me, Mom, is there anything wrong if I like her? Sooner or later, I will need a wife. I need to open my eyes and look for someone right. Soon, I will be fifteen." She said, "Next year." Then I pinched her. "I am not a Casanova, but I am Nocci, a good-looking boy." Softly, I said, "You like Diana as a daughter-in-law?" She is washing clothes, pretending she never heard me. Then she stops for a second, looking towards me, saying, with a thin voice, repeatedly saying, "She's not for you." That word from Mom hurts me so much. I didn't know what to say at that point, whether to shout so loudly or leave. I was so angry with her. If it were someone else, God, I would kick her ass. We are suffering these days. Mom is exhausted on any level. Poverty is not the right word. Other than that, we are doing our best to survive these days. After that, Mom told me Diana was not for me, she reached the maximum limit, hurting me so badly only God knows. I was quiet for a moment, hearing that from my mom. It's like I was not good enough for Diana. I didn't answer back. I pretended I didn't hear anything. Possibly, she didn't mean to hurt me like that. I changed the conversation, saying, "How long does it take to finish washing? I am tired and want to go home." After a couple of minutes, Lena spoke up. "Hey, young man, a few more minutes. Be patient." So, I sat on a large rock just a few meters away from them. I needed to be alone for a few minutes. I heard a noise like a snake moving. I looked around me. Nothing. So, I got up and grabbed a bamboo cane, which was amazingly effective in killing snakes.

I can't believe it, but a snake was under that rock I was sitting on. It came so close to the washing area. There are always people around the fountain, and normally, they won't come so close. If Lena finds out, she'll be afraid of snakes and never come here again. So, after that, I got close to Mom and Lena. I wanted to scare them off, so I whispered, "Hey guys!" But Mom jumped on me, shushing me because she knew what I was about to say about the snake. They are almost done, I said, "Okay, Mom, we're ready to go." Lena asked if there was any news about Joe and Federico. I said, "No, no, Lena. You will be the first one to know." Lena had tears in her eyes. Mom talks to her and Josie all the time. We need to be strong. She said, "I went through this. It's not easy to wait for someone. We need to be positive and pray to God, waiting for them to come home one day."

A couple of days later, early in the morning, I wondered if Mr. Bianco had left any information about this war with Father Rocco. I'm curious to know. Later tonight, I'll go see our parish. Meanwhile, I was having coffee with Mom when Lena walked in from the stables, saying, "Hey Toto, we had a visitor overnight." I said, "What, Lena?" "The fox visited our chicken coop," she said. "We got lucky. Only missing a couple." "Well," I said, "Leonora has the same problem with it. We need a shotgun! Otherwise, we'll never catch this fox if they keep coming around our house." I said to Lena, "Before it's too late, we need to do something about it. Otherwise, there will be others following them, and it will be a problem." "I agree with you, Toto. We need a shotgun in our house, heaven for our own protection."

After the morning coffee with Mom, I said to the ladies, "I am walking the vineyard today, or so the olive field. I am sure the vineyard is ready now, the olive later. We need to know as soon as possible. I am so sure this harvest will be ready before time." I walked through the vineyard and the olive field. This year they are loaded. Thank God. We will have a good harvest. As I predicted, the vineyard is ready to go. Winery time. We need to start soon. After that, we'll worry about the olive harvest. On my way back home, I stopped at La Pera fountain, hoping to see Diana. After I got there, I saw a couple of ladies from the village doing laundry. No sign of her. So hard to catch her here. Going back home, I saw our neighbor Remo's dad working at the farm. They have a parcel of land near the fountain. They only grow Rapini and fennels for later fall, located right next to ours. I stopped to say hello to him. "Mr. Falco, they left you alone this morning?" He says, "Hey Toto, what's up?" I said, "Not much, a little concerned. We've been having foxes attacking our chicken coop lately. Do you have any suggestions, Mr. Falco?" He said, "They've been a problem lately. They need to be guarded otherwise they'll keep coming back."

Mr. Falco is always alone. Poor guy with three sons, only Remo left behind to help him out. He's older than my parents, working every day at the farm. Sometimes I ask myself, if they are well off, why don't they get some help when they need it? I will not know why he sacrifices himself so much. He must be over sixty years old, working like a donkey. We need to start as soon as possible on our mini harvest, no later than two weeks from now. After my walk through our vineyard and olive field, I am worried. I hope we can manage. Starting early, I am sure we can get a couple of people better now than later. Waiting extra time jeopardizes the conflict with others. I am scared. Our manpower is not enough. I will look for help from everyone we know, regardless of how much is out there. Hoping after this winery harvest, we can slow down a little. Then another big job will start, the olive pick.

In late fall 1941, considering the time we spent at the vineyard, now we are more relaxed. The last few days, I am reciprocating the help with Zio Tom, farm work. One hand washes the other. After that, our olive harvest comes. I hope no heavy rain comes, losing good days will push us behind. I hope this weather gives us a break this year. Normally, rain always comes in the fall, a special time to do the olive harvest. Otherwise, it will be hard to work in the ravine and on the hill. Before the olive harvest, normally, we do a lot of plowing in the field for the wheat and corn seedlings. After we have that out of the way, including picking olives from the tree, the difficult work is over. Thanking God, the landlord seems to be happy this year with the winery harvest. I hope he will be with the olive harvest too. We complete all our harvesting for the year. All went well, more than we expected. Mom was so happy about it. I never had the chance to meet with Mr. Bianco after that lengthy conversation at church before he left for Rome. I am sure he brought some news about this war.

People always say Rome is a big city. Living in Roma, they are the first ones to know everything, a lot in politics. So, Mr. Bianco brought some news for us about this war. I must see Father Rocco; he is well-informed. We need to thank God; our whole family was there to help us out. Mom always says, "Who seeks, gets." Unfortunately, now we are missing the most important things at home, happiness around our house. Mom had a family conversation after the last harvest. She talked to our landlord. We are with her. We are always subject to some penance. Many things need to be taken care of. Our master, once more and more, he does have an issue every single year at harvest time. He never seems to be happy. Mom despairs because of that. I am worried she will get a heart attack one of these days. My in-laws and I worry about the farm. They have a lot on their plate, worrying about the baby and having a responsibility in the countryside. I am giving two hundred percent at the field. Like today, it was another exhausting day. Almost dark, I am here, refining soil for planting. Not an easy job. I am using our cows more and more every day at the countryside lately. A little rough for veggie preparation. This is the only way I get more work done. Dad will never let our cow work a full day under the sun or rain. Only early morning and later afternoon. Then, since my brothers are gone, they need to work. Fortunately, we have them, Magno and Violetta, two young cows, tamed well by my father, easy to drive them. God bless you, Pa. I am going home. Tomorrow is another day. Later that night, normally, we dinner after seven. Walking in the house, my mom was waiting near the fireplace. She was praying. I noticed lately she's coughing very often. I'm not saying or starting a conversation with her about the farm. I'm exhausted. I don't want to give Mom more pressure. I just wonder if I should leave everything for the end of the year. I didn't eat. I went straight to bed.

Mom came to my room. She said, "Hey, what's bothering you, son?" "Sorry, Mom, only tired. Do not worry. I need to be up early tomorrow." She's pulling the blanket over me, closing the door behind her. I stayed awake for over an hour, looking at my brother's bed. It's empty! I start crying until I fall asleep... It was a long night, a crazy dream. I was in my room, all together, Mimi, Federico, and I. We were there to discuss, the three of us joking over who would be a better farmer among us. I said, "Not me." Mimi said, "No, me." Then I said, "Joe will be gone soon on his own. I'm sure he will get his own farm. So far, we are singles. Mom needs someone to look after her." Federico said, "I will get married." I said, "No way I will move; I will stay with Mom always." I was crying. No one would go away. Calling my brothers to come back, yelling, "Mimi, Federico, I am alone, please stay here. Don't go. Come home now, please..." "Toto, Toto, wake up." "Sorry, Mom, I fell asleep. I need to go. I'm late. Zio Tommaso should be on the farm already there." For some reason, Mom held me back that day. I had a coffee with her. She opened a conversation with me. I was confused. So, I said, "All good, Mom. We'll talk tonight."

Soon I got to the farm, but Zio Tommaso never showed up. I started cleaning up around the trees where the tractor can reach, as we usually do. Today has been a long day without lunch. Normally, my mom or my sister comes down and brings something, but my sister-in-law never comes on Sundays. I forgot all about Mom needing to help out Mrs. Ciocco with Christmas sweets. I'm stupid; I didn't bring any lunch today. But no worries, I'll leave early today. Later in the afternoon, I looked at the sun; I could tell it was about four to four-thirty. On my way home, I'll stop to see Zio Tommaso first at his house to see what happened today. I'm so sure something happened; when Zio Tommaso didn't come today, I was very worried. In the last few months, I've been looking for help everywhere. I'm tired and lost. I do not know where to ask for help anymore. I want to burn everything and run away from here forever. Walking toward Zio Tom's house, as soon as I got there, a big dog on a chain was attacking me right in front of the house. A big German shepherd, a very vicious dog. Since the last time I was here, he didn't have any dog; he must have just gotten it. I called a couple of times; no one is home. "Tommaso, possibly not here," no answer. I saw the tractor sitting at the barn. I said to myself, "He didn't go anywhere today." I walked around; no sign of him. I know he owns a bicycle, a lovely one. The bicycle wasn't there. On my way back home, as I was going home, here comes Tommaso, walking with his bicycle in one hand and a small box in the other. I didn't know what to say to him. I said, "Hey Zio, all good?" "No, Toto, the fuel line broke this morning on the tractor, so I went to town to get a new one. Lucky me they're open on Sunday." With a low voice, I whispered, "Can I help you with it?" "No, do not worry about it; I'll be there tomorrow. By the way, Toto, just to let you know, we might have a problem in the near future getting fuel. So, we need to be ready for it. Nothing to worry about for now; we can start plowing in the morning the area you need the most for now." "Thanks, Zio. I will let my mom know about it."

Uncle Tom is a good man; possibly, he needs to be supported with the cost of the fuel. The repair on the tractor is costly, and he never has the courage to ask for help. After seeing Zio Tommaso, I stopped at the fountain; Diana was there washing clothes. My heart has been bleeding since Mom told me about her being promised to someone else. I said, "Hey, beautiful, did your mom let you out by yourself?" She looked at me smiling, saying, "Hey, Toto, don't go overboard." Then she said, "I always come by myself if you didn't notice before." "I didn't know; otherwise, I would be here more often." She kept washing clothes without looking at me. I wanted to say so much, but the words wouldn't come out. So, I sat in the same spot as usual, at the big rock where the snake was last time I helped Mom here. "Okay, Diana, it's almost dark; you should go home." With a thin voice, she said, "Yes, you're right." I offered myself to help carry wet clothes, but she said, "No, better you don't; it's close by, just uphill. Don't worry, Toto, I'm good. Another time, Toto." Before I left, I said to her, "I know you don't want to be seen alone with me, Diana. I want you to know I care about you." She said, "We're too young to talk about it, maybe in a couple of years." "I will be fifteen in spring; there's nothing wrong if we talk." "Oh, yes, you do know my parents." I started walking, saying, "Okay, don't worry; hope to see you at Christmas time." I enjoyed the walk back home; she gave me a smile. I said to myself, "That was worth coming this way. I was happy; it wasn't an empty trip." After seeing Diana, I walked so fast back home, like a free bird flying in the sky. With no time, I am so happy to talk to Diana, a pretty girl. I hope one day we build an understanding together. It is past seven in the evening; almost time for dinner. I was singing and screaming. I said to Mom, "Dinner's ready." Mom looked at me, "Hey, young man, what's happening?" "Nothing; I saw Zio Tommaso, and he will be at the farm in the morning plowing our land." She replies, "What happened today? He didn't come today?" I said, "No, Mom, he had a problem with the tractor fuel line." "What is that?" "The tractor fuel line needs to be replaced." Over dinner, I asked Mom, "Shouldn't we help pay for it? Possibly you can reimburse Uncle Tom for the broken fuel line." Josie said, "Shouldn't be our problem; Zio helps other people, right?" I said, "True, but other people don't know about this broken fuel line; we do." Continuing the conversation with Mom, I said, "Hope we could pitch in some cost. I'm sure, Mom, we could afford it; I do have a little savings if you need to pay for that fuel line, please." She said, "Don't worry about it; I will talk to Tommaso." Today, I learned something new from Uncle Tom. Although he helps others sometimes from his own pocket, he pays for that repair without asking for anything.

I do believe in sharing things. Zio Tom having a problem with that fuel line means a cost to his pocket. So, it would be fair if someone helped with the cost.

The ladies do not understand my concern about reimbursing the cost to Zio, which would make him happy. After Zio's conversation, I took advantage of the opportunity to talk to my family about the overall situation at the farm. Marianna, Josie, and Lena were all there. I said to Mom, "When you have a few minutes, we need to talk about something else." She looked at me, saying, "What is it, Toto?" I said, "It's regarding the farm overall. I'm happy all the ladies are here, Lena, Marianna, and Josie. This way, there is no misunderstanding; everyone can hear me out."

"Our farm is divided into many sections: the land on the hills of owls, our house and surroundings, and then the big field where we grow quatrefoil leaves for the occupants," I said to Mom. "Before it's too late, we need to let go of a part of it this coming year. We must give up a little to keep up; otherwise, we risk losing all that area. I will speak to our Lord Mr. Capo regarding the land we have at the Owl Hills. Only for a couple of years; nothing to worry about. The most important thing is we keep the good part of the land where our olive is."

After that conversation about releasing a partial part of the farmland, no one agreed. I went on explaining that this way, we can keep up with the farm work and the farmhouse until my brothers are back home. Then Lena said, "Why don't we wait until next year and see what will happen with this war? All the main work is done for this year, so why give up now? All grain seeding, granola, corn... let's wait for now, Toto." Mom and Lena were right; the major work was done for this year. Our problem remains without Zio; there's no way we would manage all this land. No one agreed with me; I'm wrong. We need to wait and see what will happen next spring overall.

Tommaso never asks for compensation; God bless him. He is the type of person who gives a lot to our family; he is a family man. We do have good friends, more than one family, who help us out. Friends exchanged manpower with my brothers when they needed it in the past. During Christmas time and Easter, Mom has been so generous with everyone, bringing them lamb, rabbit, extra virgin oil, and cured green olives, and they are always happy about it. Tommaso's wife loves our oil; most of the time, they keep saying, "Don't do this to Mom; your family needs more than us." My dad always says, thanking Tommaso for all the help we get. Without him, we need to work day and night to make up for what he does with his tractor. So, we always thank our good family and friends. Since my father died, Uncle Tom has been much closer to us; he has supported me a lot, lately, about that tractor conversation with Mom. I said, "We need to help out."

A couple of days later, I'll never forget when Zio Tom and I were cleaning up some weeds at the fountain area to keep that area clean where the ladies do laundry on a daily basis. Not only because it's our responsibility, but we like to keep it clean. He told me something that made me so proud of myself. He says, "Toto, you're a family man now; your brothers will be proud of you for everything you do at home." I said, "I hope one day they will realize all this." Then he told me, "You grew up very quickly. I respect him like my father. Keep up with it, Toto." Many times, I have taken care of things in the house, starting from the stables' work to leftovers at the farm by my siblings. All that is possible because I am the youngest of the family. Dirty work is always Toto's responsibility. Today, I will do anything to see my brother's home. I will do all over again as long as they are here. It has been a long time since my family suffered; we do not have enough to survive these days. I do not know where to bang my head anymore. Mom sometimes makes everyone happy, inventing special homemade food like pasta, special soup, bread made by corn flour, and God knows what else she will do soon. Saying, "This is better than the one we buy at the store." I ask myself, "Why can't we have a normal life like those Mangionis in the town?" God is forging us; it's just impossible. From winter to fall, from harvest to harvest, we are struggling all year long. We need to set a plan; I am running out of options. I have no alternative to support this family. The house needs serenity; our family needs help, and more supplies. Regardless, Mom keeps saying we will manage it. Four ladies, two kids... I am discouraged. Sometimes I am talking to myself like a crazy person. How can we survive if my brothers do not return soon? I do not know what to do or where to start. After my father and Mimi died, things are getting worse every day. Is it my fault or the fault of this war? One thing is certain: we must reorganize ourselves and go on all the way. My sister-in-law, they do not agree to give back a partial of the land. I said, "We need to give back to the owner partial of this land. We cannot keep going like this. Too much work, and asking for help from other people makes me feel like an idiot. A miserable life is not fair either for the others. Soon, another year is over. Next spring, we need to see which partial we can keep under our control and give back to the landowner. Our countryside is formed by several plots of property: the first part with our house and barn, including about almost five hectares of land, the second part a little less, where we have olive groves and vineyards. We need that. The third partial is where we grow wheat and corn. Possibly, we can't drop a partial of that. Everything else we could keep. Another twelve hectares, different owners. Possibly we can abandon a section of it. All this needs to be taken into consideration. It's Christmas; we need some serenity in the family. We have no solution. So many people have abandoned us after this war started; it seems to have no end. We do not know how to manage at the farm anymore. No clue how to survive in all this without my father and my brothers. The only thing I can do is keep working so hard until my brothers are back. I hope soon. Giving back some land to the owner will be the best solution. I learned from my dad.

NEVER LEAVE FOR TOMORROW,

WHAT YOU CAN DO TODAY.

During the Christmas holidays, while talking to the family, I gave them a heads-up about dropping some land. So, later next spring, we will talk again. There are a few people who will take that land; all this because of my brothers not being here. We are short in manpower to farm this land; it's impossible for us to keep up with it. Next spring, I will be fifteen years old; we all look forward to that. "Farmer at fifteen, you are a grown-up young man for your parents." My big wish is to see my brother's home, no more, no less. Mom will not agree to give up any land back; I hope I cannot convince her by next spring. We do have an area close to the fountain; we use that strictly for tomato and veggie plants. Possibly, we can give up part of that and part of the hills of owls. They require a lot of handwork; we are planting over a thousand tomato plants, which keeps us so busy from spring to the end of summer. Veggies, at the same time, we do have another area we can replace it with; the return income is not there. Tomatoes are exceptionally low income.

This morning, I saw Josie with little Nicoletta playing with a little puppy. I got close to Josie and asked, "Where did you get this puppy?" With a smile, she said, "Franz gave it to me. He came by on the weekend with it." "On the weekend? I didn't see him." "Oh, you were in the countryside, down the veggie field. He was in a hurry." "Where did he get this puppy from?" "From the village." "Possible, whoa, he's so quiet. Did you give him a name?" "Yes, his name is Friz." "He looks chubby; what breed is he?" "A Saint Bernard. He will be a big dog, Friz. Hopefully, he will be a good watchdog." "Well, we do not know that. Wait until he grows up."

Every day that goes by, we get more friendly. He starts following me wherever I go, around the house, in the field—a very nosy dog. He never barks; he must be a month old. Sometimes, I wonder if he is normal. I asked Josie, "Friz is normal!" She said, "Why? Well, the way he is acting." "Oh, give him a year; you'll see," she said. "Toto, remember, dogs not barking, they bite." I looked at Friz. "Hey, you, make sure you look after our babies, home, Mom, and our stables. Keep foxes away from here where all our occupants are."

Mom and I were picking up the latest fresh veggies. First, she wants to save part of it for the big boys in town: doctors, landowners, pharmacists, and more. Lucky for us to have vegetables until now. These days, normally November is the latest we can pick up fresh veggies. After that, we need to focus on other typical winter vegetables such as rapini, fennels, and chicory. This holiday, Mom can use all the help she can get. I am saying that because any extras she brings to a local fruit store. So, it's a big process, not an easy job. It needs to be clean and washed before she brings it to them. Wintertime, all veggies are full of frost ice. Mom never asks for a price or gift; she does that voluntarily. And she accepts whatever they give her or offer, except for the fruit store; she takes the money.

Walking back to the house, I started a little conversation with Mom about Diana. "Hey, Mom, do you remember that evening I was happy after I saw Zio Tommaso?" She goes, "When was that, about a couple of weeks ago?" "Okay, Toto, tell me. I do not remember, son. Why were you so happy?" "I saw Diana at the fountain. So, we chatted for a few minutes." "What did you say to her?" "Nothing important. She was washing some clothes, and she smiled at me." "So, then what?" "I offered to help carry the clothes back home, and she said no." Mom stops walking, and listens, "Toto, sit down here." It was a big rock; we sat on it. "Son, I do love you so much. I am telling you once forever. She is not for you, Toto. I have already told you before, and I will say it again. Listen to me, son. God knows how much I love you and all my children. The last thing I would like to see is any of you suffering because of a woman. So, Toto, please let go. Diana was promised to someone else already."

After that big chat with Mom, my silence overall gave Mom an answer about Diana. She cut my heart; no words after that, no comment about her coming out from my mom's mouth. Possibly she knew something I didn't. I will never talk to her about Diana again. Whatever will be, I say to myself. "Can that be? She is fourteen. Soon I am fifteen. I should believe what Mom just said." Sometimes, parents make big mistakes imposing or setting up kids similarly. Life is beautiful and shall not be ruined by anyone. That conversation with Mom about Diana—I do not believe anything anymore unless she knew what was going around. I am a stubborn boy; I never give up on anything. Tomorrow, I will see Father Rocco. I need to know a little about her and her family. Hoping he or so has some news about this war. Since Peter Bianco was here, after he left, Father Rocco never said anything about it. I need to ask him if he has any news or suggestions about this war. Since the time he came to see him, after that, Father Rocco never said anything about him. Normally, he always talks about things happening out there. Peter was from a big city, Rome; possibly, he did have or say something about this war. I will see him; I am curious. Hope this trip won't be wasted. I will use the excuse to confess myself.

Late in the evening, I stopped by the church to see Father Rocco; he was there. I was mentally down, and when he saw me, the first thing he said was, "You came to confess?" I said, "What?" Then, I said, "Okay, maybe, if it's not a problem, Father." We went on with my confession, and after that, I asked if he had more time for me. He suggested, "Come to the back of the sacristy, Toto, tell me what it is." I wanted to ask about Diana. I wouldn't know where to start. I like her; I've never met anyone else, and I don't believe in going to look for someone else. Can we get together with her family and talk about the two of us? He looked at me, saying, "Let her go, son. She will be marrying someone else." So, Mom was right. For a minute, I didn't know what to say. I changed the conversation, saying, "After Dad and my brother died, everything seemed so hard at home. Mom, my sister, my sister-in-law, the babies. I don't know anymore how to go on. I hope you can give me some suggestions. I know before St. Mary's festivity, there was a gentleman here, if I recall correctly. The name was Peter; he had some information about this war. When will we be able to hug our brothers again?" With simple words, he told me, "No one knows how long this will go on, only God."

After seeing Father Rocco, later in the evening, we were having dinner. I opened a conversation with everyone at home about going to the church, talking with Father Rocco, and our intention to give back part of the land to the owner. For a minute, no one talked; then, Mom said, "Toto, are you okay?" "Mom, we need to let go. We don't know how long this war will last; there's no way we can continue working like this." I started off on the wrong foot, so slowly, I changed my conversation before she got angry with me. "Mom, Lena, and Josie, so I'm not sure when my brothers are coming back. The only thing I am sure about and worried about is our landlord giving up on us." After a few minutes of silence, Lena spoke up, "Why are you saying that, Toto?" "I said why. I might be young, but I am not blind or deaf, Lena. Our landlord has been questioning us for the last couple of years since Dad was sick. The overall return at the farm." Lena said, "We need to stay together, do not complain, let the landlord come to us." No further comments; after that, I walked away from everyone. Our conversation died there. I am killing myself and sacrificing seven days a week. Mom understood where my conversation started or where I was coming from. They asked me what I had in mind. I said, "We can give back some land, as long as we retain a major part—the house, first hall with land. I was thinking the part where the granola and corn are; we can always plant it somewhere else. If we let go of that large strip, it will reduce our workload a lot." After that conversation with my family, time went by without a decision being made. We spent a quiet Christmas at home. This is the second Christmas without my brothers. The house is almost empty. I am sitting on the fireplace step, looking at the flame, with one hand on my forehead, facing down, thinking, "What can happen now? I do not know what to do anymore. God help us." The New Year is at the door; we need to organize ourselves. Father Rocco is the only person who can help us out.

Seeing Father Rocco, I was shocked; possibly, he's right overall. We do not know anything about this war—what's happening out there; God knows. I spent the whole day out; my head is not working properly. Going to the variety store to pick up a pack of tobacco for Zio Tommaso, after that, I will go home and celebrate New Year with Mom, my sister, and my sister-in-law. It's later in the afternoon; I need to stop at the store. I hope the golden-haired girl is still there. It's New Year's Eve; sometimes, she might close early. Zio Tom will be happy; he smokes a pipe. Normally, in the morning, and once or twice a day, or after dinner. He is a good family man. Tom is my dad's age; he's married to Gilda and has two beautiful daughters, Laura and Benedetta. I am on my way to the food store. I say to myself, "I hope the store is still open. Normally, she closes at eight, but because it's New Year's Eve, she might close a little early. The worst is if it's closed; I will go for a walk to Mr. P's, have a drink, and go home." Making an empty trip doesn't bother me much; I just feel bad if she is not there without wishing her a happy New Year.

Soon I got there; she was pulling the metal shutter down. I said to her, "Hold on, Bella. You will not let me in." She looked at me, saying, "What are you doing here?" I smiled, "I am here because of you." She said, "Because of me?" "Yup, I came to see you." She goes, "Sure." I said, "Then, if you do not believe me, do not let me in." She goes, "I do not believe you, but I want you to come in. I have a little thought for your mom." So, then she goes, "You always come here just to see me, like other times, Toto." I repeated myself, on purpose this time. "Seeing you is like seeing the sun in the morning." The other time, I came to see you, plus because I needed to buy something. "Why do you not believe me?" she says. "Okay, come on in." I walked in, closing the shutter behind me. She lives upstairs, owns a lovely apartment; her mother owns this building, and she lives with her. We chatted for a good fifteen to twenty minutes, plus or minus, about this war, this year's business overall, or so. People are afraid these days; our neighborhood is not safe anymore. So, she asked to be excused for a couple of minutes, possibly to grab a cigarette; she is worse than a chimney. She took some time before she came back. After she came back, she was having a cigarette. I said, "Can I have one?" She looked at me, smiling, and said, "You've never smoked before." It was embarrassing for me to say that at my age; I had never smoked, also because in my family, outside of my mother and my sisters-in-law, everyone smokes. I was an innocent boy; it was the first time in a situation like this. So, I hardly whispered, "No." She got close, saying, "Here, try one." I got even closer to her, lighting my cigarette. I was getting close to her, so my heart was beating a thousand. I did not understand what was going on. I wanted to hug her, but I was afraid of how she would react. She kept talking; I was not listening to her. The only thing I wanted to do was get close to her, so I caught another word she said, "What else have you never done before?" That was embarrassing for me to say, so I answered her back, "No, I didn't." I didn't want to say I had never been with a woman before. Slowly, she started teasing me until I kissed her. In that moment, I remembered my brother's phrase, "Catch immediately when it comes, before she changes her mind." So, she was taking my breath away; there was no stopping until we made out. It was a crazy idea; for me, it was paradise. I was above the clouds, for the first time in my life. For the first time, I experienced what making love was all about. It was a crazy idea; she is older than me. For the first time, I was above the clouds, seeing some stars without being outside. I said to myself, "Why didn't I do this before? It is a first time for everything." Now I know what making love is all about. I had never been in that situation before; I had never thought she would do that. Considering a young boy like me, fifteen, in the next spring, she is about twenty-five. Then, I needed a little time to catch my breath. God, where was I before?

After that, we continued talking. I wanted to leave again, but she said, "Slow down, have a cigarette." I said, "Can I have a pack? I like to smoke occasionally. I started smoking lately; I just don't like to buy it." She started laughing, "You want to learn to smoke?" I said, "Look, I know how to smoke. My whole family smokes, as you know. So, I want to start smoking." I said to her, "You pay for the first pack." She laughed, saying, "Toto mio, you are a fully grown-up boy now." After a few minutes, she said, "Okay, only this time. Next one, you pay for it, or you don't smoke. I made myself clear?" I said, "Okay, deal." It's late, past midnight; I must go. "You live upstairs; I need to walk for half an hour to get home." I gave her a kiss and left. It was past midnight; I said to myself, "Welcome to 1942." I was singing like a bird. Every boy likes to sing. An opera of Giuseppe Verdi's Rigoletto (1851) I loved. This was unforgettable!!! After sending her kisses, saying, "I will see you soon. Happy New Year," it's past midnight. My mom, for sure, wonders where I am; she never goes to sleep if we are not home. Mom always wants to know where we are or what time we will be back; she worries about it. She does the same thing with my siblings. Regardless of how young or old you are, she does not sleep. I am rushing home; I want to take a shortcut, going through the mule track. Because of many rumors, I figured it was better to stay away from there, so I went to the gravel road. As my dad always used to say, "Better safe than sorry." Since Dad died, I have kept his spike knife with me. After that big story about werewolves, I am careful at nighttime, especially in later nighttime. I want to be home as soon as possible. Approaching the crossway near the church, it is a spot where you can see lights in the cities of Pescara or Francavilla, our town. So close to the church of St. Mary, I stop. I just remembered for a minute, looking all around me; something came to my mind. My brothers always used to talk about this place; they are ghost crossways. I say to myself, "This is possible?" Here I am in the middle of this; I see no one. So, my brothers were wrong about it; possibly a couple of hours past midnight. All this will happen anytime between midnight and three o'clock in the morning. I said, "No f...way this is possible." As much as that spot is so open, you will enjoy seeing if anyone is coming from anywhere. It's a legend from everyone.

It's not a good spot to stop. I look around me more than once; I see nothing. I just wonder if it is just a legend or if it's for real or like everything else. Dad used to talk about a werewolf in our neighborhood. So, I sit for a little while; all this gives me chills. I wait and wait, looking down to the city; the fire crack never stops. Slowly, I walk away from that crossway. I am possibly a little drunk; I did have a couple of glasses of wine there. I said to myself, "If all that is true or if it's another man's invention." I am a young man; being afraid is normal, but being afraid of ghosts? No way. I could also believe it if it were an animal, like my father used to say, about a werewolf. A sick man it could be an animal and not a man who changes into a wolf. I am ready for it; to see something. I want to know; I was anxious to see something, anything, a flash, or a person's shadow. As long as I can convince myself of it. So far, nothing. This is a legendary story like anything else. Sometimes, we need to experience things to believe; otherwise, we never learn the right way.

Standing in this crossway, I never see anything or hear something. I walk away slowly, turning around like a sea crab, here and there if anything will follow me or pop out. Whistling like a solitary guy, I reached home. It must be easy; it's two in the morning. I see nothing. All this gives me more self-confidence; to myself, I do not care what people say; I believe what I see. Sometimes, others exaggerate. New Year's late night, approaching the house, I see a light in the kitchen. We normally use oil lamps; it was kept low. I said, "Can Mom still be up at this time?" From her, anything is possible. I hope not; if she's waiting for me, it's trouble for sure. Soon, I got there; Friz came out from the barn and started barking. I said, "Shut the F...up, little one. You never bark; now you start barking. What's happening to you? All together, you come to shout; you want to wake everybody." He kept barking behind me, like someone else was with me or following me. I stop; I went down to my knees, patting him, talking to him, asking, "What's the matter, boy? It's okay; it's only me." I remembered Zio Tom always says!

Toto, your most fears live people, Not the ones that are dead.

I had a feeling someone was following me, but I never saw or heard anyone. It was a chilly night, and Friz stopped barking. In a couple of hours, it would be daylight, and at that moment, I thought to myself that someone might have been following me, which I didn't notice. I brought Friz inside with me. Normally, we keep him outside, but he sleeps in the barn. We're afraid for him because of coyotes or foxes. He's only a couple of months old, just a puppy. In the barn, it's warm and safe for him and the cat.

After I let him into the house, I started talking to him, saying, "Do you want to sleep here in the kitchen, near the fire? Luckily, everyone was sleeping; they didn't hear anything. They must have gone to bed early. I thought they would wait until midnight to celebrate the new year. Normally, when my dad and my brothers were around, we'd stay up late, sometimes until three in the morning. Now, it's like we play solitaire. After a few minutes past midnight, everyone goes to sleep. I would be sleeping too if I didn't stop at the market store by now. I said to Friz, "Stay put and no barking, okay? Otherwise, you go back outside." He was quiet, with his front feet stretched forward, his head resting on his leg, looking at me as if he wanted to say something. I said to him, "I am going to sleep now; you better be good and no barking." I stood by the fireplace for quite some time, thinking back to Tina. I asked myself, "How can it be possible? I am almost fifteen years old. To make love to her, she's possibly twenty-five." Friz looked at me. I asked him, "What do you say, boy?" The only thing he cared about was sleeping near the fireplace. I wondered if she would talk about us with anyone. I hoped not. I worried about Mom. If she knows, she'll surely have an illness or a heart attack. The next time I'm down at her store, I will have a little chat with her. This is not about me; it's more to do with my family. So, if she's okay to go to the open, or close the book, we need to talk about it. It's almost three a.m., and I need to go to sleep. I said to Friz one more time, "Stay quiet; otherwise, you will get me in trouble."

New Year's Day, 1942. I never thought I would be celebrating without Joe and Federico. I predicted they would both be back by now. My projection was having my brothers home. We could look forward to programming our work on the farm. Having my brothers here by now would have made my life easier, but unfortunately, they're not here. All my hopes have vanished, gone with the wind. After my visit to the church, and talking to Father Rocco yesterday, we have no hope to see our brothers for a little while. God help them, wherever they are. I hope they will be home soon. We all need to survive this economy. I have no clue where to start. It's New Year's Day, very cold. I finish cleaning and feeding our inhabitants at the barn. Today, my freedom starts now. I will take my own initiative to do everything I need to be done without asking anyone—no Mom, no Lena, or anyone else. I went back to the house, and Mom was up. She says to me, "You just got home." I start laughing. "No, Mom, I just finished at the barn." She looks at me with a mining look, saying, "Who let Friz in?" I said, "I did." Then, Mom said, "Get him out."

Without arguing with Mom, I asked Friz to get out. He didn't listen; he kept barking at me. So, I got close to him and said, "Hey, it's time to go outside, mister." He barked again. I picked him up and brought him outside. Going back to the kitchen, Mom said to me, "Where were you last night?" I was pissed off, so I said to Mom, "Okay, first of all, last night, I stopped to see Father Rocco at the church. Then, after that, I saw Tina at the store. She gave me something for you, a gift. After that, I went to the bar for a game of cards. So, please, Mom, I am asking you, please stop controlling me like a little boy." We bickered for a while, and then I said to her, "Starting from today, January first, from now on, I will make my own calls. Please, stop arguing with me. I will always tell you everything, only if I need to. So, stop questioning me in the future." A little freedom on my own from now on. She never stops asking, "Did you stay at the bar all night?" I said yes. "You can ask Mr. P." She asks me, "Who was there?" I didn't want to tell a lie, but this one was. She could go and ask if it was true. So, I said, "The usual. Nicoletta." I needed to close that conversation as soon as possible. I said to her, "Mom, soon I am fifteen. So, stop. I do have farm work to worry about. I need to run my own life sooner or later, right, Nicoletta? I am a young man; I need to go out sometime." She cooled off, saying, "Franz, Leonora, and the kids are coming for lunch today. Do not disappear again."

After lunch, with Franz, my sister, and sister-in-law, we started a conversation about this war and how we will handle it. Soon, we might get visitors from town to find out who lives at home, what we have, all our features, where our food comes from, what we produce, and who are the masters of the countryside. We'll see what happens when that happens. I don't believe anyone will come, but if someone does, we'll say we are farmers and we don't know anything. We're just working on other people's land since my older brother was dealing with the Master, and now he's gone to war. We don't have much information about them. January is a special month for farmers, with little work to worry about.

December was a cold month, and I'm sure January will be worse—snowing and even colder for the entire month. The fields are very wet. Talking to my mom after Franz and Leonora left, discussing new plans for the coming year, she's worried—not only about the farm but also about Marianna becoming a young lady, and Josie and Lena with the children. I asked Mom what she suggested, but she didn't know what to do. I gave everyone my opinion, so now it's all up to them to decide what to do.

Later on New Year's Day, I went for a walk, taking Friz with me. I stopped at Zio Tom's. Everybody was home. They have two young ladies, Laura and Benedetta, Marianna's age. So, I was having coffee with Zio Tommaso, and I asked about Mom's concern regarding our young ladies. With all the movements around Francavilla, it could be dangerous for our young ladies to become victims of assault or abuse by some animals—God knows from where. Then he said, "I do have a shotgun. I will shoot anyone who comes close to my daughters or my family." I laughed at him, saying, "They have automatic machine guns, Zio." He agreed, but he's not worried for now. We hope or assume this will never happen. Otherwise, we need to see what we can do about it. Then he rephrased himself, saying, "This summer, I will send both of them up to my cousins in Villamagna village near Chieti. There, they will be safe."

I remembered our master telling Mom not to keep too much reserve in the warehouse, so I went back and asked Zio if he had any cans to store or transport oil or wine, maybe five to ten liters or less. He was lost for a minute. I said, "Like the ones we use for transporting milk or small fuel tanks." Then he said no, he only has a large fuel tank in the barn. I thanked him.

Walking away from Zio Tom's house, Friz following me every step, I was about a thousand meters off the gravel road near Pera fountain, hoping to see Diana. As usual, it's hard to catch her here. No luck. I will keep an eye on her. To me, she will be my future. I cannot see that. I've never seen anyone talking or seen with her around. Maybe she might get confused, saying, "Diana's not for me." Mom told me that she's promised to someone else. It cannot be only rumors. Unless she had heard that from someone else before. I need to reopen this conversation with my mom soon.

It was a cold week. I'm walking back to the Nocci house, my mind thinking about how to save supplies for a rainy day, where to hide them so they won't go sour. We don't have a special hiding place. After talking to Franz and Zio Tom, I thought it would be good to save some supplies. I will visit this abandoned cave close by, a little small forest ten minutes from our house—perfect. No one will go there.

This place, no one knows about it. In the old days, they called it "vampire refuge." I hope it's just a fairy tale that no longer exists. It's almost dark. I wonder if I'll be able to see anything there at this time of the evening. This mini forest possibly belongs to the owner of the olive plantings at the hills of owls. I know there's a large bush prior to getting in there. I will go another time during daylight, not because I'm scared, I just need to see if there is another way to get in.

As soon as I got back home, Mom asked where I had ended up all afternoon. I said, "Sorry, Mom, I went to the countryside for a walk." I asked Mom if we would have dinner soon. She said no, I need to arrange it myself for once. "Okay, no problem, Mom." I looked at Friz and said, "Are you hungry?" He barked at me, which meant yes. We toasted some bread with oil and homemade salami—a great snack. After that, I asked Friz to go to the barn; it's time to go to sleep. He barked again. He didn't want to go out. I said, "No, just because I let you in last night doesn't mean it's all the time. So, here we go; stay there." After taking Friz to the barn, I went back to the kitchen. Mom was there near the fireplace, with her chaplet, praying. I said to Mom, "That day we spoke about Diana, you were joking with me, right?" She didn't pay attention to me. I noted that when she prays, she does not want to be disturbed. It's New Year's, later at night, almost bedtime. Looking at Mom, praying with her head down, like she's sleeping, I said, "Mom, you know it's January first today." Then she looked at me and said, "So?" I said, "If you pray on New Year, you must pray all year long."

CE UN DETTO, SE'' PREGHI A CAPODANNO, PREGHI TUTTO L'ANNO.

THERE IS A SAYING, IF YOU PRAY ON NEW YEAR'S YOU PRAY ALL YEAR.

She never answers me. I left her praying and went to bed early. I asked myself if these prayers would surely be for Joe and Federico, who are away from home. In the later morning, without going to the field, on a freezing and humid day, after finishing cleaning up the stables, I found myself talking to myself again. Friz looks at me, wondering what I am saying. Sitting at the board of the cow feeder in front of Mangia and Violet, our cows, I'm thinking ahead about this war and where my brothers might end up. Since Federico left, we have no clue. Only a little work can be done in the field at the moment. I now have time for other things to do here at home, a small job in the stockroom.

In the middle of the day, I wanted to see that cave, if it's accessible, before bringing anything in there. I will need containers to store and protect anything valuable. I'm going, but I'm not telling anyone about this. We have some residents in the barn—animals, I call them—our inhabitants. Starting from a dozen sheep, two goats, one pig, over two dozen hens and chickens, many rabbits, two cows, Mangia and Violet, and finally, a little donkey, Pippo. Dad used to call him "asinello americano." I do not know why. We do have space for more inhabitants, like a couple of horses or more pigs or more cows, but unfortunately, the cost is high, so buying more is not possible. Not everybody can afford it. Mom loves them; there she is, feeding chickens first before anyone else, as usual, for Mom can't live without the occupants in the barn. Every day, like a foil, I greet my mom before I leave home, no matter where she is. I will look for her and say, "I am going down to the farm; do you need anything?" "Yes, Toto," she said. "Stay home; it's a chilly day. I don't want you to get sick."

Going to that special place in the mini forest, there is an abandoned cave about five hundred meters from the country road. Full of trees, it's a mini forest where no light will come through, only a mixture of trees protecting the sun from coming through. There is still a small trace from the old days. Certainly, it must have been years since someone came here. This place is spooky. God help me; I wonder why they call it the Vampire Forest. I hope I will be safe. Lucky for me to find a gold mine here. It was not a clever idea to come here. There is a large hole with an old gate. Who knows if it works? Trying to open it, nothing happens. It would take a tractor to open it—an old iron club style. I will come back; possibly with a crowbar, I will open it. I need a lamp or something to see inside this place.

Going back home, I stopped by Leonora's house for a coffee. She was alone with the kits. I asked where Franz was, and she said he was in the village, seeing someone, possibly the Lorenzo family. I said I had never heard about them and asked if all was good. She looked worried and with a thin voice, she said, "Okay." So, I didn't want to go further. After the coffee, I left, hoping everything was okay. Unfortunately, I have an intuition for things, and looking at Leonora, I was sure that she was worried about something. What I do not know. I hope it is nothing. Sooner, I will come back and talk to her.

A few days went by since New Year's Day. Not much work can be done at the farm. My major concern is preparing the soil where the veggies go. That area is flat and has poor drainage, so it takes a long time to dry up. My other worry is that I never followed up with Leonora about the last time I was there. I had a major concern seeing my sister with a long face. She was worried about something. Normally she always smiles with no worries. Tomorrow will be two weeks since I was there, and I need to see if she is okay. At the same time, I need to see that cave. If it is suitable for a storage area, I am not sure. But I think that wooded plot is at the border of the ground where we have our olives, next to the hills of the owls. So next time I am there, I want to see if there is a track to exit at the olives field. I hope that the bush's partials belong to the same owner of the olives at the hills of owls, to Mr. Capo. It's a chilly day; it's below zero. I don't remember winter being this cold. I brought Friz inside the house. Soon it's dinner time. Mom doesn't like to see the dog in the house; she always says, "Bring him outside." This dog is intelligent. As soon as Mom talks, he starts barking at her. Considering he never barks, he understands when Mom complains about him. I said to Mom, "He likes to play with you." I said, "Okay, after dinner, I will bring him outside." Mom doesn't like talking during dinner time. So after we finish eating, I said to Mom, "We have extra replenishments. We need to go through this winter or longer." She asks why, and I say, "Just curious, Mom." She said, "Possibly two quintals of wheat, four sizes of bushels of flour, a hundred and fifty liters of oil, and very little of another supplier." I asked about beans, and she said, "Since you are interested in our food supply, ho mom, just I like to know about it. Do not worry." I need to take advantage of this weather; not much work can be done at the farm. So I can organize that storage for our surplus foods. It's a chilly night. After that chat with Mom, I took Friz out to the stables, spending a little time with him. He's growing like giant steps, and it is so quiet inside the stalls. All our inhabitants are nice and quiet. Walking back to the house, it's about two hundred meters. We have a small bench next to our front door, made by an oak tree split in half, about two meters long. Our farmhouse faces southwest. We can enjoy the sunset on a daily basis. Conversely, in the morning, to see the sunrise, we need to go to the side of the house, close to the barn. Sitting on that wooden bench, I have leftover half a pack of cigarettes since New Year's Eve, from Tina. I light one up, enjoying the thousands of stars. It's almost a full moon; it seems you can grab them with your own hands. A beautiful night.

This morning, after finishing at the barn with my occupants, I asked Mom if she needed anything from the variety store, saying I was going there, and afterward, I would stop by Pietro's house.

She says no, only to be safe. I wanted to take Friz with me, but he's only over a month old—too small for such a long walk. She always worries about us; sometimes, I wonder why so much fear. After I left by myself, as usual, I passed in front of Diana's house to go down to the main road. I never see her outside because there are trees that block the mirror between the house and the road. With my luck, no chance to see her. On my way back, I will stop by to say hello to them, an excuse for the New Year. As soon as I got to Tina's variety store, she was busy with a customer. I waited until she was free. As soon as she was available, she came outside, saying, "Hey, Toto, has the New Year been good to you?" I looked at her and said, "What about you?" She said, "As usual." "So, tell me, Tina, you talked about New Year's Eve." "About what?" she said. "About us," I replied. "I do not remember anything except your family being my best client and you a good friend." I didn't know what to say. I asked about a pack of cigarettes. She laughed, saying, "You have twenty-five cents." "Okay," I said. With a big smile, I paid for the cigarette and left without turning back.

Chapter 5
Boy struck by lightning

After I had freed that burden on my conscience, I thanked God. She forgot a ready New Year's Eve, less than two weeks. After that, I stopped at Pietro's house. Nuccia was there; she said, "Let me make you a coffee. Pietro will be back soon." I said, "No, I need to get going. I have a couple of stops to do before I go home." Walking up the gravel road, I saw a jeep with four military soldiers heading toward the church. Normally, they never come this way. I was curious if they would stop at the church, but they didn't, so I stopped at Diana's house.

When Marianna opened the door and saw me, she was surprised. "Toto, what are you doing here?" For a minute, I didn't know what to say, so I just wished them a happy new year. Standing in the middle of the door, she seemed to lose her voice. I said, "I'll come in for a minute." Then she said, "Of course, come on in." Her husband was not home, but Diana was there. I said, "Happy New Year, young lady," with respect to everyone. Marianna offered me a coffee and homemade cookies. My heart was beating fast—like a fast car or a strong wind. Diana was there, and her siblings were there, but Diana didn't say a word. In my opinion, Diana's mom understood why I was there. It was the first time I was at Diana's house, and my heart was pounding. All I wanted to do was get out of there as soon as possible.

January 1942. I am losing my mind. I can't find a small solution to collect all the vegetables concealed by the cold. I had to do it before the Christmas holidays. We'll see how to solve the frozen vegetables. We have a lot of fennel, escarole, and radishes. So, now, collecting them is hard. Removing the straw from them will be hard. Unfortunately, before Christmas, we protected them from frost with straw. Now, removing it needs the hand of God.

As soon as I got home, I went straight to the stables to see if anyone looked after our inhabitants at the barn. Thank God, someone did. I asked Mom who looked after the animals, and she said Lena. I asked why she didn't wait for me. For the first time, she said not to worry about it and told me to take advantage of this day to relax more. Soon, it will be hard work at the farm.

Talking about the farm with Mom, we need to cave the veggies before it's too late. She says not to worry; as long as we do it before the end of January, it will be okay. After that, I said to Mom, "I stopped at Marianna's house to wish everyone a happy new year." She looked at me and said, "You crazy son." I said, "Okay, Mom. You want to talk about it, or should we close this conversation now?" She stopped talking. Josie was there, so she said, "You like her?" I replied, "Nothing to worry about, Josie." I said goodnight to everyone and went to sleep. Mom mentioned dinner, but I said I wasn't angry and told her not to worry.

I went to my room. It was before dark. I pulled out Mimi's box and started playing the accordion, putting notes together. I began to sing, but it didn't sound so good. I need to write down something better. It's time to go to sleep. All that without mercy. The ground is frozen, so there's no way we can do any work at the farm today. We need to let it go for a little longer. I will concentrate on barn work and my new discovery: the shelter and how to renovate that cave/shelter for security in the future.

All our options are gone. From now on, Lena, Josie, and I will be in the field. There's no time for breaks or days off. Josie needs to come and help out. Marianna will look after the inhabitants at the stable. Mom will take care of the babies and housekeeping. We need to complete our winter vegetable harvest as soon as weather permits. We also need to clean all the bad grass and weeds, ready for spring sowing. Soon, our vineyards need to be taken care of. It's a chilly day, plowing the land where most of our veggies go is not easy.

I have been working with Mangia and Violet, our cows, for two years now. I am lucky; they listen to me. Since Dad died, I am the only one who can go around them. It looks like they've known me forever. We do have a wagon and a small wood sled to transport goods from the field to the barn or other places. With the wagon, it's safe because it's equipped with all safety features. The wood sled, not so much. It's very dangerous, especially downhill. There are no cables for a handbrake or a way to stop when sliding down. Dad built a small iron bar, about three cm thick by fifty cm long, which can be used as brakes. By making two holes at the rear of the wood sled, it was enough to insert it into the two holes, which slowed down the slide by touching the bottom of the earth when we went down the hill.

Being safe with that is impossible. I am paranoid when I go down the hill. Our cows or our donkey—they complain when they see me using the wood sled, like they know all about it. Our wood sleds are built in such a way, like snow sleets. Less than two meters wide by three meters long, very well built with two wood beams at the bottom from an oak tree, possibly 35 cm laminated like a boat style. On top, the wood platform is very sharp at the front, curved up for easy sliding on the ground. We use it a lot in the countryside, transporting straw, hay, grass for animals, and it's extremely useful.

Since Christmas has been so cold, always below zero, I would start with fennel. It's hard to clean. I said to Lena, "I am going down to the field, to the veggie camp. I must take out the fennel first. After that, it needs to be cleaned, washed, and placed into the boxes. If you and Mom come later, they will be ready for a final wash. When you guys come, bring Violet or Pippo with the wood sled trail to bring home the goods. Surely, it will be ten cases overall." I need my tool supplied with a hoe and an iron fork. I left for the field, reminding myself, "Not before noon."

Friz followed me to the field, chasing birds all over the place. I said to him, "You'll never catch them. Don't waste your energy." Thank God, the ground was not frozen. Removing the straw was a piece of cake. After that, I started digging partial fennels. After that, I will go to the escaroles. Possibly, the market store will take a couple of boxes each day of them. We must do this for the next few days until we're done with it. Normally, we do this before holidays, but unfortunately, this time, we were late. The weather cracked on us, and we only picked up what we needed for the house.

Later that day, Mom and Lena came down, washing all veggies, ready to be packed in the boxes for the market. We had about seven boxes overall. After we were almost done, I asked Mom if she wanted to take some rapini or so. We had space for one more box. She said, "Why not? They are good." We packed a box of rapini. They are the most requested veggie these days. Later in the evening, after I delivered all the veggies, on my way back, I went by to the Hills of Owls. It was very dark where our olives were. I had Pippo with me, our donkey. So, I walked through the end of it where the bush started. I wanted to go to that cave and see. It was dark, and I didn't want to leave Pippo alone at the side of the bush by himself. Not a good idea—there are always coyotes around. I need to do this in daylight. Going back to the house, passing by La Pera Fountain, I heard some noise at the fountain. I said to myself, "Possibly someone is doing laundry or washing clothes at this time of the night." I didn't have a watch, but considering how long I had been out there, it must have been past eight or nine o'clock. In the wintertime, it's late.

Walking away from La Pera Fountain, I was curious about the noise I heard, so I decided to go back. I wanted to see if anyone was there. It's located about 250 meters from the country road. I said to myself, "Our women come here sometimes in the evenings, but not this late in the winter." I needed to see if anyone was there. I saw no one at the fountain. I heard what sounded like a cubed voice—possibly an animal. It wasn't late, but immediately I thought of werewolves. With Pippo, I couldn't run, so I slowly walked away without making a sound. I was sure I had heard noises before. Possibly, I was wrong. My head always thinks about werewolves because of the stupid legend Dad used to talk about. I wanted to make sure no one was there. Stupidly, I went back to check it. The only noises I heard were the water noises coming out from the big torch leading to the big vessel where women do their laundry.

Winter 1942. It's been almost two years since my dad passed away. I remember when he told me about some animals, including werewolves. In life, there are things you don't forget easily. I learned that from my parents. All families have traditions that are continued from generation to generation. Other concerns are antiquity, which brings experiences and gives us advice. So, like my lessons from Dad about the werewolf or ghost, God knows what else, because it happens in our village. It makes me worried about things that sometimes enter your mind forever, like a disease that can't be cured until you die. Almost home, I saw the light on; Mom was waiting for me. First, I placed Pippo in the stables. Then I went to the kitchen where Mom was waiting. As usual, she said, "All good, Toto?" I said, "Yes, Mom, all good." I asked for anything to eat, and she answered, "Yes, son." Then she asked me if the greengrocer had given me anything. Mr. Storto said, "You'll go by tomorrow, and he'll have it ready for you." She was worried. She said, "I'm going to sleep. Please clean up after you finish, Toto."

It's been over a year since we've been so tight with money. I wish I could help in other ways, but unfortunately, there are things that we cannot produce here in the countryside. Sometimes, we need to buy. We have Luigi and little Nicoletta, who are first on my list. The most important thing is baby necessities, then everyone else. Our family has been going through many problems—from Dad's death to my brother Mimi's. Further to that, we've been seeking help from anyone. Oh, God, why this miserable life? The next morning, we had snowfall again. Luckily, I only uncovered the veggies we needed and picked up yesterday. Then, today was another wasted day at the field. This morning, after I looked after our inhabitants, I went to that cave. I needed to open that gate. After completing the work at the stables with my farm boots, I used to plow dirt, I went to the shelter. I had with me an iron crowbar and an oil lamp. I hoped this place would be suitable for great storage. Looking at this gate, it must be over a hundred years old. Otherwise, with rust buildup, I wouldn't be able to open it. I hoped I wouldn't need the torch. After wasting over an hour just trying to open it, I needed to be heated. Otherwise, this gate wouldn't move. This place is on a rapid hill with many mixtures of burning wood trees. It's extremely hard to walk through. Looking at the shelter, I said to myself, "It must have been here for a century." This mini forest must be over fifty hectares of land, connected to the Hill of Owls. I walked back toward the olives farm—a little long stretch to get there. The good thing is there's no mud walking through this tree. I will create a walking track from our olive field to the shelter as soon as I have time.

After my visit to the shelter, on my way back, I talked to myself about whether I wanted to keep this place a secret or if I should talk to my family about it. Either way, it would be a big job to transfer our goods there. As soon as I got home, Mom was gone, possibly to see Mr. Storto. I looked at Lena; she was playing with Luigi and Nicoletta. They are two years apart, growing together. It's nice for the two cousins. Nicoletta is more aggressive than Luigi; for sure, she will be mischievous. I asked about Mom and Josie. Lena said they went to town. Mom didn't want to go alone—you know the reasons. I opened a light conversation with her. She said, "I hope soon the boys will be back." I said to her, "Don't worry; they will be back soon. I'm so sure you and Joe will start a new life after this war."

My sister-in-law is right. There are many reasons for us to worry about them who are at war. We lost a brother; I don't want to lose anyone anymore. I am crying just thinking about it. God knows where they are—alive or dead these days. Lena was focused on the babies, saying, "I do not know, Toto, if it will be a new life. Since I married Joe, we talk a little; it's like I am not existing for him." I was so shocked I didn't know what to say to console her. Finally, I said, "Please, Lena, do not say that. Joe loves you so much. He is different from us—typical person, or I should say strong characters, like Dad. You remember Dad." Laughing, she said, "I do remember. The first time he saw me, he said to Joe, 'Where did you find this little rose?' He takes me for a small rose." So, I said to Lena, "Joe has many enormous qualities. He's a talented person. Just his personality is a little different, which other people envy him. So, give it more time. You know his character, nothing more. I'm so sure when he returns, it will be different. And don't forget little Luigi. He will make him go crazy with joy."

Early February 1942. I asked Mom about Marianna going to Villamagna with Zio Tommaso's daughters as soon as they go, possibly later in the summer. So, we should send Marianna with them. Staying here is dangerous for a young lady. After the last time I was at Francavilla, I saw many unfamiliar faces and a lot of soldiers around. I am scared for our women in the house. You, Lena, and Josie with the baby are a little more secure, but I worry about Marianna. She said, "Okay, Toto, we will talk to Franz." I asked why talk to Franz; Marianna is my sister, not Franz's sister. Then she mentioned your brother Pietro. "Give me a few days before we make any decision." I don't know how, but I want Mom to understand the risk of keeping girls here. We have no protection. So, I said, "We'll see if that's possible. We can ask Marianna's godfather at Chieti. She'll be much safer there. It's a quieter area, and it's close to home." I said to Mom, "Nothing is close to home. Regardless if she goes to Villamagna, it's much further from Chieti, almost half a day's walk from here." After we talked about the possibility of moving the women, I said, "Nicoletta, please, soon we need to make a decision." She reacted, saying, "If they stay here, they will not go anywhere." I did talk to Tommaso; I believe Laura and Benedetta will go later in the summer. If this war is not over by then, they need to go. Or we will send Marianna with Tommaso's daughters.

My biggest worries overall are all these soldiers in town, and lately, they started going around our village. I saw them going by near the church. So, regardless of where these soldiers are coming from or what races they are, I cannot trust them. So, Mom, please, let the young ladies go away from here. Keeping young ladies unprotected at home is a risk for everyone, including ourselves. Walking away through the hills of Owl, a shortcut from home, about a fifteen-minute walk, that little forest sits behind a small main farm road. It can be noticed only from the main gravel road going to the village. No one will hazard to walk in there. This cave, after so many years, now has a new occupant. "It is here, Toto Nocci. No one will find this place." This shelter has a name, Vampire Forest, so the shelter I will give a proper name from now on will be Toto Cave. After I left that shelter, I said to myself, "That place is perfect to hide anything. Enclosed by trees, with tiny light and stretches of sun coming through, very relaxing." Soon, I will find the owner. I will ask if they will gift it to me at no cost. I will open for hunting in this mini forest after the war is over. Here I am now; we will open this gate. It took me a little time to open—a fair-sized gate. I will need some oil to loosen the hinges of the door. It's very rusty; otherwise, I cannot fit some boxes or other containers. This place is a tunnel, very solid, all stone. It does have some qualities. It can be used for many things. I am so sure this has been here for a long time, possibly since primitive days. I am sitting here and enjoying the forest air for a good half-hour, having a cigarette inside the shelter. I am smoking three cigarettes a day. I am too young; it's not good for my health. Well, all my brothers smoke, or so my dad, long he was alive. There is no man in our neighborhood who does not smoke. I say eighty percent are smokers. At the same time, I am thinking about what I can hide there—possibly well-protected containers, a barrel of oil perfect for wine barrels, and some homemade tomato sauce bottles. No wheat; it will feed the mice. We'll see what else we can store.

As soon as I got back home, Mom jumped on me, shouting and yelling, asking where I was all morning. I said, jokingly, "At Diana's house." She said, "Bullshit." I said, "Why don't you believe me?" She wants to know, or for some reason, she keeps an eye on me, this day, since that night out of New Year's Eve. My biggest worry is Mom does not trust me anymore. I always play dumb with her. So, I asked Mom, "Do you think I will lie to you sometime?" Talking to her, I asked her to remember she hid things from Dad once. "Can we talk about it, tell me more?" She said, "Then, yes, Toto, I will one day. Sometimes, people think without knowing they are hurting other people's feelings. Remember in life, do good to anyone, forget all about it. Do bad to someone, think about it." Mom made it so clear; we do have an open account with someone out there.

The Nocci family has been known in the past to be aggressive people. Possibly before the eighteenth century, they too were peasants, as much as their ancestors. Sometimes, a little thing you do builds a story behind you, and that remains or stays in the family forever from many years ago. Since those days, God knows what happened to our great-grandparents. Sometimes things do happen. Unfortunately, the story never dies, remaining forever with families. The only thing she says is not to get in any trouble out there, and to stay away from unnecessary arguments. After that, she says, "I only have you, Leonora, Pietro, and Marianna now. Any more sorrows in my life will make me suffer more." Someday I will tell you more, Toto. She holds many grudges in her life, and she doesn't know who to talk to. Telling me about her youthful life and what she went through truly makes me cry.

We are in the late winter of 1942. The war continues. Few people are working in the countryside. After that little story of my mother, it worries me a little. She has suffered a lot in recent years. Losing your husband and a son in the war in six weeks is not easy to suffer and survive all this. Mom grew up without parents, serving other people—difficult days for her childhood. Since I remember, she's always given us the best a mother can give to their child, a thousand one percent in everything. She never had a good life—seven children to worry about. She's worked since she was a child, never knew what it meant to be a free lady, always under pressure from others. I never forget when she said that to me. "I met your dad; it was a new day for her, something to lean on, someone to protect her from fears as a woman, or I should say as a child." In those days, the late eighteenth century, life was worthless, living without having someone to tell you the right things or reassure you of your fears, teaching you what life is all about. Difficult for a young girl without parents to accept things you don't know. Being afraid is nothing wrong; the only thing is if you have someone tell you what it's all about, teach you what life is, and walk you as you grow up.

Mum for us is like a hen for her chicks, with many roles—she can scold us and tell us what to do or not to do in our lives, but she always dedicates her whole life for us and for all the other things she loves. Mom always gives us her all, talking about good things and sad things. Dad was, I would say, cruder. He was a man who didn't give satisfaction to others, a man who took without giving. He was a guy who pretended for no reason until he got what he wanted out of his life. He presumptuously obligated you to give or do what he wanted in his own way. I asked Mom how she knew so many things about our father or his family apart from the life she lived with him. Then she said she knew Dad before they got married, so she said, "A quiet bet since I was working at the cemetery, twelve-thirteen years old. After meeting your dad, we became friends. We used to live close by. Slowly I met the rest of the family, and I got to know more about all the Nocci after I got married to him in nineteen-o-eight (1908). I am happy to become part of the Nocci ancestors." I wanted to ask for more, but she wasn't too happy to talk about the family, so I played a game, saying, "Look at what a beautiful product you built with our father." She said, "What did I build?" So, I said, "As you don't know what you've built." She said no. So, I explained to Mom that she gave Dad seven beautiful children.

Later in winter, working in the field, many times I ask myself if I do the right thing for my ladies at home, and if they are happy with my work. I am worried so much about them; I don't know what to do sometimes. Many times, I don't know if I'm right or wrong, or if I'm wrong about what I do on the field and home. This war never ends. I am so worried about my sister Marianna. She's a woman now, or so my in-laws, they are young ladies; we need to think about their safety as soon as possible. I walked down to town a couple of days ago. I saw what was going on around the town. Next time I go, I will see better what is happening. Since Mom wants to bring some fresh veggies to Mr. Santoro, it will be a great idea to look around. She asked many times to do that; the last time was Christmas day. I will try to go down before the Easter holidays; we have time for now. Many farmers have lowered production lately after the news about needing to contribute to this war. Many people worry. No one needs to support this war. Peasants collectively took many forms in our days to contribute to WW2. Our family was lucky never to be raided or obligated to support military actions. I am a young man, worried about many things from farm obligations to family issues. As much as it's on my agenda, it's all in my daily bread.

March 12, 1942, early afternoon, a coincidence came up. I sat down to have a little bite, just a sandwich. After that, I lay down on the ground for a couple of minutes, with my hands behind my neck, relaxing. I fell asleep, dreaming of having a bath in the small pond where our water creek is. We have a small pond where we wash all our veggies. Such a stupid dream—from the water, a werewolf popped out. I said it can't be; we are in full daylight. Normally, they are only around at nighttime. I was drowning in such a little pond. Then, thunder woke me up. Friz was lying down next to me. I was scared to death, sweating like a pig, as if I had taken a bath. Without wasting any time, I left to go home before this storm hit us. I said to Friz, "We better rush home; otherwise, we will get wet."

I said to myself, "Two years today, my dad died." The sky is black, scary thunder and lightning; big rain will come down soon. A few meters away from us, it starts raining. I said to Friz, "We better move; it will rain hard soon." I am two minutes away from home! Heavy rain; I am running like a rabbit. Soon, I got to the barn door. I stopped to catch my breath. I was there for a minute, at the stable door, lurking in the door frame, looking at the big thunder flashes, a big lightning. I said, "It's scary," as it seemed to crack the sky in two parts. The next one, even bigger, coming down. "Ho, Fu... I hear calling my name, 'Toto, hey Toto. Can you hear us?'" I see my mom talking to me, or so Franz. I was looking at everyone. Hardly, I could hear their voices. I was stunned, lying on my bed, with great pain in my head. They were talking among themselves, saying, "He needs to rest."

Later that night, I got up. I asked what happened. Mom said, "You got hit by big lightning. We found you on the ground near the stable. Thanks to Friz; he was barking like crazy, so we came out from the house to find you on the floor. The toilet has been demolished to zero, including the tree next to it. You've been lucky to be alive." Mom asked if I wanted to eat anything. I said no; I waited for dinner time. She said, "It's past dinner time, son. You've been sleeping for over five hours since we found you at the barn." I said to Mom, "Can that be? I do not remember anything." Meanwhile, my head went on like two drums, boom, boom, like someone hitting you with a hammer on the head.

The next morning, I woke up early. I went to the barn; hardly I could walk. I saw Friz sensing around. I said, "Hey, come here; we'll go for a walk." He started barking at me, like he wanted to tell me something. I said, "Do you want something from me?" I did five hundred meters; I had to go on slowly. I came home; Mom was there, making coffee as usual for everyone, asking how I felt. She asked if I wanted to go to see Dr. Cicca. I said no for now; we'll see. I stayed home a couple of days, working around the barn. My head still spinning; a couple of weeks went by since I was hit by that lightning. I am much better now, not a hundred percent.

I do get a few small blows as if someone pinches you on the head, nothing serious.

April 5th, 1942, Easter Day. This year, we didn't reenact the Passion of Christ with Zio Tom and Toto. They never asked, and I didn't volunteer. Regardless, there was no way I was in condition to do so. I am not recuperating one hundred percent so far after what I went through. It might take a little longer. I am back to the field. I never went to Marshal Santoro's to see if anything happened about my brothers. I doubt they can help me with it. Mom has been quiet these days. Normally, we have a little tradition for Easter—some homemade cookies that taste good. Every region has its own tradition. Mom always has a couple of styles using the same mass of flour. Typically, donuts, in horseshoe-style format and a doll with a boiled egg on top, or Tarallo-type donuts. Sometimes, jokingly, I ask if she will get me a horseshoe-style cake. They are good for dipping into coffee. I did join Mom for Mass. Only a few people attended Mass. After exchanging Easter greetings, I saw Diana. She is looking great— tall, almost my height, long hair. She is a star. Saying hello to her, the mother without hesitation called her, saying, "We are running late; we need to go home." Mom looked at me. She felt like ignoring us. My mom said, "Do not worry about Toto; it's not your fault." After Mass, I asked Mom if I could stay behind. I needed to talk to Father Rocco. She said, "Be home for lunch." After Mom left, I sat at the last bench of the row, waiting until everyone was gone. Seeing our priest after Mass is like going to see the doctor. As soon as everyone was gone, I asked Father Rocco if there was any news overall about this war. We sat at one of the church's benches together chatting. First, he asked me how I felt physically. Then he said, "No, Toto, all this is not looking good. This is a world war; no one knows what will happen. Let's hope the Lord sends it to us." So, I asked about this guy who comes around sometimes, a quiet person, tall, big guy. I never see him in the village, only here at church sometimes. Father Rocco couldn't figure it out. Then he says, "You talk about a built guy, tall, middle-aged." I said, "Possibly, Father Rocco, yes." When he went on telling me he is okay, he lives a little far from us, at the bend of the provincial road. So, he does come once in a while. Nothing to worry about him. Toto, his name is Attilio. That made me feel a little better. Going back home, I walked together with an old friend, Donato. He lives in Cetti neighborhoods. We walked about five hundred meters together. He is older than me, has no school, and no work. He helps a small contractor, repairing chimneys in our town. He was telling me if this war doesn't end soon, he will join the partisans. I said, "You're crazy..."

After that, I stopped visiting the villagers' old people. I said to myself, "Every weekend, this war took all our brothers away. I need to go straight home; otherwise, Mom will spank me for being late for Easter lunch." Later noon, we were all sitting at the table having our Easter lunch. Josie asks, "When is this war over?" Mom says, "Figlia mia, this war never ends. No one can tell. We hope soon, or remember for us peasants, life is always a war. From when you are born today, you die. We never stop suffering until our Lord says so. After that, we go for a better life. Possibly, no one agrees with me, liked or not. It is reality." We were enjoying Easter lunch. Later, I will go down to see Pietro. I hope they are all okay. I said to Mom, "Possibly, I will be late. Don't wait for me until later in the evening." On my way down to Pietro's house, I wanted to stop at Mrs. Ciocco's house to see if all was okay after that rush from the church this morning. I am curious if they were in a rush because of Easter Day or if she didn't want Diana to talk to me. I started believing Mom; what she said to me, to stay away from her. I need to have a good talk with Diana soon. One of these days, I must do that; you do not want to believe everything you hear from others, including Mom.

In spring 1942, after Easter lunch, I went to see Pietro. Everyone was there. My niece was happy to see me, saying, "Zio, we got a doll for Easter." Pietro and Nuccia did the impossible for this girl. We chatted for a little while. They asked about Mom and everyone else at home. They also asked me to stay for dinner. I said yes; I would love to spend time with my brother. I had dinner with them. I was happy to chat with my brother and my nieces. They are big girls, ten and twelve. Before I left, I asked Pietro about this war. Nuccia started crying. She said, "I hope I am wrong, but there are rumors Pietro will be called back to the army soon." Tears were in her eyes. She said, "Can't they do that? They have a family to worry about—Franz with three kids, and us two and one underway." I had no words to tell Nuccia. I said, "It's only rumors, Nuccia. We pray to God that never happens. Do not worry for now. People talk without knowing what they say. Do not think about it for now; just relax. If one day he needs to go, I am here. You can come to our farm and stay with us if you want. We can manage together, so don't despair now; we will wait and see."

Pietro says, "No, we're okay for now. We'll see what's happening down the road; time will tell. Hopefully not. If we need to move out, I'll go near the cemetery where Nuccia's family is. They have a good space there, and we can stay with her mom." "Thanks, Toto," he adds, "You guys are three families there. We don't need another one, so don't worry; we will be okay."

After thanking Nuccia for dinner, I said, "Okay, brother, we're always there for you if you need us." I left later in the evening and didn't stop anywhere; I went straight home. It was dark, the main road without streetlamps. You can imagine our countryside without streetlamps—only in our dreams do we have electricity. After passing by the famous crossway, I said to myself, "It's early, but I want to go by the fountain. Last time I was there, I was worried because of some noises I heard. Even though it's early, I'll go straight there to see if anyone will be there so late." As soon as I got there, it was so quiet, only the sound of water coming down from the tube source. I sat at the edge of the concrete bevel where ladies do laundry. So peaceful. We Italians say, "Not even the spirit of a living soul." So silent. Here, you can sleep without anyone disturbing you. I had a cigarette, enjoying a few minutes of the beauty of this place. I said to myself, "I don't know where, but I did read a sentence somewhere: 'In life, you can build something beautiful even with the stones you find in your path.' Well, it's late; time to go home." Slowly, I walked home, without worries or thinking of anything else. As soon as I got home, Mom was there waiting for me. Normally, she never goes to sleep before this time, always past ten. Lately, I've seen her more relaxed, I should say more energized. It's been months since I've seen her like that. She had the fireplace going, always kept for later in case Josie or Lena need to do something for the babies.

I wanted to talk to my mother about Diana, but I didn't know where to start. So, I said, "Mom, I know your feelings for Diana. Can I ask you something, off the record? Mom, what do you think about her?" She says, "Toto, all mothers want good things for their children. Certainly, the love we have for our children cannot be replaced or changed for anything. But sometimes, we make elementary mistakes as parents—advice or telling our kids certain things, such as how to get married or what to do. Unfortunately, we do that only for the children's love; hardly we want to hurt our kids or their feelings or run other people's lives. It would be the worst thing a parent could do. Diana is one simple example. She's been promised to someone—a guy you possibly know. His name is Brunetto." I said, "Mom, what are you saying? That guy is Mimi's age. God bless your brother—I didn't mean to name your brother." Mom is too old for Diana. Or so he's not here; God forgive me—possibly he'll never come back from the war. "I will talk to him when the time comes. We need to break off that marriage; there's no way this guy will marry Diana." Mom got upset with me. She's right; I shouldn't have said that. Correcting myself, I said, "Mom, I will talk to him when he's back. He will understand. Diana is too young for him. So, I will tell him to leave Diana alone. Finito. I hope he comes back from the war. I will settle this score on my own."

Mom reacted to my words, saying, "Toto, first of all, limit your bad language. And second of all, you stay away from them." I said to Mom, "It's my problem, not yours, Nicoletta. Who cares about

Brunetto or anyone else? Listen to me, Mom; we are a poor family, but respectable and honorable people. So, Nocci is well-known to our town. I will do something about it." She didn't like it when I said that I would do something about it. She screamed at me, saying, "Listen to me; sometimes, love plays bad tricks on people. That's why you stay away from that family." She closed the conversation about Diana; possibly, she won't talk about it anymore after tonight. She went to sleep, leaving me by myself next to the fire, alone on a chilly night, to think about what she said to me. I stayed up late; possibly, I won't sleep tonight. Normally, I don't sleep much. I made myself a coffee, lit a cigarette, and called Friz inside. Looking at him, he will be a big dog. Five months old, he's like a newborn calf. Since I let him in the house that night, he loves sleeping here near the fireplace, only if Mom's not around. After this Easter break, we need to organize farm work. Slowly, I am recuperating from the lightning strike. It would be better if I saw our family doctor. It's been bothering me lately; I have a continuous headache, something in my brain like a pinch. Possibly it's just the stress, also the pressure of responsibility that is in the countryside. Soon, we need containers for preserving homemade foods. This time when I go, we do need some containers. Or so, I will go to see what they look like. We do need to store some olive oil and some wine or other goods we have at the warehouse. I will go visit our Marshal at the Caserma; after that, I will go to the consortium. Or so Sunday, my fifteenth birthday. I hope Mom will do something special this time. It's been so long that we haven't celebrated a birthday—for one reason or another, it's always been forgotten.

As soon as I got home, I asked the ladies if our occupant had been looked after. Mom said yes, nothing to worry about. "Just come and eat; otherwise, it'll get cold." I looked at Mom; she was cleaning up near the sink basin. We have a homemade concrete sink. Sometimes, she washes other minor kitchen tools or even clothes there—small stuff. Before I sat down for my dinner, I noticed she ran out of water. I said to her, "I will go, Nicoletta." I asked her if Friz had eaten; she looked at me, saying, "Friz is bad." I asked, "What did he do now?" She said, "Do not worry; I will fix him up." As soon as I got out there, here he came barking at me. I said to him, "You got Mom upset. Can't you stay a full day without me? You got in trouble with Nicoletta." I started playing with him; sometimes, he goes crazy when I am gone for the full day. Possibly, those are the reasons he barks; otherwise, he doesn't like barking. After I picked up the water, he followed me into the house. Before Mom said anything, Friz barked at her, like he wanted to tell her something. She said, "Why is he barking at me?" I said, "I don't know; possibly, you did something to him." She said, "Get out." I said, "There you go, Ma'; he knows you don't want him in the house. That's the reason he barks at you. Be nice. He knows you do not want him inside the house. Only sometimes do you let him in." After we finished dinner, I told Mom about getting a headache on and off. She said, "Possibly too much stress." I said, "No, Mom; I am worried about that strike from the thunder. I hope that didn't damage my brain." She came close to me, saying, "You don't worry about that; you will be okay. You see, give it time; all will be good."

Spring 1942, later in the morning, as I was heading down to the field, I saw Zio Tom. I said to him, "Are you here to help me today?" He replied, "No, Toto, it's been a busy month. Maybe next week I can give you a couple of days." Our vineyard needs care. I asked Lena to lead Josie and Marianna to look after the branches that hang down as soon as possible. They need to be tied to avoid damaging the fruit stem. Additionally, Lena, please make sure to pick up any weeds built up around the trunk or the base of the plants. Any dead leaves or too many branches without fruit produced in the low area need to be removed. Lastly, let me know if there are any broken wires along the Capanelle. After my long talk with Lena, with my suggestions, they will have work for some time. Me and my cow will work on plowing the area we didn't seed this year. I want to make sure no weeds grow; otherwise, it will be harder next year to clean up.

Working away my day, I realized that this coming Sunday is my birthday. I will ask Mom for a cake to celebrate my fifteen years of life. I am always thanking God for it, for giving me life. I've been working in the field like Pippo, so a little song came to my mind. I started whistling it with an easy joke, saying, "Affaciati bella mia, I am dying of nostalgia. Take il ciestello andiamo via, tra Fiori e monti di maiella miaaa, viviamo questa vita lontano da qui. Su Montagne Verde che aspetta noi, incluso l'Abruzzesella miaaa. Affaciati bella mia, che muoio di nostalgie, il mio cuore piange di allegria, senza te non andrà via."

After a full day in the pit, both me and my cow were tired. They needed rest and food. Going back home, I saw Remo, my friend, near our veggie field where his dad has land. I stopped for a few minutes and asked him about his friends Gianni and Roberto, if he saw them after that day we met down in the town. He said yes, we see each other here and there. I asked if he had any news about the war. He said, "There is nothing, Toto, only worries. People are starving in the city. Our leaders are losing control of the situation. We hope by the end of this year it will be over. Otherwise, our country will be in a lot of trouble. And God knows, you and I will end up on the front line soon."

As soon as I got home, the first thing I did was look after the animals. I freshened up Violet and Mangia, my cows, giving them a good clean-up. After that, I brought them to the stable and gave them some fresh grass. I made a cauldron of broccoli leaves cooked with flour and ground wheat for them. They loved it. I do it once in a while, especially when we've had a long day in the field.

As the day was almost dark, I sat on the front door bench, having a cigarette and looking at the sun disappearing behind the mountain. It was a beautiful red sky. I wished I could capture it with my mind. I wished I had a camera. I never saw one or touched one with my hands, only in my dreams. One of the teachers when I was at school had a photo showing us a camera. It looked like a little box to me. It was in my second year of school. She had a lot of patience with us, explaining what a beautiful instrument it was or what it looked like. As the saying goes, there is always a first time in life for everything. I'll never forget; Dad always said to all of us, "For every living person, there is an opportunity in life, as much as there is a way for everyone." In my options, there are none; there is no other way or source I can hold on to. From now on, I will take one day at a time. Tomorrow is another day.

Early morning, having coffee with Mom, I asked again about Marianna. Should we send her away or keep her here? She said, "No, Toto, I want to keep Marianna here with us." After Mom's decision, keeping everyone home for now, I am not comfortable sending her anywhere. I said, "Okay, Mom, but remember, if we see any strangers come around, they all go, including Josie, Lena, and the kids." She said, "Okay." Then she asked why I was so worried about all this. I explained to her about bad dreams or what I saw in the city, including the last time I went to town. Then I asked her when the last time was she went to town. She said, "Possible when we had your dad's funeral, almost two years ago." Today is completely different. Later, Mom mentioned that there is an army in the streets, which is why I am worried. Moreover, I saw military jeep trucks coming to the intersection near the church. After Mom said, "Okay, we will look for a place soon, but don't forget something," she tried to make me relax, saying, "They are like your brothers, serving the country, so we should not worry. Please, do not think about it, Toto."

Later in May, my head is not working. Sometimes I am experiencing some headaches. I should say, small sharp pains. Mom wants me to see a doctor for it, but I said no. Maybe later if it doesn't stop. It's been a little better lately, so I'll let it go for now. After we cut down our veggie plantation, we can relax a little. More time for our vineyards and tomato plants. We have a lot of tomatoes this year to worry about. I never had the chance to go down to the consorzio place to see what is available in small containers. This coming Sunday, I will go. I need to discuss with Mom if she has a few lire to spare. That way, if I find the right ones, I can buy them. At dinner time, I said to Mom, "How many bottles do we have for tomato sauce for these years?" She said, "Not much, about two hundred." Then she said, "We will need new corks for them." I said, "Maybe we need more this year. This coming Sunday, I am going to the consorzio to see what they have. So, I will look for the corks." We need to hide house supplies. Otherwise, we need to start looking for a safe place for our ladies to stay if this war does not come to an end. Soon, I need to tell Mom about the containers. My savings possibly are not enough to buy all of it. I wonder if she will agree or not. We are going to need it soon. She said, "Can we manage with what we have without spending money?" Lena never says anything. Then I said, "Mom, if we want to save some oil, wine, and other things, which you keep in the jars with vinegar or oil, such as dried tomatoes, peppers, sauces, and pork fat, they last from two to three years minimum if kept in a cool area."

Lena liked my idea of saving some of the extra stock we have at home. The only thing she said was, "Where will we keep the preserved items, and will they last a couple of years?" I said, "I have an idea. You guys live that with me, okay, Mom?" We stayed late. It was almost dark when we left the field. Mom never said yes or no about the containers. "Chi tace consente," there is a saying, "who is silent, allows." So, I believe Mom will agree with it. Going down to the consorzio on Sunday, for sure, I will take Pippo with me, our donkey, to help carry back our needs. If I purchase the containers, I will put the saddle on him. That way, we will bring home all we need. Otherwise, there's no way I will be able to carry all on my own. Possibly, I can take Lena or Josie with me. Going always to the town, they will be dead tired. I will ask my friend Remo to go with me. It will be the best solution. Before I spend Mom's money, I said to myself, I need to make sure the cave will work and who owns that little forest. So possibly, Zio Tom knows who the owner is. I will ask him next time we are together. It's been two weeks since I planned to go to the consorzio to pick up what we need to store tomato juice and other things for the future. I never had the time. We've been so busy on the farm site every day of the week, from sunrise to sunset, including Sundays. There was no time for anything else. It's been so hard to stay on top and keep up with the most important work on the field, seasonal committed work, from the vineyards to the vegetables, without forgetting the wheat harvest coming up. This coming Sunday, I must find the time to go there and get tomato corks and containers before it is too late. I hope I find what I need for it. This day is not easy to get what we need.

This year, we plan to bottle about 300 liters of tomato sauce, hopefully enough to last two years. The surplus we can sell; I hope I'm right, and we will produce over five hundred boxes of tomatoes. That will give Mom some extra money to carry on until next winter. We have the wheat harvest coming up. I will talk to Mom about keeping only what's necessary to stretch to next year and giving the balance to our landlord. Hopefully, we can pay off that promissory note we have outstanding from last year. The wheat harvest will not be enough to pay back one hundred percent of the loan, but we will at winery time. We need to clear those debts before the end of this year. I am cleaning the area around the barn to make space for the grain to be threshed soon. Mom came down, and she says, "I will help you with it, Toto." I say to Mom, "This is very dusty; it's not good for you to breathe in the dust at your age." She says, "Don't worry; dust will not kill me." I saw her looking so sad, like someone without hope in life, as if to say, only the desire to die. I got close to her and said, "Are you okay, Mom?" She said, "No, all this is killing me slowly. Since your dad died, and then Mimi, two of my sons... only God knows where they are. This war without an end... no, Toto, I'm not okay."

Summer 1942, we have no more strength left to go on in this life. I don't know what to say to Mom to make her believe that one day all will be okay. Unfortunately, life has been sour for all of us. All we can do is pray to God and wait for Joe and Federico to return home one day. Then I said to her, "About little Nicoletta, Mom, she looks like you. And don't forget little Luigi... looks like Joe. What can you say about the little ones?" She gives me a little smile, saying, "You're right; I should not despair and have faith in God. One day, my family will be back together again." This morning, we had a downpour, heavy rain. The only reason we are at home without going down to the field is too bad because today is Saturday; otherwise, I could go to the consorzio. I hope it clears up later so we can do some work in the field. It stopped raining about an hour ago. Working around the house is okay; going down in the pit is not possible. This afternoon, if it does not rain again, I will go. Since that lightning strike I had in that storm, now it is scary. I don't want to be struck again. I am not sure, but people say that a couple of spouses got killed long time ago by a thunder. So, I do not want to think about that. Shit happens every day; today to me, tomorrow to you. So, I will wait a little longer if I need to see our doctor, I will go. Going through some of Dad's old tools, I found an old hatchet, an old tool to cut the reeds in the woods. It's a typical axe on one side and the other side like a scythe, a powerful tool. It needs to be sharpened and a new wooden stake. Later today, I will take it with me. I need to cut a few branches to make a little track to walk freely from our olive field to the cave. We call that place the vampire shelters. Soon, I need to use that place to hide some goods. After that, I am so confident that place is perfect for our needs.

I saw Mom hanging outside around the stable talking to our occupants. I got close to her and asked what she was bitching about. She says, "Nothing, just talking to my chickens. They are all over the yard, making a big mess." I said, "Nicoletta, leave them alone; nothing to worry about. They will not go anywhere." Then I said, "Hey, Nicoletta, I have a request. Can you make pasta e fagioli neri di casa? I meant homemade pasta and black beans. The homemade pasta is a special shape, done by hand, cut into little square pieces, about two cm squares each." She replies, "What desire came to you today? You know that for children, it's heavy black beans." I said, "You separate the pasta for them. Hey, Mom, we eat late today, not before eight. I need to do a couple of things on the farm. Do not forget; I like it made with a lot of tomato sauce, quelli pelati, and tomatoes without the skin." After my request to Mom, I fed Pippo, our donkey. I fixed the scythe, getting ready to go to the Owl Hills. I will need oil for the lantern and rust release for the gate. On my way down, I need to stop by Tommaso's place to see if he has some lubricants for that old gate.

I thought I had some, but we didn't have any. He possibly does, otherwise next time.

As soon as I got to Zio Tom's, it was just past lunchtime. He was at the barn, working around the tractor. I said to him, "What are you doing, Zio?" He said, "Oil change. Soon, we need to do some serious work, so I like to keep fresh oil ready to work." Then he said, "What brings you here?" "Oh, I need something. I wonder if you have some lubricant for the old hinges on the door," I said. He says, "Yes, I do. It's a new product, an additive oxidation. It will last a long time." Then he asks, "What do you need it for?" I lied to him, saying, "For the barn door; it's getting rusty." Then it came to my mind when Dad lied to the brigadier. I said to myself, "Why did I lie to Zio?" Well, it's too late now. Going to the owl hills, I stopped by the Pera fountain to see if Diana was there. As usual, no luck. Still, I have an open diary about Diana's boyfriend. After what I discovered by Mom, I want to talk about it with her directly. All these rumors... I do not like. In our country, rumors are like a disease; they will attack you like cancer and never leave you alone until you die. I do not want the word to be spread that she is engaged to that person. Otherwise, we are in trouble if that happens. I do know the old man, Mr. Faro, Brunetto's father. I will see them sometime. They are not too far from Diana's house, just below our church, a noticeably quiet area. I finished early today. I will stop by half an hour's walk from the hills.

Looking at the mini forest, I said, "I will walk to the northwest of this bush. At the end of this bush is the hill of owls, perfect. Going to the tunnel from here is a piece of cake. Get to work, Toto. There is a minor donkey track space going into the tree without cutting any branches. No one will notice this walk-in away if someone comes by here." Looking up, I can see almost our house. I never noticed that before, so it is an easy way in. This track is perfect to get to the tunnel. A little long this way, it is safe; no one will see me in and out. Later afternoon, cutting small branches, I left the front of the cave as it originally was, so it looks like no one was here before. I oiled the old gate before I left, hoping it will take off the rust buildup. I hope the liquid Zio gave me will work on that old gate; it is so heavy to open halfway. Next time, I will work on it. Next time I come here, with my donkey, I will carry anything to be stored.

Going back home, I said, "Now I will visit Mr. Faro." Soon, I got near the church, I tied Pippo at the side of the road. No one will see; I am lucky that this donkey never brays. I left Pippo 500 meters away from Faro's house. Soon, I got there, he had a dog, a small retriever. Possibly, he used her for hunting. So, before I knocked, she sniffed me out without barking. She's very friendly. After I knocked, the old man came and opened the door. He knew me, saying, "Son of Luigi, Nocci, yes, you know us," he said, "Who does not know the Nocci family?" I either said jokingly, "It is a compliment or an offense to us." He said, "No, please, come in for a coffee." Apologizing, he said, "I am sorry for your father and brother." So, I said, "Do not worry, Mr. Faro. Do you have any news from your sons in the war? We do not hear anything for so long from my brothers. I've been asking around; no one can give me news about it. My mom, she is going crazy because of that." The entire village has no clue about it; he says no one brings home any hopes. We pray to God they will be back soon. Then I said,

"Okay, we will see each other again; hope they will be back soon, Mr. Faro." The guy didn't walk me out; I was on my own. They have a big property here, a lot of stuff. God bless him; what luck. I walked to the rear of the barnhouse; I saw a godsend, a full serrà of hay of the first-degree type, all impaled with iron ropes, protected by a roof over, protection from rain or snow.

After I saw Mr. Faro's house, I said to myself, "My sister, they are starving for a shortage of hay for their animals, and this guy has so much surplus. This guy is loaded, overflowing with it." Without thinking, I grabbed two bundles, taking them with me. Almost dark, no one will see me. As soon as I got to Pippo, my donkey, I said, "You can carry more; I will go back and take more." So, I went back, grabbed two more bundles, and went to Leonora's house, half an hour walk. I did go, a quick delivery. As soon as she saw me loaded with hay, she wondered where I took that from. I said, "Do not worry; you're good for a couple of weeks. After that, we'll see." I am heading home; it has been a long day. Even Pippo is tired and hungry, passing dinnertime. As soon as we are home, I will look after you, donkey. Early Sunday morning, I woke up Mom, asking if she will go to the town with me or if I need to go by myself. At the same time, I need to take the donkey with me to bring back the supplies we needed. After I finished at the stable, I asked Mom again if she was coming. She said no, to ask Lena; she said, "I am going to mass." I said, "I waited for you after mass." She says, "No, it's too much of a walk for me, going always to the consorzio." I said, "Okay, Mom, I will go by myself."

Mom gave me some money, not much, a few liras for corks. After I arrived at the consorzio, it was quiet, almost deserted, no one there except the owner and an old man picking up some seeds. I asked for some corks or tomato jars and what the cost would be. The gentleman said, "I don't have much." Then he asked me if I was Luigi's son. I said yes; you knew my dad. He looks at me, saying, "Yes, you do look like him a lot. I knew your dad since the old days. He used to live up at Ponte Zelis before." So, I asked again, "Sorry, I didn't catch your name, mister." He said, "It's a difficult name. My name is Jacob, but everyone calls me Giacomo." After a little chat, I said, "Do you have what I asked for, Mr. Jacob?" He said, "Not much. I have some jars and two demijohns of 50 liters each, corks as much as you wanted. If you take all of it, you will give me a good deal." He said, "Give me a minute." So, if you take all of it—five hundred corks, two demijohns, four dozen jars, and ten gallons with lids—I said yes; he gives me a good deal overall. I loaded poor Pippo like a mule with a backpack. I said to myself, "I hope Mom will give me the money to finish paying Jacob; I owe the guy two hundred lira." I do not know how to manage it. By the time I got home, it was later afternoon. Mom looked after our occupants at the stables; Marianna was not home. I asked Mom where she went; she said, "I believe over to La Peras people for a coffee." Jokingly, I said to Mom, "Hope she's not in love with Biondo. He's too young for Marianna." Mom says, "You always think for the worst." I said, "Only cooked broad beans cannot be born; the rest, everything is possible." She doesn't like my concern about Marianna. Believe me, she is a grown-up young lady; aggressive, I feel sorry for any man who will marry her. Mom's conversation about Marianna made me think about Diana. I said to myself, "I should take Diana now. At her age, even if she was eighteen, I don't want to lose her."

I am cleaning up the warehouse, going over some supplies we store here. I did find Dad's old WWI tools. The gun is a piece of junk, but the sword I liked, and I will keep it in my room as a memory gift from Dad. There are many other items, mostly junk. I stayed late at the warehouse; I want to see most of our suppliers. Now, the most we can spare is olive oil, possibly two hundred liters of wine, and 500 kilograms of wheat. Luckily, Dad kept the wheat in metal containers so mice can't get to it. Everything else is normal daily reserves. After the wheat harvest, I will take all our wheat stock to the mill. They will give us the necessary flour when we need it. I am always thinking ahead, as I have four ladies at home and two babies to worry about. It's better to have some reserves in place before it's too late. Mom helps me out with the money owing to Jacobs, paying off that small balance. Now, we need to focus on our summer harvest.

Just before the wheat harvest, Mom asked Zio Tommaso if he would come and do the cutting for us, making it easier for us to collect behind the tractor. It will save time without asking too many people to help us out. Many times, we thank Zio, always quick to help on the farm regardless of what we need. He never says no. Early morning and late at night, Tommaso is always there, helping us out. On the second day of our wheat harvesting, we are having a light lunch for everyone in the field. Just past noon, sitting below a tree's shade, I asked Zio if the ladies will go to Villamagna, as we talked about earlier. He says, "Toto, we haven't decided yet." Then he asked about Marianna, Josie, Lena, and the kids, if they will go away later in the summer. Mom joined the conversation, saying, "No, Tommaso, for now, we stay together until the end of the year. Possibly I will send them to Marianna's, up north of Chieti. We need to see what is going on with this war. Hopefully, it will be over soon. Otherwise, we all need to go away from here." After that conversation, we went back to continuing our wheat harvest, without stopping until the end of the day until it was dark.

Working on a collection is not easy. Sometimes there are consequences of many types: space, containers, help from other people. It's not a game. Most of the time during our harvesting, we are working from daylight until later at night in the field. With our poor manpower, we need to give all our efforts to the harvest, giving it one hundred percent attention by the full family. Many times, Mom comes; she takes the baby along with her to help us out in the field. We went on for a full week to finish the wheat harvest. Afterward, we need to have it threshed and disposed of as soon as possible. This time we made a deal with our landlord to keep for ourselves only twenty-five percent of it and pay down that promissory note we have. We had a decent harvest, possibly bringing our deficit down to fifty percent. I never asked Mr. Monte about it; I am sure Mom will see Mr. Monte if he will rectify that note.

After that, we did our corn harvesting, nothing to share with the landlord. It's all for us, just enough for our needs. Soon we will start with the large tomato harvesting. I hope we will get some return from there. Mom likes to keep only the leftovers after the first and second selection are done. The people buying from us want suitable selections for wholesale purposes. Any leftovers we use to make sauce for the house. I need to set up the place in the cave as soon as possible to keep all the extra supplies we have: wine, oil, tomatoes, and other products made by Mom, preserved in bottles and glass jars. After that, only the tomatoes need to be saved. The shelter is perfect for holding these products: mild temperature, quite dry, like a cold cellar. Without any worries, inside, including on the floor, are rock-stone. I need to create a couple of shelves for the bottles and jars to keep them off the ground. If there are any animals coming inside, I am keeping the gate closed. Sometimes there are foxes or coyotes around, so this will keep the bottles and jars safe.

Lately, I am helping Zio Tom; he needs to clean up around the firecrackers building. There's extra land they don't use and belong to them. Unfortunately, because of the need to meet a distance from any close residences since this war started, he has had problems with them. His house is near that powder keg, and we know the land belongs to him. Renting it to those firecracker people was a terrible mistake. Loaning all that parcel of land many years ago was a bad deal. Since then, it has been giving him only problems. Many times, there have been sabotage in that place. I told him to let them go, tell them he needs the land. He explains, "Not easy, Toto. The town will support them because of the type of work they do. They build firecrackers for too many organizations, including major town festivities. So, it's not easy to let them go. Having people in the house who are strangers, you risk being robbed and bribed. When he gave this land away for so many years, he did not consult any legal advice, and now he has a problem. I hope he will solve it as soon as possible; otherwise, it is cooked for a few more years to come."

Later in the summer of 1942, soon we have our winery harvesting coming up. This year, there's much less than in years before. In the past, we always had extra to sell to the vinoteca. When Dad was alive, he sold part of our share to the wine cellar, keeping part for the house. This year, there is no way we will reach that quota. For some reason, I don't believe this harvest will give us enough to send to the wine cellar. It's less work for us, but there's no squeezing a little for the house. We will drink less; my house ladies do drink a lot. So do I; I love wine. Regardless of red or white, most of our vineyards have Montepulciano red grapes. Mom wants to keep part of it for the house. We do have a couple of demijohns left from the previous year, so this year, we can cut down a little. It has been so quiet; you see no one around. Many people are afraid to leave the house, including my brother-in-law Franz, with three kids; it's better to stay home safe.

Sometimes, I wonder about all the sacrifices we make without any return. There is no satisfaction. I remember in my third year of school, I was reading an Italian comic book, a short paragraph about two monkeys. I read a small paragraph, a comic book named Bil-bol-bul, an old book in the school, damaged, possibly from the twenties, maybe even older. Two chimpanzees, possibly brothers, a small one and a grown-up one. The little

 one stole a banana from the garden; the mother graced him, possibly because it was the first time. So, the big brother saw that, changed face for anger, the color of his face, saying, "If it was me, I would be punished." I am saying it's God's way of punishing poor people. I do believe in God, or so I believe all peasants who farm land believe in God. Like Mom, praying every day. Christ loves them the most. Not because they are special people, but because they pray more for a better life. God gives without asking. Possibly more results on the farm without praying every day, like Mom does. What I learned from the doctrine is that we need to pray for our soul, not to obtain something from God. Our Father says, "Give us our daily bread," or others will pray for our sinners. Something I remember, as much as I am not a good Catholic man. Julius Caesar says, "King of Rome, give me what is mine," or so he said, "Give to Caesar what is of God." He meant all belong to God in the end. There is no such thing as yours or mine. I was right with Mom; you pray on New Year's Day, you will pray all year long. So, I am saying, Mom, please stop praying on New Year's Day.

As soon as we are done with our last harvesting, I am visiting Compare Mario. They are located near Chieti, and we need a safe place for our women. I do not trust the strangers buzzing around our city. I will go in the morning and will be back before the end of the day. Mom wants to keep Marianna home, but I will insist on moving her to Compare Mario, whether she likes it or not, before it's too late. After seeing that military jeep near the church area, I don't feel comfortable, especially with few young ladies left from the village, especially younger teenagers. Over the weekend, I will go to Francavilla to see if everything is good.

After the fall rush, I visited the town this week. Looking at our seacoast, it's full of military personnel. I don't know why or where they are coming from. Mr. Santoro, our marshal, is not around. One of the brigadiers told me that the situation is critical. There is a possibility we need to move out from here. Possibly, he refers to moving from where they are now to another location. I just don't know what he is talking about. This is our town; we live here, and we will stay until we die. I need to stop at one of the old churches, Santa Liberata, in the main road center of Francavilla. It's a few steps from the post office, a cathedral built in the late eighth century. This church was built in honor of Santa Liberata after a miracle in Francavilla. So, there's an old story about a monk who came from far away. He was attracted by a mermaid at the seaside who lured him into the water. He would have been killed if it weren't for a miracle by Santa Liberata, who appeared with angels smashing the siren. So, the monk was saved. After that, he made the vow of chastity in honor of Santa Liberata. Just a little story about our church of St. Liberata.

Talking with my mom after my visit to the town, we are very worried about what the brigadier said, or seeing so many soldiers around. I am so sure our country is in a lot of trouble, especially after the request for even younger people to be called to the army. I am so sure that, as the brigadier says, we need to watch our daily steps, where we go, or what we do. I am convinced the ladies need to go away soon. The only place I can think of is Compare Mario near Chieti, a small village. I will need a full day to go there and come back home. We need to relocate our young ladies as soon as possible. Finally, Mom gives a sign of understanding, agreeing to have them go away from here. This coming year, we are keeping the sowing exceptionally low until this war ends. In winter, we always review all our options, what we need at the barn, if we have enough supply for our occupants. The major animals to feed are the two cows and Pippo, our sheep, and donkey, who need less. Mom always takes great care of our little animals, which often die of hunger during the winter. Many times, we pick up fresh grass from the field site. The only problem is it all depends on the weather permitting. Sometimes, in late December and January, we get frost, and there's no way we can pick up any fresh grass from the field. In less than a month, it's Christmas holiday. Without my brothers home, God, tell us they're okay. Let them come home soon. Christmas is not the same. I will go for a walk in Chieti. We need to place Marianna, Josie, and Lena in a safe place and relocate them there.

After our last olive harvest, I spoke to Mom about the tunnel. She wonders what I did with it. I saved over two hundred bottles of tomato sauce, about fifty liters of oil, and two demijohns of wine so far. No other food or preserved food. We are very short lately with everything. Mom asks if there's anything else we can save there. I said, "Anything protected from small animals, Mom." She wants to see the place, but I say no to her; otherwise, she will go by herself when she needs something. Going there by herself is out of the question. Not only is it uncomfortable for her to walk back and forth, but it's also an uncomfortable trail for her to carry anything. I explained to her that I will go with Pippo and pick up what she needs when she needs it. Unfortunately, we only have oil, tomatoes, and wine there. Anything else, I ask Mom if she wants to go to the church with me tonight. It's a chilly night, possibly too cold for her to come. I am going by myself.

It's a surprising night; only a few people are here. After midnight mass, I asked Father Rocco what's happening. I didn't see many people at mass. He looks at me, saying, "Toto, people are scared of going out at nighttime these days." Military personnel are coming around every second day. Then he says, "Toto, I don't like what's happening in our town. I can smell troubles. We need to stay alert with so many strangers around our city. Tell your mom not to worry about the farm too much; first, ensure the safety of the family." After my chat with our parish priest, he made me worry about our family and its safety. Walking back home, I walked through our village. I didn't see a light on; it's completely dark. Christmas night, this is not a good sign. I got home almost at two am. Friz was lying down at the front door without barking this time. I sat on the bench near the front door, saying to him, "It's a chilly night, my friend. Do you want to come inside?" He's just a year old, and Mom trained him well. He knows he's not permitted in the house, so she takes him for a walk.

Christmas day, possibly, we are all together. I will talk to my ladies about moving out soon; it is important. Between this holiday and the new year, I will go to see Compare Mario; they are in Chieti. Weather permitting, I will go, but it's always colder there than here, sometimes with heavy snow. I didn't sleep all night after my chat with Father Rocco last night. I am distressed by the situation here in Francavilla and what may happen in the coming months. I better look after our occupants first this morning. After that, I will go over our situations with Mom. I am sure she will come up with a solution. Later in the morning, after I was done with our stables' work, I stopped by Leonora and Pietro's house. I need to see if they are considering having women and children move out from the house. They are much closer to the military activities, but we are a little safer here. Today, no one is taking into consideration how risky it is to live along the Adriatic coast, full of foreign soldiers wherever you go. My brother Pietro is afraid even to send Nuccia and the kids over to her parents northwest of Francavilla near Leonora. There's less traffic there. Where they are now, on the other hand, Franz will not move; he wants to stay home without going anywhere.

Christmas day, lunchtime, as soon as I got home, Mom wandered where I was all morning. I said, "I went to see Leonora and Pietro, stopped for a coffee at the village bar, and here I am, all yours, Mammina." However, she gave me a special look, knowing I was about to say things she wouldn't like. After lunch, I asked my house ladies if we could talk about a couple of things, regarding this war and their safety, for everyone's benefit at the house. Lena was the first one to say yes to it. After that, Mom said, "Yes, Toto, what is it?" I didn't know what to say. Our town has become dangerous, flooded with military personnel. I won't know what's happening. Regardless of what I think, we are close to the seacoast, and don't forget Pescara is a big city guarded by the military, most of them Germans. I don't feel safe for anyone to stay here anymore, except for Mom and me. So, as soon as I find a place, we need to go away from here as soon as possible. Mom did not agree with me, saying, "You see a ghost down the town," then she said, "We are not going anywhere for now. I told you, and I repeat, stop bothering me. I want to stay here in my house."

I was incredibly angry with her. I wanted to shout like a madman. She doesn't realize what is happening in Francavilla and

Pescara these days because she is a good person, expecting everyone to be the same. I said to Mom, "Please, you and I need to go down to the seashore to realize for yourself what happens there on our seacoast." So, after that, she said, "Okay, we will go after this holiday to the town to see what is happening. Remember until then, I don't need to repeat myself about this." Telling Mom last night at church no one was there, the church was almost empty, which tells you anything; people are scared to go out these days. Other people left the village this holiday. God knows where they went and stayed. We need to find a place first before we can move. If we stay here or go and stay somewhere safer, I assured Mom I would stay here and look after our occupants this winter. If they want to go, I am sure I will be okay alone here, plus I have Friz with me, a good guarding dog. So, Mom says the only place I can think of is Marianna's godfather. They are near Chieti, not too far from home. I can stay with you for now until late spring. Mom's idea was great, so I will see Marianna's godfather tomorrow to make sure they are okay with it. Lena and Josie didn't comment on it; they are also scared these days. They know what's happening out there. It will be the best thing to do these days, move to a safer place north of Chieti or farther than that.

The next morning, I left early to go to Mario's place in Chieti. I took Marianna with me; she will be happy to see her godfather after so long. We left about seven, and if all goes well, we will be there before lunch. I hope she will remember the place. I've only been there once before this war started with Mom and Dad. I was in school at that time, so it's been over four years. We brought along some Christmas gifts for the godfather, hoping he will like them. Mom prepared them last night specially for them. Fried sticks, with flour, eggs, and sugar, are Mom's specialty for Christmas. On my way up to Chieti, it is a chilly day. We were halfway when we saw a farmer with a horsey wagon catching up to us on the main provincial road. The old farmer asked, "Where are you guys going?" I said, "We are going to Chieti, visiting our godfather." He invited us to get on the wagon, giving us a lift for a few kilometers. So, we did get a break. Overall, we got there about ten.

Our godfather was not home; only his wife Maria and his son Tonino were there, along with some strangers. There were about five of them, plus three kids. Marianna was happy to see the godfather, even though she was not her godmother; only her husband was. After giving her the little thought Mom gave us, I asked when the godfather would be back. Maria said he would be around lunchtime. He went to Chieti for some personal reasons. I said Marianna and I would wait for him; we want to ask him for a favor if it's possible. We chatted for a while about this war and the area they were in; it seemed to be noticeably quiet. Maria said not really; Chieti is busy, with a lot of people moving up from the seashore area. Showing Maria's Mom's treat, she said, "Oh my God, my favorite Christmas sweets." She was happy about it, commenting on how Nicoletta always has a good touch over cookies for special occasions. We had lunch with the godfather. In southern Italy, when you sponsor a kid, they all become part of the family, as compare or commara! It's an old way of respect for the entire family.

I asked Mario if it would be okay to host Marianna, Josie, Lena, and the kids for a little while at their place until this war is over. He looked at me, saying, "Compare, we can keep only Marianna for now. We do have a family from Ortona since late summer. They are Maria's relatives, and everybody, for now, is having problems. Many people are in the same shoes as us," he says. "We are not so sure how long we can remain here the way things are right now." "For my little commara Marianna, we will sacrifice a spot one way or another. For everyone else, it's impossible to accommodate everyone here." We had a long chat, and I felt sorry for Mario; poor guy, he will do anything to help in these situations. We need to find another solution for our family. Marianna is nineteen; she understands staying here will be a big responsibility for our godfather. We left about almost three in the afternoon. Probably we will be home by dark. It's a long walk from here to our house. Before New Year, we need to see where and how we resolve this situation. Marianna and I are close in age compared to all the rest of my siblings. On the way back home, we talked a lot, so I asked her a couple of things. She went to Lapera's house the other day; was there any reason to go there? She didn't want to tell me the reasons. I said to her, as a joke, "You know, Biondo is too young for you. Mom will spank you if she finds out about it." She says to me, "Mind your business." I said, "Okay," then I said, "You know he's much younger than you."

We made it back home with good timing, ready for dinner. Mom started asking questions about the godfather and family. Marianna did all the talking. The first thing she said was, "I am not going there. I will stay home with you guys if it is, Mom." She looked at me, saying, "What happened?" I said to nothing, Mom, "They do have a family from Ortona, and the spaces are limited." So, they don't mind having Marianna. Our full family is impossible. Marianna says, "Mom, I'm not going anywhere, regardless of what is happening here in Francavilla or Pescara." Mom, with a short comment, said, "If we need to go, we will go, whether you like it or not, young lady. This is for your safety. No more comments about this. We will figure something out soon." After that comment with Mom and the rest of the family, I am worried about them overall. Possibly this winter, we will stay together here without going anywhere. So far, we have no other option. After this holiday, we will decide what route to take for the safety of my family. Since all these soldiers invaded Francavilla, it is not easy to stay safe with three young girls in the house, plus my mother and children. Only me, a man, can protect them. It's best to secure them as soon as possible. I'll ask around where they can go: in Villamagna, where Uncle Tom's girls are, or I'll find another place. There's a good place in Caramanico, but it's far away. I'm sure something will come out.

New Year's Day 1943. After tending to the occupants at the stables, I walked down to Mr. P's bar. Pasqualino, in his late fifties, is a good man, solidly built, a typical bartender who can manage non-behavioral people if he needs to. I enjoyed a coffee there. Remo, my old friend, stopped by. I asked him why he never left to join the partisans in northern Italy. He laughed and said, "Soon." Then he asked about me. I replied, "No, I will stay with my ladies at home until this war is done, with the hope that one day my big brother will be home." After I left, I stopped by Pietro's house nearby. I asked Nuccia where the kids were. Pietro said they left them with Nuccia's parents this holiday. The situation here is not that great, Toto. Possibly Nuccia will go there soon. I sat next to my brother for a few minutes. Then I asked what was going on. Pietro didn't talk. Nuccia said he had been called to go back to the army soon. I hugged him, having no words for him. I asked Nuccia if she wanted to come and stay with us. She said no; she would go with her kids to Miglianico. Walking back home, I asked myself, "All this is happening now, over four years since this war started. We are praying to God for it to end soon. The entire world suffered from this war."

Our family has been damaged by this war so much. We lost our father, then my brother Mimi. We don't know where Joe and Federico are. Now Pietro needs to go. A big family in the hands of God. Not a great New Year's Day to give to Mom. I don't have the courage to talk to her about it. She has a head full of negative memories. I can't give her any sadder news. On my way home, I stopped at St. Mary's church. I needed to light a candle for the dead. It was past mass time, and no one was at church. It was completely empty. I sat there for a few minutes, looking at Christ on the cross. I said, "Only you can do something about this war, no one else. Please, God, let our siblings come home one day safe and sound." I left the church later afternoon. Our church spot is perfect to see what is going on around the seashore, including our town. I wonder why the soldiers come by here so often lately. They can see the entire coast without navigating the entire area. It's about a two-kilometer, twenty-minute walk down the hill from the church to the coast.

Later, winter 1943, we received a visit from our good friend, the Marshal from Francavilla. Mom was happy to see him but apologized for not visiting him during the past holidays. He said, "Don't worry, Nicoletta. I am here to warn you guys. It's time for all of you to go to a safer place. We are informing the villagers to move out. If they stay, it will be risky. Please find a place to go." The Marshal was clear; we need to move out from here. We do have a couple of options: Roseto, Silvi, or Atri, northwest of Pescara. Small towns, are much safer there. He said, "If you guys have any people there, you might know someone there." We knew that was coming. After Pietro went to war, Nuccia moved to Miglianico with her mom. I am so worried about our ladies. Three of my brothers are in war. Looking at Mom, she doesn't have any tears left to cry about. Mom suggested Atri. There is a family Dad knew there, La famiglia Pavone. He always said to Dad, "If you ever need help, come to see me." Dad knew Mr. Pavone since WWI. After that, we saw him only once or twice. It has been a long time since we saw them last time. I don't know if they are in Atri or nearby. I've never been there. Mom started screaming like a crazy person. She was going crazy these days. I left; she needs to calm down before we go anywhere. Going to Atri is about a day's walk, with kids and our wagon of supplies loaded. It could be much longer. God knows if there's another option close to our home. Now we worry about what will happen to our farm. Possibly I will stay back. I will do what I can by myself without my ladies. I will prepare myself for it. By Easter, I want them to go to Atri, whether they like it or not. There's no turning back.

After consulting with Mom and Lena, I said, "Guys, our territory is getting bad. Possibly there will be an invasion by other countries or a big fight on our seacoast. No one is safe here anymore. We need to move out as soon as possible." Mom wants to do the summer harvest before we go away. I know she worries about everyone. We don't have much to take with us, leaving everything behind, hurting our economic position. So, I said to Mom, "I will come back and deal with our harvest as needed."

Church Parkette over 300 meter above sea level, twenty-minute walk to the shore, beautiful mare Adriatic view.

Easter Sunday, April 25th, 1943. Many people have left from our seaside, only a few farmers are around. Our family never left, but tomorrow we will go. I am all ready; I boxed the chickens to take with us, and Pippo. We brought our sheep to Zio Tommaso's friend in Villamagna. I hope we can get back after this war. They have a lot of sheep there, over a hundred. Zio's family is there for now. We don't know if they are safe or not; we'll see. I visited the cave to pick up over fifty liters of oil and all of Mom's preserved food in the jars to take with us, leaving behind some oil, wine, and tomato sauce for later. Going to Atri is about thirty kilometers, over eight to ten hours walk. There's no way Mom and the kids can do that, so I sit the kids in the wagon, Mom walks with us. We are taking side roads; it is much safer. I tell Mom we will go via San Silvestro, to Villa Raspa, Montesilvano Colle, Città Sant'Angelo, to Atri. We will do three stops, hoping all will be okay, guys. We left so early without saying anything to Leonora;

they said they will go to a friend's house they have in Roseto Abruzzi. Daiana and her family left for Silvi Paese, nearby to Atri, where we are going.

The last few days, many people have been evacuated since last autumn when Zio Tommaso told us about it. I say to Mom to let Marianna go away; she refused to do so. Since then, many others left without being told. There are rumors our city will get bombed sooner or later, and we are under fire from being hit. We are the few left behind. There are many farmers eventually; they don't want to go anywhere, taking a chance to stay home was out of the question. I wanted to stay behind also, but I wanted to make sure that our family is safe and sound where they stayed in the Atri area. This place we are going, I've never been there before; I hope it is a safe place. Staying with the Pavone family, I am so sure they are in good hands. The only thing we know is it's a safe place for now; we'll see. One thing is for sure; as of now, there are no soldiers or bombs, according to our Marshal Santoro. We left early; we wanted to make it there before dark. We've never done this road before; I hope we don't get lost. Walking for over two hours, we just passed Villa Raspa. The next stop will be at Madonna Della Pace. After we arrive there, we need to take a break; my head hurts, and I am getting some pinching on my back like someone hit me with a hammer, so we better stop for a few minutes. The next stop will be at the next village, Tre Cimminieri. We arrived there just after noon.

All this because of this war. We stopped for a few minutes; the babies need attention. Lena and Josie will look after them, and Mom will assist. I lay down on the ground under a beautiful oak tree, a big one. Friz is next to me; he wants to be pampered by me. I said, "Sorry, my friend, this is not the right time." Possibly we stopped for a good twenty minutes. We had some coffee and Easter cookies made by Mom, Dolci di Pasqua.

This road is completely away from Pescara; we stayed away from the seashore. It is a little longer stretch to go up to Atri, but at the same time, much safer than the main roads. I am talking to Mom, saying I will go back home after we settle at the new place we're going to. She told me, "I am coming back with you, Nicoletta. I want you to stay with Josie, Lena, and Marianna all the way. I can't leave them alone. I will go back by myself." Since we left this morning, I am worried about the farm. We left without checking everything. Not only that, we have so many veggies and other goods without giving them to anyone to take care of. I look at Mom; she is walking at the front, pulling the cow's cord on her hands. Lena and Josie take turns sitting on top of the wagon with the babies, so I ask her to go and sit on the wagon with the baby and let Josie or Lena walk more. She's been walking since we left home without taking a break. Going to the wagon will relax her legs for a little while. Mom is a golden lady, never complaining or grumbling about anything or contradicting another person. In life, she has much love for everyone. Continuing our road to Atri, soon we reach Città Sant'Angelo. As soon as we get there, we will stop for half an hour to feed our animals and take a good break for ourselves.

Chapter 6
Displaced by the war.

Thank God, we finally decided to move out. It weighed heavily on my heart, especially with Mom opposed to leaving home. Convincing her wasn't easy. Later in the afternoon, after a brief break at Citta Santangelo, we were getting close to Atri. The trip had turned out to be longer than expected. I wondered if we were still in Abruzzi. We had been walking all day since we left home. From here, I could see the Gran Sasso Mountain. After a full day of walking, one day I will go up there. It seems like a dream! Dad's passing comes to mind.

Here we are in Atri. From here, we can see the Gran Sasso mountain. Just under that, we have our protector, St. Gabriel, a young shepherd boy who became holy. God blesses him with so much confidence. We Abruzzese believe in him very much. We arrived just below the town. I could see a rapid ravine to get to it. I decided to stop here. We needed to see where this family lived before moving on. There was no one around. I told Mom to wait while I went up the hills to see if anyone knew this family. Friz always follows me regardless of where I go. Just before we walked into the village, I saw a priest coming down. I stopped. A priest was perfect. I turned around, and we waited for him. Mom asked him about the Pavone family, who lived far from where we were. The old priest stopped to chat with Mom, saying, "Signora, you need to go back. You've come too far. I will walk with you guys. They are located about half an hour from here, going back toward Città Santangelo, about three to four kilometers back, in a small village called Collo Petito." The old priest invited himself to help us out. After a little conversation with Mom, asking where we were from and how we managed to get there from so far away, we learned his name was Don Ambrosio. He was the parish priest for St. Gabriel Dell'adolorata in Atri. There were many churches in Atri, and we were lucky to find this priest.

After a brief chat with the priest, we asked if he knew the Pavone family. He walked us there. We were dead tired, and it was almost dark when we reached the farmhouse. Soon, a lady came out asking who we were looking for. She was around Mom's age. Father Ambrosio never came in. He left us at the entrance gate of the farm, near the main road. As soon as Mom explained the reasons we were there, the lady recognized Mom. They had met before in Francavilla. The lady was courteous enough to let us in and relax for a few minutes. It was almost dark. La signora was so kind to us. Mr. Pavone knew my father from the old days. By any chance, if he's around. She said she would be back later and told us to relax for now. She asked Mom about Francavilla, a beautiful town we were in. Mom said she had been there once, during a big festa of saints. Mom wasn't sure which one, saying it was on top of the hill, near a pretty cathedral, a popular name. The lady went on talking about the beautiful church in Francavilla. She talked about other places, saying she couldn't remember now. I said to her, "San Franco?" She agreed, saying San Franco was a beautiful church, with a bell tower and a sea view, one of the best. We celebrated there every year from August 15th to the 18th, during Ferragosto.

Ninuccio came in, and he looked at me, saying, "You are Luigi, Nocci's son." I was surprised; he had never seen me before. Then he asked, "Where is your dad?" Mom started crying, so he figured out that Dad was dead. After a little family talk, I asked Mr. Pavone about staying with them for a while and whether there would be enough space for us and the animals. His wife said, "We have a room for the two kids and their moms. You can share it with Nicoletta, yourself, and your sister. We also have an old kitchen next to the stall; you guys can share that. Unfortunately, we don't have much; this is a small farmhouse." I said it's perfect and invited him to help me unload the wagon and everything we had on it. After spending a couple of days in Atri, settling my family there, including the animals, I had a little talk with Ninuccio. It was a great evening. He said many things about Dad. Then he said, "We haven't spoken since WWI. Thank God we're here to tell the tale. After the war, we never saw each other again, only once or twice. That time I met your mom and your siblings. The minute I saw you, I knew who you were. You look so much like him. And about your mom, I find her aged. She's the same age as my wife, close to sixty, right?" I said, "Not yet, a couple more years." She's been through a lot in the last few years. We lost Dad and my brother Mimi. It's been three years since our losses." He went on, "I saw him only once, over ten years ago, where you guys live, near the cemetery. After that, we never came across each other again." He said, "I knew your dad very well. Dad was a mean person to deal with, a very strong character." So, he asked how he died. I said, "He was sick for a long time, since after WWI. Mom says he was never the same after he came home from the war. He always suffered from small attacks, heart problems. The day he died, I didn't know what would happen, Nino. He seemed to be getting better that week, recuperating slowly. He had been sick for years."

That morning, Mom said he went out for a walk to see Leonora, my older sister. Possibly he had a heart attack or stroke. I don't know what will happen. So, can we help here at the house or the farm? Maybe we will be here for a while. We brought some food supply along with us. The only thing we need is to look after our cow and the donkey. We didn't bring any hay for them; I hope you have some. One last thing, Mr. Pavone, I am going back this coming week to Villanesi. There's so much left behind to be looked after on the farm. I need to be there for a few more weeks. I hope you don't mind if I leave the women here without me to worry about. We settled in a small hamlet of Atri. They have a mini-farm, good enough for a small family. Thank God, things turned out this way. Mr. Pavone's house is perfect for us to stay here. I got to know everybody, his daughter Maria, and his wife Linda. They're nice people. I need to thank God for finding them. As soon as we're settled with Mr. Pavone's family, I will go back to Francavilla to the farm. Mom insists on coming back with me. We don't have much food there. I can manage by myself, but it will be more difficult with her going up and down if I need to. Going back home from here is over an eight-hour walk. Now that we know the way, it might be a little less. We hope this war will come to an end soon; otherwise, all the farm work we did this year will go to waste. Without my mom, my sister, and my sister-in-law, there's no way I can save some of the harvest.

Talking to mom, I said to her, "There's a cooperative group who come and collect everything like the one mom talked about, so in the worst scenario, we will give to them. But they give back only fifty percent. How they do it, I don't know. Where they get the people, I won't know. As long as they do it, then we'll see. First, we need to take all to that stage ready for harvesting. After that, I will talk to the Storto people; they know how to contact for it."

It has been three days since we've been here. I need to go back home. I said to Mom, "I will be back in a week or two. Do not worry about me. If all is good, you will come back to the house with me." So, I took Pippo and Friz with me and left to go back to our farm. The road we took on the way up was great and safe but a little too long. Ninuccio suggested taking via Tre Cimminieri; it's much faster. After that, I will take the same road we came from. So, I am going that way to see about it.

My first stop was at Tre Cimminieri. It took me over two hours. I asked an old man how far Villa Raspa was. He asked where I was going. I said near San Silvestro. He suggested going via Madonna Della Pace; it's much faster than going to Villa Raspa. After that, I was home in less than an hour. I said there's another half-hour to forty-five minutes from San Silvestro to the house in Villanesi.

Later in the afternoon, I am home. All our neighborhood's farms hardly see anyone; it's very quiet. After I fix Pippo at the stalls, I finish cleaning up the mess we left on Sunday from my occupancy in the stable. I take a walk down to the veggie pit; there's a lot of work to be done. It hurts just to look at this good of God, left to rot, now almost abandoned. I will continue to do my best to keep up with it; I hope I can save some of the vegetables for our fruit store this spring.

Saturday is my birthday. I will be celebrating by myself. I will be sixteen. One more year without my family. God, hope this will be the last one without my brothers home.

A couple of days went by; I am playing solitaire at home with Friz and Pippo, my donkey. The house is empty. Yesterday was my birthday; no one was around. It is depressing. My brother Pietro left for the military, and I never had the chance to see where they ended up, nor anyone else. Our village only has a few people around. I am despairing. I didn't see Zio Tom since when we took our ship to Villamagna. Later today, I will go to the church to see Father Rocco; possibly, he will give me some suggestions overall.

I stopped by the cave this morning to pick up a couple of liters of oil, some tomato sauce, and some wine. It will be good for a couple of weeks. We do have some flour at home that mom keeps in a large metal container; we normally used it in the old days to store milk. It will protect it from any insects or mice. Those are never missing at home, especially in winter time. Now you don't see them, only some flyers.

On my way to the church, I stopped at the famous fountain for a few seconds. Normally on Sunday afternoon, it's always busy, but now no one is here. I am going to Diana's house; all looked up, no one is here. Possibly, no one has come back so far. I know they went to Roseto of Abruzzi before us. So, everyone else.

Soon I got to the church; it was locked. Normally on Sunday, Father Rocco stays here all day, and the church is open. I waited for a little while. I had Friz with me; he's particularly good and never runs away when I go places. As soon as I got to the church, I saw a military jeep with four guys on it, not too far from the church in the parkette. I walked over, asking them if the church was closed today. One of the guys said no one came today; we never saw anybody. I asked how long they had been there. One of the guys in German said, "Ganztägig." I asked what, and then the other guy said all day. They were Germans, and one of them spoke good Italian. I didn't ask anything else; I just walked away. Walking back home, I went through our small village; there were people here who never left. I did go to see Mr. Falco; he was home by himself, poor guy. I asked for Remo, and the old man said he left for the mountain. I asked what to do, and he simply said, "To get killed." I said to myself that he joined the partisans. I thought he was joking when he told me about it. I could not believe he did that, so I asked him if he was okay, if he needed anything, please let me know. I am home; just stop by. I left, talking to myself; he meant to do so. He's seventeen, turning eighteen. What a crazy guy.

Going back home, I felt a minor pain develop in my head, like a sharp pinch at the back of my head. It was very painful. I just wondered if it was because of that thunder strike or just a normal migraine. As soon as I got home, after checking that Pippo was okay, I prepared something to eat. There wasn't much in the house. I looked to Friz and said, "What are we going to eat?" He barked at me. Now he takes possession of the house, always inside, just because mom's not here he takes advantage of it. We had some dry beans we cooked, adding just a little oil and salt. We had no bread or other food we could eat. Friz was not happy about it; he didn't eat. Then I said, "Either the soup or the door, my friend. Your choice, Friz. I'm not crazy about it, but for now, we need to eat something."

Early in the morning, after feeding Pippo, I went to our veggie farm. We don't have much this year; we reduced our planting, down to lettuce, radicchio, eggplant, spinach, potatoes, and green peppers. No tomatoes or zucchini this year. I will keep up with this and bring some to the Market store as they become ready. I will seek someone who can take care of the wheat and vineyard this summer. There's no way we will manage it. Possibly I will pick up mom and Lena for a couple of weeks to help me with weed cleaning. I will bring Violet back for soil scratching until later summer; after that, they can go back to Atri.

I stopped by Zio Tom's house; no one was there. After that, I visited The Miller people near Chieti. It's over an hour walk. Normally, we use the guy in Francavilla, but it's too dangerous now, so these guys are better. Dad always used to come here. After I got there, it was almost dark. I asked for the owner, Mr. Rovente. I had never met the guy before; normally, my brother and my dad dealt with them. After he came out, an ugly guy, mean, he said, "What do you need, boy?" I said, "First of all, I am not a boy. I am from the Nocci family, and I wonder if you have anyone who wants to do our wheat harvest." He asked about mom and everybody else. I said to him, "We moved for security purposes, so here I am. Can you help us?" He said, "Leave all to me; I'll see what

I can do." He asked me to come back in two weeks; there might be a small group harvesting for other landlords without farmers. They only do this work: wheat harvests, grape harvests, and olive groves, the largest ones. But it will not be easy these days.

Coming back from the provincial road, there is a shortcut to Villanesi, which is used only by farmers. We call it LaFonte di Pizza, a short stretch of road with many trees, most of them oak, perhaps over a hundred years old. The road has a deep ravine down; after the creek, there are small hills. After that, it clears up, and you can easily see our village from our house. This road does have a history of local farmers. Down that hill, there is a washing tub where people do laundry. For some reason, they say many ghosts occupy that tub; possibly another legend from antiquity. God knows. To me, I never believe all this stuff or see anything. I said to Friz, "Do you believe in ghosts?" Dog is sensitive, he started barking at me as if he said yes.

We got home almost at midnight, and I wanted to eat something. A little polenta will do, from wheat flour, as we don't have cornflour as usual mom does. It's been over a month since I came back home from Atri, farming by myself. Our land owned by others cannot be abandoned; it's a big responsibility. I'm hoping my brothers will return soon to help me out. Lately, I haven't seen Franz or Zio Tom or any other farmer since I came back from Atri. I will see Mr. Falco this coming weekend; since I came back, I didn't go there. A few more days after that, I want to go up to see my lovely family in Atri.

Possible bring mom back with me, working through the summer here will give us a lift. Our land is not fully abandoned, hoping this war will come to an end soon. I am working through the summer; it will give us the opportunity to keep our land in good condition for next year's harvest.

Saturday night by myself, I am sitting on the solid bench next to the front door, having a cigarette. It reminds me of one night long ago when dad woke me up well past midnight, saying, "Toto, come with me to the mills." He had the wagon loaded with a few sacks of wheat, ready to go to the mill near Chieti. It was possibly 3 a.m. in the morning, and he wanted to be there by the time they opened. Going from the side road through the LaFonte di Pizza, the small country road I took the other day, at that sharp hill, dad said to me, "Look behind us." Someone was sitting on the wagon; they were coming with us. I looked to the wagon loaded with wheat we were carrying; I saw no one. I said, "Dad, you are dreaming. There's only the bag of wheat on our wagon." Then he said, "Okay, you're a lucky boy. You can't see what I can't." I know, don't worry about it. I will tell you later. After that, he never said anything to me. I didn't want to ask him about it; possibly he was dreaming. Walking away, I said, "All this doesn't make any sense. This old story about ghosts, werewolves, vampires, makes me worry sometimes, living in the house by myself, with Pippo and Friz."

Sunday morning, I wanted to go to Atri, then I changed my mind. Possibly next weekend, I will wait. I need to go to the town first, see the Military headquarters, or our Carabinieri. I want to make sure we are safe here before I bring Mom back home.

Without risking anything, I did take a walk at the seashore. I can see troubles; no Italian soldiers around. I am so sure something is wrong. For some reason, I have a feeling there are problems here. Without going to Francavilla, I went back to the farmhouse. Working at the pit alone, I am killing Pippo, doing the cow's work. We have a single dirt plow for one cow to pull, which we used for a single animal like a horse or donkey to work with. I am using poor Pippo; he's a strong, big donkey, a little smaller than a horse or, I say, like a mule. Mr. Falco stopped by today, saying, "Leave the weeds behind, Toto. Focus on the vineyards; they need the last coat of spray protection. If you want to use my big pump to spray your Capanelle, it will be much faster before it's too late." He's right; I never gave the second coat of spray this spring, to protect against fruit diseases. After that, I will come to the open land cutting these weeds.

Later in the week, I stopped by Mr. P.'s bar. No news about the war; no one says anything. Just a big worry by everyone. Only a couple of people were there. Then whatever will be, will be. I'm going back home. I am on my way to Atri; it's been a little while since I came home. Our village has been so quiet; nothing to worry about. I will bring Nicoletta back, or so I need a cow to do some plowing. I will take Violet; she eats less. Going to Atri, I got lucky. From San Silvestro to Madonna Della pace, a guy with a chariot with a horse gave me a lift. A well-off gentleman, he moved his family there, or so he says. Since last Christmas, he's been playing a tourist person, going back and forth until this war ends. After I left him, I saved over an hour. I got to Collo Petito at lunchtime. After spending all afternoon with my family, I said to mom, "We need to go back home. In the morning, we will leave early, just the two of us. Lena, Josie, Marianna, and the kids stay here. So, we will take Violet with us. If we move, we will be home by lunch tomorrow." She says, "Something happened there." I said, "No, the only thing we can do is some work at the farm like others. Otherwise, all our year's work is wasted. Are you okay, mom, to walk back home?" She was happy to come home but not happy to leave everyone else here.

I wake up about four in the morning. I said to myself, "We need to get going." So, I called mom. After getting one cow, Violet, ready, we left. The road was deserted; we only stopped once. We got home later in the afternoon. After feeding Pippo and Violet, I went to relax a little. Afterward, I went back to the stables to clean up. I didn't see Friz; I had forgotten all about him. I was looking for Friz; he was not around. I asked mom if she saw Friz; she said no. I said to myself, "He never goes anywhere without me. I wonder what happened." I called many times; no sign of him. I did leave him home to guard around the house; it's impossible he left on his own. Someone must have picked him up. The next morning, he was there at the front door. I yelled at him, spanking him several times not to leave the house without me.

After that, I left, working down the farm. Later that day, Zio Tom showed up. I was happy to see him. I asked when they were back; he said yesterday. I came by the house in the afternoon, no one was there, so I took Friz with me. I fed him. This morning he was gone. I hope he comes home. I said, "Yes, I spanked him because of that. Yesterday when we got home, he wasn't around the house." We chatted for a little while. He said the full family is up with their friend in Villamagna; they will stay there for now. I let him know our family is in Atri; Mom and I are home looking after the farm for now. We'll see what will happen later on. I asked him if he wanted to stay with us until his family is back. He said no, he will be going back the next weekend. So, don't worry, Toto, just stay alert. Our coast isn't looking so good; it looks like we might get bombed soon. God, why all this penance? It's been over three years we suffer. Let this war end as soon as possible. Mother and I have no more strength to go on. Let our brothers return home as soon as possible and be reunited with their family.

Crying about this war will not change anything. So, we are away from the town, a little safe here. We will wait and see if anything happens in town or our city; we can see it from here. Soon after I got home, Friz came to me. I cuddled him for a while. Then I said to myself, "It was not his fault, but he must learn not to go with anyone." Mom had dinner ready; she made homemade pasta with potatoes cut in little squares like soup. It was great. Then she says we need some food for the house; there's nothing here. I said I know, Mom, I will go this week and get most importantly what we need. I don't have money or anything to sell. I will go to Tina and pick up what I can; I will pay her later. Mom gave me verbally a list of a few things she needs, possibly over fifty liras, possibly more. Later that night, I couldn't sleep. No cigarette, no coffee, tired. I looked at the small shelf we had where we keep souvenirs. There is Mimi's box, my book, and dad's personal old weapons from WWI. Good for nothing.

Later in the week, I saw our miller man regarding the wheat harvest. He had an arrangement made with the harvesting group people; they would do or so the grape and olive for us. I asked what the terms will be; he said better than letting it rot in the countryside. So, I didn't say no; possibly we have no choice. Let them take care of the harvest. Since I keep coming back to the farm, I am reskinned to get killed. I want to save some products for later in the war. I am so worried about my family; without my brothers, I am so worried I will not keep up with my obligations. Our farm produces over five hundred Staio of wheat per year. After seeing Mr. Rovente, he said before you go, we have some flour here; you can pick it up anytime. I said yes, we know about a hundred and fifty kg; possibly next time. That was the little we asked for; the landlord left it for us last year.

Summer ran away so quickly. Later in August, I only visited our family in Atri once a couple of months. Possibly after the Ventemmia, after the grape harvest, I will go up bring some flour and more olive oil to the Pavone family. We kept about 100 kg of flour from the wheat harvest, selling to the miller group the balance of it. Or so we kept partial at the miller's house, the balance of it; soon they will come for the vineyards. I hope we recuperate over fifty percent; not like the wheat harvest; they only give us fifty-fifty. So, I asked Mom when she wanted to go back to Atri; she said no, I am staying here with you. Then she said, "When you go, bring me back my chickens."

The next day, I was cleaning the stall a shocking surprise came. A group of German soldiers, about four of them with a big dog, a German Shepherd. I needed to lock up Friz; otherwise, they would go after him. I was worried about Friz; I never saw him fighting any other dogs before. I asked if I could lock Friz in the little cage we have next to the chicken coop; they said okay. So, I said to Friz, "Stay quiet in here; these people are impatient with people; can you imagine with dogs? You don't want to get shut." I walked back to the house a few meters away. I said to mom, "They are showing up at our house like that; we were not expected to see them always up here. This was the first time they come always here." After they inspected the entire premises, one of them, he knew our language, then, asking mom where our house supply was. I stepped in, saying, "We have none." The guy didn't believe me. They searched the entire house again and the warehouse, saying we are smart not to keep anything around. They found ½ bag of our flour in the kitchen, some potatoes. We had little in the house, just enough to survive. After they checked everything, they asked where the rest of the family was. My mom explained our family condition; one son died, so my husband and two other sons are in the military. Only I have this young boy home with me. Please don't hurt us.

One of them said something in their language to the guy speaking Italian. So, the guy said to mom, "There is a cow and a donkey in the stable. We will take the cow." When the guy said they would take the cow, I went crazy. I jumped on him, and his dog attacked me, biting me in the upper left arm, just below my shoulder. The soldier hit me repeatedly without stopping, all over my body, including my head, cracking my forehead. Mom started screaming and yelling, begging them to let me go, saying I was only a boy, with pity and repeating to take what they wanted. "Take the cow, please, take anything you guys want," she pleaded repeatedly, begging them again and again to let me go. For a minute, I thought they would kill us both. For a second time, the soldier hit me on my head. I was bleeding all over the place, on my head and my arm until one of them said, "Let him go; he's just a country boy." He had broken my head, okay, and there was a small cut on my arm just below the shoulder, where the dog bit me. Then the guy said to me, "You don't want to live long, young man." I didn't react because of mom, so they let us go, thanking God. Mom cried out to the soldiers to let me go free, asking for mercy many times. They let me go, taking our cow, Violet, and some supplies from us. I was crying about Violet. They didn't touch Pippo, our donkey. I was bleeding hard. Mama bandaged my head and my shoulder. The dog took a piece of meat off my arm just below my shoulder. I lost a lot of blood, so I needed a little bandage to stop the bleeding on my forehead.

After that, I did follow them. Soon I caught up with them always through the village, going down to the church parkette. They have a little base there, possibly temporarily in the little square. Not too many soldiers. I saw where they kept all the animals. Possibly they will take them away later, to the town or to the slaughterhouse. I said to myself, "I will come back later tonight and take back my cow, Violet, from them." I was so angry without knowing what I was doing. These people are heartless, like animals, without mercy. They take and destroy everything they want. Mom was worried. I had a bandage on my forehead, and I was bleeding badly. I went back to the house, took Pippo with me to the cave, picked up more supplies, ready to leave in the morning. I never went to sleep. About midnight, I prepared Pippo, ready to go. I said to mom, "Please change my bandage to black;

the white bandage was full of blood, or so noticeable in the dark." After that, I said to mom, "Get ready; we need to go." As soon as I came back, possibly an hour later, I needed to pick up something at the cave. I said to Friz, "You stay here with mom; don't move."

I went back to the German compound. I was scared to death, about two hundred meters away, very dark in that church area. All together, a siren coming from the city and our town. It was loud. I wasn't sure if it was from Francavilla or Pescara. It was so strong; anyone could hear it, like someone needed help or was having a big party. A few soldiers left immediately, going down to the main road. I was so scared, afraid, but I needed to take Violet. Approaching the animal, there were no guards. I was shaking underneath. I was afraid of the German dog, the one that bit me. Slowly, with the small rope I had with me, I put it around Violet's neck. Then there was a little calf, so helpless. It was so quiet, so I didn't hesitate to catch her too. I walked away down to the ravine where La Pera fountain was. It was a very dark night. I knew a little passage that led me there, without being seen. I managed to take both away, thanking God. As soon as I got home, Mom was ready. I didn't know the time, possibly three in the morning. She was crying. I said to her, "Why are you crying? We need to go now, Mom; no time to cry." She said, "You lost a lot of blood; you need to lie down for a couple of hours before we go." I said, "No, mom, we need to go now." We took Pippo, Violet, and the calf. Friz was barking at the calves. I said to him, "You shut up." We left at once. I was bleeding on my left arm and the side of my head. That German dog took a good bite out of me. I washed with a little wine, bandaged, and moved on, taking Friz with us. By daylight, we reached the area of Madonna Della Pace, northwest of Pescara. We heard some bombs over the coastline. It was hard to say if it was Ortona or Francavilla. We were scared, walking as fast as possible. Mom and I were exhausted. We were scared to death on the way here, especially when we were close to the suburbs of Pescara.

That skirmish with the Germans yesterday taught me so much, many things. Now I know more about what type of life my brothers live away from home. We are all praying to God when this war comes to an end. After we settled in, I said to Ninuccio, "I have a gift for you; come, I'll show you." So, he saw the small calves, no more than three months old. He said, "That's for me?" I said, "Yes, after I will tell you how I got that." He went to get them some milk. I said, "She eats like the others; you don't need to be babysitting anymore. She will be a great cow, Mr. Pavone." Two weeks later, my family was suffering, and we were so sad. We did not see tomorrow being a better day. A war without an end. We are a big family, but unfortunately, the most important pillars have been missing. Without my brothers, there is no peace. I am keeping my family's spirit up as much as I can. I lost all desire to move forward in this life of hardship. Soon, I need to go back home. I need to see if it will be possible to save anything left on the farm. Otherwise, everything will be lost. Mom does not want me to return to Villanesi for now. It is extremely dangerous, but we need to see what is happening back home. That is our house. I must go soon and see our place. Someone can or will take advantage of it sooner or later. Dad always said to me, "In the world, there are two types of people: those who work for a living and those who work to steal from others, living a life on the backs of others." He was referring to people who steal or abuse others. Marianna wants to come home with me. She's a lady now; soon she will be twenty. Mom says no; she's much safer here, no place for a young lady in Francavilla.

The next day, Friz and I left all our animals at the farm in Atri for what we have left. Lena and Josie are helping at the farm with the family we are staying with. I brought some supplies every time I came – oil, tomato sauce, salt, coffee, and sugar for everyone, to keep everyone happy for a little time. At home, in our storage, we have, soon we will run out; there's not much left there. I hope this coming Oliveto harvest will give us some oil back to be stored. I will do what I can by myself, without asking anyone else, like I did with the wheat and grape harvest.

I got in late, without walking around the house; I crashed until later morning. I walked through our house and the barn to make sure there was no damage. In the house, there were some mice droppings; possibly they are coming from the front door. It needs to be fixed at the bottom. We are lucky there's no food in the house; we only keep a small supply of food around the house locked in small containers for safety. There are mice, flies, and insects to be protected from.

Later in the day, I wanted to see Zio Tom if they left to go back to the Villamagna area, or else I needed to go by the church. After I did a trip over to Zio and the church, everything was locked up, no one there, or any damages. I stopped to see Mr. Falco, the old man, possibly by himself. Talking to him, he said,

"Toto, there have been bombings along the coast. It's dangerous to stay around here. Go away, son, from here." Then I asked him who has remained in the village these days, and how they live without help from anyone. Now I know what mom was referring to: working a lifetime to build something, so they want to stay home, not go anywhere. They are old people living in this small group of homes, like Mr. Falco. I asked if he heard from Remo these days; he said, "No, nothing. Do not worry about anyone, son. We will manage without any help, just to be safe."

Working at the farm, cleaning weeds and rubbish accumulated over the summer, I'm here like a scared sparrow, alone and without food. I'll stay a few days, then I'll go back up to Atri. I wonder what condition our town is in. I better not go there; if they catch me, they will put me on the wall. But I must go to Mr. P; I'm sure he's there without going anywhere else. Going down the main gravel road, I stopped to see if anyone was at Pietro's house. I walked down to Mr. Pasqualino's Bar; I was right, he was there. Asking him why he never moved, he said, "We will soon, before we get killed here."

Later, on Sunday, I went up to my sister-in-law Nuccia's parents' house to see if they were there. No sign of Pietro or his family. The old lady says they left for Caramanico. I don't know where that is. I looked around, seeing some farmers who never left; they were risking staying at the farm.

After a few days, I said to myself, "Possibly I can use some help." So, I will pick Mom up from Atri; I can use her here. It takes a lot of work to clean up around. After picking mom up from Atri, we started the two of us collecting olives. Just mom and I. We did well. The countryside is almost deserted; you don't see anyone working. Going towards Chieti, there are people farming without fear. Over here, no one, at the farm, in our neighborhoods. We did well, Mom and I, picking olives for almost two weeks. Every two days, I am loading Pippo and delivering to our oil mill near Chieti. I am risking my life going to the mill; this war will last for a long time, God knows. There is no other way; I must do this without fear; otherwise, all will be lost in the ground. Lately, I have seen a few farmers come back and clean up; we hope this war will be over soon. There's a disaster out there; we don't know what will happen along the Adriatic coast.

Lately, I've never seen our landlord; it's been over a year since they were here last time. I hope they are okay; safe living with a Jewish background isn't easy these days. After this olive harvest, we will go back to Atri for the rest of winter. Mom was curious about the shelter; possibly she's never seen one before. With the fireplace going and Friz laying down on the floor, I remembered something and said, "Mom, remember when you were talking about dad and the problem you guys had with the vegetable people? At the end, you stopped talking about many other issues. In your life, you had those days; you want to talk about it." Mom looked at me and said, "I don't want to talk about it, Toto. Sometimes words hurt more than they should." Leaving, I said, "Sometimes it is good to talk about it if it has been bothering you for so long, regardless of what it is, mom, good or bad." Without saying anything, she went to sleep. Soon, we will go back to Atri and celebrate Christmas with Marianna, Josie, and Lena, together with the kids. I hope for next Christmas, my brother is back home.

Since we came back from Atri, it has been a long time; we need to go soon. By Christmas, we'd like to be with our family in Atri. Pescara and Francavilla have been destroyed; it's been a disaster the last couple of months. I went down to the main road a couple of times for groceries; it's so hard to get anything. We've been living with restricted supplies - mostly veggies, wheat flour, and some preserved food saved over the last couple of years. Going to the main road along the coast is like winning a lottery; if you get caught, the risks are high. So, I am taking all necessary precautions possible when I go down to the sea coast. I'm not afraid of anything; I've been down the main road many times. I do know my way around, using side roads. After the September bombing, the seacoast has made it impossible to find suppliers we need – groceries, cigarettes, salt, sugar, and coffee. Most of our resources are gone; there is no market where we can get credit or go these days. Any small grocery store is closed. I was worried about the babies mostly. The only place I can think of is this guy my dad uses for things you can't find at the store; he has contacts in the illegal market. I know we need to pay more for it, and in advance - possibly double the regular price. Dad calls him strozzino; I never knew his real name. Everybody calls him Strozza-Cani (dog choke). For me, I would call him a throat-cutter to people. Unfortunately, everyone makes a lira over someone else these days. As the saying goes, the more you do, the more you've got to put in the pot.

On Christmas Eve, I need to go and look for this Strozzacani. The only thing I know about him is that he lives near Sain Silvestro, at the border of Chieti and Pescara. Well, I need some shopping for mom, or so we know that is not his name. Regardless, we need him now; the price, we do by most importantly needs for the house. I want to help older people or so in the village left behind by family members. A lot of them can't walk longways, or they don't want to leave the home where they were born. I hope they have food and water; far we know, Germans have taken over many sources and prisoners over our city, including some Italian soldiers. Big rumors are going around; we need to be careful. Civilian people are getting killed; God help us out. Talking with a few people, we don't know what is happening to our country. I do know one thing – we need help to free ourselves. Since they opened to new allies to protect our country, it's been a disaster. We are getting killed like mice, with no reasons, just because our governors screwed up; we are paying the price here. Strangers invade Italy; we don't know anymore what to do or what is will happening out there.

Early in the morning, I asked mom if we go back to Colle Petito, or if she wants to stay here this holiday. She said no; she wants to be here for Christmas, in her house. So, I said, "I am going to Villamagna to see Zio Tom. I will be back before dark; I need to see if our sheep are good and hope to say hello to Zio and his family." She didn't want me to go; it can be dangerous always going there. She knows I'm stubborn, so I went, taking a pack of tobacco with me for Zio Tommaso. I am sure he will love that. I said to mom, "I will go by myself; Friz will keep you company until

I return. Please don't go anywhere; stay safe." Going to Villamagna is over three hours walk, taking the shortcut. I will be there by lunch and back here by seven. Walking along the river Alento to shorten my way, to Villamagna, I am near Ripa Teatina. I find an old lady's bike abandoned; it's very light and a little rusty. I could grab and take it with me with one hand, so, I said to myself, "I can fix this for myself; need a new chain, both tires flat. I am so sure Zio Tom will help me out with it." I carried it always to Zio's place. I was dead tired when I got there; they were happy to see me there. Gilda, Benedetta, and Laura were there. I chatted with Gilda for a little while; she offered me some meal. After that, I said I need to go soon; otherwise, I will be late to get back home. She asked me what happened to my arm; I had a band on it where that German dog bit me. She said, "Let me look at it." Seeing a big mark, she said, "I have some cream we can put on it." She did; medicated for me, cleaned, and banded it again. Or so she said, "You will have a beauty mark there like a cicatrice," she meant a scar. I don't want mom to get scared or worried; I need to go. If she doesn't see me return by dark, she will get scared. So, I asked if I can leave the old bicycle there; otherwise, I will never make it back with it. She said no problem; Zio Tom went to Chieti, possibly won't be back before later afternoon. Then I asked if they need anything – food or other home needs. I come back in the new year and bring some groceries if they do need them. I gave Gilda the tobacco for Zio. After that, leaving, she said, "Say hello to your mom, and if you do come again, bring some barley grain to do latte with it." I said, "No problems."

As soon as I left Zio Tom's family, I said to myself, "This family does so much for us since dad died; they're always helping out. So, this is the minimum I can do for them." On my way back home, I need to be there before dark. It's not an easy road for a young man by myself, for many reasons. Walking along the river Alento, there have been many unpleasant episodes, so it's better to avoid the dark alone. There's a history in the past along this river; the Alento river flows down always to Francavilla, and many little creeks join this small river. I just want to avoid problems. I got home not too late; mom was saying the Rosary with a long crown provided by who knows to her. Since I remember, it's always been the same one. I asked if she prepared anything to eat. Looking at me, she gave me a sign to wait. I went to check our stable; only Pippo was there. Not much work for anyone for now; we left everything at Colle Petito. I hope after Christmas, we go back and spend New Year with our family there. She's convinced to stay home and die here; for her, it's not a problem. Since Dad died and then Mimi, her life is so different; it no longer makes sense for her to live. If she won't go, I am staying here with her; I will not leave her all alone. Living in a farmhouse by herself is like locking someone in jail and throwing away the key. She's my mom, and I will look after her for the rest of her life.

Soon, it will be New Year; it will be five years since my brothers are gone. I will go and visit the village people. I asked Mom for some money if she had any. She wants to know why. I said, "After the visit to the village, I will stop by Strozzacani for coffee beans and orzato for Gilda. I promised her to get some." She didn't want me to go; it's a long stretch from Leonora's house to San Silvestro, or so dangerous. "Don't worry, I'll stay away from main roads, Nicoletta," I assured her. Later in the morning, as soon as I got to Leonora's house, it was all locked up. On my way to Pietro's place, I saw an old relative of Franz's. I said, "Mr., you didn't go away with the family?" He says, "No, Toto." Then he said, "Regardless of what you are doing around here, you know how dangerous this area has become these days." I asked, "Bucci, why is it dangerous for me and not for you?" Tears were in his eyes as he said, "I am sixty years old; you are sixteen, big differences, Toto. Yesterday was a disaster for our neighborhoods; the Germans killed over twenty people – all peasants who have nothing to do with this war. Innocent people; they live today for tomorrow to live. They only understand hoeing the ground." I said, "How did all this happen? Poor Italy, where have we arrived? May God forgive us our sins. They are peasants; civilians people are not to blame for our national mistakes. A massacre, son," he lamented. "I am so sorry, Bucci; I do not have words of support for you. I hope God will punish those responsible for this disaster."

December 31st, 1943, tears in my eyes, I said to him, "Do you want to come and stay with us for a short time?" He says, "No, I need to stay close to these people's families. Possibly, your dad knew all of them." "Just go home, Toto," he advised. Then I said, "If we can do anything for their families to help, I can come back tomorrow and help out." He says, "No, go home and stay away from here or near Francavilla." He said they killed a lot of people; no one knows why. It never happened before. He keeps saying, "Just go home; stay away from this damn area." Before I left, I asked if he knew where Franz and Leonora moved with the children. He didn't have a clue; possibly the suburbs of Chieti. They are a little safer there. I explained to him that mom and I were still in the countryside, while the women and children are in Atri, a very safe place.

After I left the St. Cecilie area, I didn't stop at Pietro's house; I went straight to Strozzacani's place to pick up salt, coffee, and orzato for Gilda. New Year's Eve by ourselves, mom, and I. I didn't tell mom anything about the disaster at S. Cecilia. We were playing scopa, a card game. These cards pack must be over twenty years old; we call them carte Napolitana, Napoli cards. As we played, I said, "So, Nicoletta, about that little story before I was born - was dad being a bad boy or was he a good boy?" She was in a good mood for once; she says, "You want to know if your dad was cheating on me with another woman." I stopped, looking at her, and said, "With whom did he make you the horns? I will kill her." Later at midnight, I said to mom, "I didn't want to tell you; I can't keep this inside me. Yesterday, a terrible thing happened in our old neighborhood where we used to live, mom. At the area of S. Cecilia, over twenty people got killed by the German soldiers. They were all peasants." After seeing Bucci today, he was destroyed by what happened there yesterday. They are possibly some relatives of us there. Then she wanted to know who the people were that got killed. I said, "I don't know, mom. God knows why and who they are." I asked mom, "Please, we need to go from here, as soon as possible; we should not stay here any longer."

Pescara and Francavilla have been slaughtered by bombs, and the worst is yet to come, Nicoletta. We must leave as soon as possible. Telling Mom, she can't stay here by herself, I said to her,

"You know very well I will not leave you here by yourself, so you must decide; we need to go." In the morning, we will wake up early and go. I woke up early; she had already cleaned up the stable. It was about six in the morning. I said to myself, "This war never ends; it will get worse." Mom is right to stay here and let our fate decide what will become of our life. Later in the morning, having coffee with her, she said, "Toto, we will go this week, okay? Soon we'll have a milder day; it's too cold for me to walk for a few hours to reach there." I was happy she made the right decision. "Okay, Mom, we'll go later in the week; there's not much we can do here." I convinced Mom to go away from here. I want to see Gilda; I promised her to bring some Orzato before we go to Atri. Mom will not agree with me, but I need to go; otherwise, I'll feel guilty if I don't. I decided I will go and bring Gilda coffee and Orzato; after I come back, we will leave for Atri.

December and January, we always get this kind of weather until early February: cold, sometimes a little snow or rain. Two months of penitence for us farmers; a normal time we manage some work around the house, but with this war, we feel like doing nothing. After my trip to Villamagna, we stayed a few more days here at the house. We've been lucky; no one came by the farm. The last time we saw soldiers was the time when I got beaten by the Germans. In the village, there are soldiers going by sometimes; they did move from the church park. I didn't see them there; thank God, our small village has not been touched so far. Normally, I go by the village to see old people if they need anything. I do my walk-through on a weekly basis. All that makes me feel good; if anyone needs anything, I will get it for them; otherwise, I will carry on. I will come back every month. Soon, we will go back to Atri; regardless, I will come.

Early January 1944, we left to go back to Atri. I said to Mom, "In Atri, we will be much safer." When Mom and I got back to Atri, I said, "Thank God, it's so quiet here; everyone is well." Little Nicoletta, she started talking; she walks, talks. This year, in August, she will be three; I hope her dad will be back. I need to teach her to call him dad. Having a conversation with Ninuccio about Atri, he's telling me the town has a big history. Built before medieval times, it has existed since the Roman Empire with so much to enjoy as an old town with characters and beauties. I said to him, "God bless the many churches, or so." This town is sitting on the top of three pointed hills, hovering on the Adriatic Sea, with the majestic Gran Sasso in the background. Not the beauty of my small town at Francavilla, but I can see people love living here. Later in spring, I returned to the farmhouse a couple of times. This is my fourth trip this year. Taking a walk around, giving our place fresh air, cleaning up any spider webs or weeds around the house. Not much I can do by myself. All land is mostly abandoned; I am doing my best to keep our house livable. Vineyards and olive trees are full of weeds; I kept the veggie field as clean as possible; all other areas, nothing has been done. This year will be no harvesting; hope next year. I am discouraged just looking at our beautiful property. Also, the village is abandoned; over seventy percent of the people are gone. Our town and the city of Pescara, many houses have been destroyed, or people got killed. As many times as I come home, I never go down to the seacoast; I do not want to risk getting killed. We know people remain in the town without moving out. Only God knows the disasters this war is doing to our country. Many times I am thinking about my brother; hope they are alive. I am seventeen; possibly soon, it'll be my turn to join the army; we hope for the best. Since I have been going back and forth from Atri to the farmhouse, the road I used to take has become dangerous. More than once, people tell me to stay away from west Pescara; there are allies who control the area. This territory along the coast is well-controlled; many soldiers circulate in the vicinity of Pescara. Last time I went back home, I took the road from Villaraspa, a full day to get back to Villanesi. I will cut down coming back to the farm for a little while; I will stay up to Colle Petite with my family.

Two months went by; I said to Mom, "I am going back home; possibly I will stay a couple of weeks there. Also, I will check on the old people in the village; I need to make sure everyone is okay." Everyone says not to go; I need to make sure the house is okay; we have so much in there to worry about. Only the house and the barn. I am worried most about the straw and hay, which someone can set on fire. Our occupants will be left with no supplies on our return home. Because of this war, there is so much vandalism these days all over the country; people take advantage to steal or damage properties. It's not a joke; so it's better I go and check it out. I am taking Pippo with me; I can use him to distribute a little manure in the countryside where all the vegetables grow; it will be good for the soil, ready for spring to be plowed and planted as needed. Possibly we will be back home long after this war is over. I did spend time at the farmhouse for over a month; I did visit the village. Only a dozen families are left there; most of them are gone. I asked around where they are; no one knows anything. Soon, I need to go back to Atri. Staying there through the summer is risky; I will be back later in the month.

Since I came down to the farm, possibly by now my mom and sister are worrying about me. I had warned them not to look for me; I said to them, "Regardless of what is happening, you guys shouldn't move from Atri." Knowing my mom, she is capable of coming down by herself, so soon I need to go back. I do need to eat a warm plate of pasta; since I am here, I've been starving. I have no bread, only salad and preserved food from the cave. We don't have much left there, only some wine, oil, tomato sauce, some preserved green olives, and dried tomatoes. We've been lucky in our neighborhood; no damage from the bombardments. We are safe, a little far; otherwise, we would have had it. We are away from the seacoast, a little safer from there.

Before I leave, I want to visit the elderly in the village again; who knows if anyone needs something. After that, possibly I will not be back until later summer. After my visit to the village, I left this morning early to go back to Collo Petito in Atri. I am halfway there. The last visit to the village reminds me of a phrase from Father Rocco: "Endure those in need, which will last forever." I said, "The quietest pleasures are the most lasting to me; I'm so sure about that; people will not forget about it."

Going the longest way back to Atri, I will stop at Santa Teresa, a small village way north from Pescara. After that, I will get to Collo Petito, four to five hours later, walking through the countryside. I noticed not too many people traveling these days, some farmers working here and there. This northwest of Pescara is quite; beautiful countryside. Possibly a good hour or two from Pescara, driving with a scooter or bicycle. I hope Zio Tom will fix the bicycles for me one day; as soon as this mess is over, I can ride around like others.

I am to Collo Petito, almost dark. Mom will be happy to see me; after walking all day, I am so sure I will have a good night's sleep. After dinner, thank God, I said to mom, "Possibly I will stay longer if it wasn't for you guys worrying about me. I was afraid you would come down to the farm by yourself," she said, thanking Ninuccio; otherwise, I was coming. I am going to sleep; see you in the morning.

A good night's sleep, early morning having coffee with mom and Marianna, little Nicoletta looks at me, saying, "Papa come." She remembers I taught her to say, "Papa come home." I said, "Yes, Piccolina, Papa will come home soon; you'll see. He will bring you a nice gift, special for you." After that, mom starts crying, walking away from the table; she knows only God can tell when if he's coming home.

Chilly day here in Collo Petite; we are so close to the mountain; temperatures here are much colder than our town. I cannot believe this temperature. Accommodating ourselves in the small kitchenette at the side of the barn, where mom and Marianna sleep. When I am here, I share the place, sleeping in one of the old rocking chairs. I did build a curtain wall next to mom; they are sleeping. Mom and Marianna liked the little divider; three people in a small kitchen room; better than getting a bomb on top of your heads.

Francavilla and Pescara are destroyed; we always thank God to be here away from our town, or so, thanking this family for hosting us. Without them, who knows where we would have gone. Ninuccio and I walk to Atri, meeting some new people. One of them with a familiar last name, Dimusciano, saying, "Soon this war will be over." I ask the old man, "What makes you say that?" He said, "No war will last this long; it's been years since we are fighting, others without political reasons." I ask him if any of his kids are serving the country at the moment; he says no, thanks, God. It was an enjoyable conversation with Dimusciano; I learned one thing from the old man: "All comes down to politics; the world is all politics, and I am right that one needs to be in politics to gain power." Ninuccio never comments on Dimusciano; I can see he is a typical man like my dad; a quiet person doesn't talk a lot.

It's later afternoon; we are walking back to the house. We stopped, picking up some sweets, a place doing homemade cantucci; they are an old tradition of this town, so delicious. As soon as we got home, I said to Mom, "Have a look at these sweets." She commented on it, saying, "The ones she does are better." I said, "I knew she would say that; to make her happy, I said, 'Anything you make is better, but sometimes it's good to taste other people's homemade things like these biscotti's. You need to know other people's favored or cuisine." We are on our own, without bothering them every day, minimizing disturbance, always thanking our Lord, to have this safe place for now. Going back to the farm is difficult; the road is dangerous; no food. I am lucky to have water with me every time I go up and down. I'm saying to myself, "I need to make a final decision; possibly I will stay there without coming back so often."

This is my fifth trip since we've been in Atri. Everyone is starving, but the most important thing is that they are surviving safely these days. It's late fall 1944, and I need to go back. It's been a little while since I was there last. With winter coming up, I am worried about the old people in the village. This time, I will take Pippo with me; it will give me a break going back to the farmhouse, and I can write a little without getting tired. Our donkey is a responsible animal; he knows how to manage the weight we put on him. Sometimes he stops and goes down on his front knees, which means he can't take anymore. He's like an intelligent human animal. We use him for many tasks on the farm, and without him, more would be on our shoulders.

I woke up early this morning; mom was already up and ready. I asked if she wanted to come home with me to Spaccanocci house, or if I should stay here with the family. I said to her, "I am going back there to work at the farm until my brothers come home. So, if you want to stay here with the family, I am okay with that." She says, "No, stay here; I need to go back." I said to mom, "Next spring, I will be eighteen; possibly my turn will come to go to the army's. I like to be home." I am sure the farm is a disaster by now. We need to cut down weeds, and our fruit trees need to be pruned; otherwise, soon they will become a forest. War or no war, I will be at the farmhouse, regardless of what happens in the future. As Mom said before, "This war never ends." It's been over five years since my brothers are gone with no news. Mom decides to come home with me. So, we had a good chat with ladies Marianna, Josie, and Lena, and we left for Villanesi, taking Pippo and Friz with us. We went via Citta Santangelo, the safest way possible. Taking mom will be a little longer, but safer. We arrived home late in the evening; it had been a long day. We found a disaster in the house; mice and spiders had a great party since the house was empty. At least no one abused our homeless place. We just relaxed; in the morning, we worried about getting dead tired.

I said to mom, "I will get you a few buckets of water from the well. You can clean up around our rooms and the kitchen; I will worry about the barn." Without discouraging ourselves, we did what needed to be done to put the house back into livable condition. Later in the day, I went to the village to see if any neighbors needed anything. Not too many people were around. The last stop I made was to Mr. Falco. The Adriatic coast has been taken over by the Americans; I hope soon we can bring home our families. I stopped at the church, walking through the little park, looking down at the seashore and our town of Francavilla. It looks like an abandoned cemetery; only rubble remains, a dead city destroyed by the war.

Going back to the house, I stopped by La Pera fountain. The water in the tub was nice and clear. Possibly no one has been using this place for days or months. Soon, I need to cut down some tree branches; a little clean-up will help keep this place ready for the ladies. I stopped by the cave, picked up a couple of jars of tomatoes, a large bottle of wine, a little demijohn of five liters, and a small two-liter can of oil. Possibly, we need more for the house; I can only carry so much with me. I will be coming back this week for what mom needs at the house; we'll see. Soon, when I got home, I wanted to write a couple of words, but my book disappeared. The last time I wrote something was here. Mom was preparing something to eat. Soon, we need almost everything here at the house. She made a potato soup and a loaf of bread with old granola flour she had locked in jars on the kitchen shelf. Lucky to find it untouched. Thank God we do have a lot of wood for the fireplace. We can keep it on day and night without worrying. Since dad was alive, we always had a big pile of wood. Now we are running short. Soon my brothers will be back, and we need to restore the quantity we keep all the time for winter and summer use.

Dad always says, Fire is good winter and summer.

This morning, I was looking for my book but couldn't find it, so I asked mom. She said no, she didn't take it; it's possible you left it somewhere else, she said. I insisted, "No, I kept it at the top of the shelf where Mimi's box was. I know we took the box to Atri, not my book." She replied, "I will look in the morning; now it's too dark to search for it."

It's late fall, and the days are getting cold. Not much is left at the farm from the previous year; a lot of crops reproduce on their own without seeding. I decided to check if anything is left at all. Early in the morning, taking Pippo with me, I went down to the veggie field. There wasn't much to pick up; only weeds and dead plants. We need to plow the entire area before we can plant anything here. As the saying goes, duty first. So, first, we plow all the land where the vegetables will go. I will prune the vineyard as much as I know, and then the olive trees. Mom came down with a little lunch just past noon. I could see the sun turning southwest, signaling that I need about three more days here before all the plowing is done.

My mom is getting old. I asked her what she needs at the house these days to survive for a while. She said, "Not much, Toto. Some flour, salt, sugar, and, you know, coffee." Then she said, "I found your book under the bed. Unfortunately, the mice did a number on it; not much left. You'll see when you get home tonight." After dinner, I looked at my book. Only a few barely readable scratches were left. I cried over it. Over eight to ten years of notes in my book, gone. I was so hungry for it. I threw it into the fireplace. Mom was upset with me, asking why I did that, saying, "One day, you will regret not keeping the few notes left in that book."

It was almost midnight, and I couldn't sleep. Mimi's box we left at Atri, my book was on fire, and my brothers, I don't know where they are. So, I asked God, "What's tomorrow? Can you tell me, or do I need to wait overnight? Maybe a dream will tell me what's next." God never talks to anyone, possibly only to saintly people, and I am not one of them. Maybe I will change with time and become a better person later. All this is not possible. It's like telling someone you love, "Give me a thousand kisses, and then another hundred, and then again." It will never happen. Grandpa used to say, "Get married so that you are nice and warm." Then when you are married, he says, "Now stay cool, my son. The wife is a heartbreaker, don't you ever forget, Toto."

Doing this pruning now in late December is no good; I hope the plants won't get damaged. I will do the minimum possible, and next fall, we will do it properly. I hope by then, I will have a feeling my brothers will be back. Our countryside needs to be cleaned up before snakes and lizards take over. Before the holiday, I will go back to Atri to check on my family to make sure they are okay.

Christmas holidays, mom and I went to Atri, and we had a mild week, spending Christmas and New Year with our family. After that, I went back by myself. It was so stressful for my mom. Later in February, I needed mom to come back here. So, late at night, I left for Atri. It was Saturday night, and I got there before noon. She was happy to see me. I said to her, "Tomorrow, we go home. Get anything you have here; you're not coming back here. I am the only one coming here when this war is over to pick up our family."

After we got back home, slowly I transplanted some vegetable seedlings. They will grow slowly, enough for my family's house uses. In the barn, they will stay warm, possibly be ready by late March to be transplanted into the dirt. The chilly winter is over; I can see fruit trees starting to bud. Soon they will bloom. I am so happy about it. If we hadn't come by now, this place would be a mess. Soon it's Easter; I hope we can bring back our ladies with kits. The farm side seems to be safe; there hasn't been any bombing lately since we came back here. I would love to see Francavilla and see how bad it is. No one knows in the village what is happening; the only thing we know is our coast is occupied by American and English soldiers. I am happy to be here without anyone telling us what to do. Our landlord disappeared over two years ago; there is no sharing to be done and no promissory note to be signed. Our village is deserted. I am visiting a few families—Falco, Mancini, Sarraiocchi, Di Giuseppe, and I went to see Mr. Faro—if they are okay. There was no one there. There are other people in the village; possibly they have their own family looking after them. Then I have done enough; I need to worry myself from now on.

Soon, my eighteenth birthday is coming up. Without my family, there's nothing to celebrate. God knows how much I want my family back together. It's been too long since our life has been a struggle of penance. I don't see my brothers, afraid of being killed, seeing our mom despair every day. Our life doesn't have any meaning anymore. No future. God, when will all this end?

April 1st, 1945, not a Fool's Sunday—it's Easter Sunday. I will walk to the church; maybe I'll see Father Rocco. It's been so long since I saw him last. I asked mom if she wanted to walk with me to church. She said, "How come so early this year?" I said, "Based on our village people, this year will be early, mom. Don't ask me why." She said, "You know, April 1st is a fool's day; people make fun of other people." I laughed like a madman, telling her, "Who could take us for a joke? It's just me and you, mom, here." On Easter Sunday, we walked to the church; the door was open, but no one was around. After mom said a prayer, we left and went home. I said to mom, "Come; we will go toward the hill of owls." As we walked, I said to mom, "I hope Joe and Federico will be home as soon as possible." I said to mom, "I am very tired of all this, mother. The land, family problems, suffering hunger. Luckily, I eat a little less. Then there's this headache that attacks me often;

the world is falling on me." She said, "You don't eat enough; you need to gain some weight. You look like a tall, skinny, dry poppy. Listen, I will make you

a special diet from tomorrow; you need to follow it." We reached the end of the hill, and I said to her, "Follow me into the mini-forest." As soon as we got to the cave, I showed her the place. She was surprised by it. She said, "How long have you known about this place? Now I know why you didn't want me to come here by myself." I said, "There's an old story about this place, so please don't come here by yourself." After she saw the place, she said, "As long as you've found it." I said, "Long story, mom. When you need anything, I'll come. Take a look at what we have here—wine, oil, tomatoes, all the good stuff you preserved. Anything I hid here, soon the family will be reunited, and we will bring it all back home." She kissed me on the cheek, saying, "God bless you, son. Your dad would be happy and proud of you if he were here today."

Walking back home without taking anything, I opened an old box of worms, asking mom about an old story she didn't want to talk about before. I insisted, so she said, "Then, the Nocci family were unlucky in the past. They do have a history, Toto. It's been years. When I met your great-grandfather, I was a young girl. His name was Luigi, like your dad. Many times my in-laws talked to me about family misfortunes and the life they lived in the late 1800s. I do remember your grandfather Antonio, including your grandmother Anna Domenica." Mom asked me to be worried about the family. I asked why, and she said, "There's a history behind our family's son..." Then she stopped, saying, "I don't want to be telling you these bad old memories, Toto, so please stop asking me about them."

I asked mom, "Why do you guys call me Toto, not like Nonno Antonio or another name?" She said, "Your dad's brother died at war, so he wanted to name you Toto like his brother. So, we call you Toto because everyone used to call your uncle Toto. Your real name is Toto." After that, I noticed tears in her eyes. I stopped questioning her without asking anything else. Sometimes we can only see things that we love, simply accepting life the way it comes, without looking at who we are in life. So, being a Nocci, we are carrying a load on our shoulders, many stories in the past. I hope one day we don't need to talk about our name anymore, except for good things.

I said to mom, "Our future needs to be as clear as crystal. With my siblings, we will make sure our family name will be protected and become better than before. I want our family to be the best of the best. Farming without anyone telling you what to do, it will be nice, beautiful." I said to mom, "This morning, we planted some veggies and a little tomato plant for this summer. This way, if my siblings are back home, we can have fresh salad of tomatoes and cucumbers." She gave me a smile. "I love tomato salad with oil, salt, and a little basil. Homemade bread, fresh broad beans. Or so, we see our vineyard coming back, Mom. I have a little hope that by the end of this summer, we can harvest our grapes." Mom and I have been in the field every day, doing our best to keep these two harvests going—the vineyard and olives—the most important for now. Our strength is minimized. Mom seems to be coming to an understanding with her life. She never asks when or how the family will be back together again. As the saying goes, tomorrow is another day.

On Easter day, I asked her if we wanted to bring back the ladies from Atri back home. Now it seems noticeably quiet here. I saw a couple of farmers working lately in the fields. She wants to wait until later summer before reuniting everyone. Possibly, she's right. We don't know anything about what is happening out there right now. I hope this war comes to an end soon. Since Christmas onwards, mom looks like it. She was resigned to this crappy life which we farmers live today for tomorrow. Since dad died, she's a different lady, accepting day-to-day life the way it comes. Sometimes I ask if she's okay. I believe that the great bitterness that she carries with her inside will never die. After the death of her husband and her son, I do not see her calm. I hope that when Paul and Frederick come back, she will change. It's been so long since I saw Diana, more than two years have passed since I saw her last. Who knows if she has changed, become a more beautiful woman, or stayed the same? With mom, I do not talk about her at all. God knows what I will do to see her. I hope she is safe and returns home soon. She's a young lady now; they are so well-off. We are happy about that. Unfortunately, sometimes we all demand more from our life.

Chapter 7
End of WWII Family re-united

Later in winter 1945, Mom and I, including Pippo, have been working hard in the field every day. Poor animal, he's doing as much work as a cow. I hope soon I will bring back our cow and the rest of our occupants home, including my family. As I walk in our village, I see unfamiliar faces. Finally, I think, people do want to come home. Going down the gravel road, approaching the church, I stop at Diana's house. Still, everything is closed here. So, I stop at the church around ten am. Father Rocco is back. I was so happy to see him back. For the first time, I hugged him. He was happy, saying, "Family all good, Toto." I said, "Yes, Father, we're all good." Then I asked, "What's going on? I see a few people in the village." He says, "Possible you don't know, like everyone else, we believe this war is over. The Allies control our country. I believe soon everyone can go home to their own house, provided that it still exists since they left, because half of Italy has been destroyed." Today, finally, one piece of good news. I discovered from our priest, possible this war is over. So much suffering, hunger, pain, creating death and discomfort in our community. Finally, we can walk on the roads, destroyed by bombs and tanks. God has mercy on who did all this.

Walking back home, I took a different route. There's another fountain north of the village, a little long stretch to go home. I did see wild fruit in the past. I can pick some for mom. This road is on the opposite side of the cave. As soon as I got there, I saw the Roseberry not ready, or other wild fruit, no good, birds did a number on it. I did stop at the Catena fountain, closer to the village. Lately, I got a severe headache, right on my temples. I almost fell to the ground. I sat for a while. Got a little late. I said to myself, "I better go home now. Mom is worried about me." Walking home near the creek, I saw fresh fava beans, ready to eat. So green, with bread and oil. So, I took some to take with me home. I grabbed mom, lifted her from the floor, and danced with her. I said to her, "The war is over, Nicoletta. We can bring home our family anytime we want." She didn't believe me, saying, "You know what you say." I sat down on the bench, with my big headache bothering me. I said to mom, "I went to the church. I saw Father Rocco. He was there, giving me the good news. And I saw people in the village coming back home. I'm telling you, the war is over, Nicoletta." She said, "We'll wait, possibly until later June."

"We need food and other supplies," I said to mom. "I will not go to Strozzacani this time. There are other places close to here. I suggest Chieti or San Silvestro or a small market nearby. Going to Francavilla is very dangerous. We need to go northwest from here if we need anything." For the first time, I need to visit a new zone north of us where dad used to go to the bar. About a good forty minutes' walk from here. In the past, dad kept us away from it. I know over this war, they never locked up, business went on as usual. A small district on the main road going to Chieti, Fondechiaro, with many resources, food, salt, tobacco, plus the solid bar our father often talked about. Later that week, I did take a walk at Fondechiaro, picking a few things for the house. I met an old friend of dad, Mr. Baglio, a well-educated person from a well-off family. They live in the neighborhoods. I asked if this war was overall over. He didn't comment much. He said, "Yes, for us it is over. I don't know for our brothers out there." Now we standby and wait to see who will come home, Toto. We won't know until later this year. Going back home, I always used the short way, La Fontana di Pizza country road, where for centuries, they say that place is the residence of witches. Who knows where they live, because I don't see houses in that place, only trees and bushes and a small fountain where people go to wash dirty clothes. It's a legend. If that existed hundreds of years ago, to me, today, it is a told fairy tale, like Snow White and the Seven Dwarfs, Little Red Riding Hood, or Cinderella, like comics we read. More, thanking God, I never saw anything similar. But I would like to meet one of these old stories one day, which the old people used to talk about...

Later in spring 1945, I am ready to pick up my in-laws with their kids and my sister Marianna. Mom insists to wait a little longer. This coming Sunday, I will go and bring everyone home. I said to mom, "Hey, Nicoletta, I am going this Saturday to Atri. I will be back later Sunday or Monday. If you want to come, please let me know. Otherwise, I will go by myself." She took me by my hand, sitting on a bench in front of the house, next to the front door. She said, "God bless you. I cannot make such a long journey in two days. If I go, we must stay a few extra days there before we come back home." Saturday early morning, possibly she wants to come to say thank you to Ninuccio and family. At the same time, she's afraid to walk all these kilometers in such a brief

time.

After feeding Pippo, I am ready to go to Atri. I asked mom if she wanted to get ready. She said, "No, you go. I am okay here. Just leave Friz with me. I will look after Pippo and keep Friz inside while you are gone. I will be okay." I left for Collo Petito, going up using the short way. I saw many people in the suburbs of Pescara. Possibly, I will be there by later afternoon. Normal walk without stopping too many times takes eight to ten hours. Walking up, I do not believe my eyes. The disaster created by this war, abandoned countryside. That makes me so sad. Poor us, we must do it all over again, starting from the weeds to the pruning of the fruit trees. All to be redone from scratch. All this makes me so mad. We peasants are like slaves, looking for an opportunity to improve the state of life. Soon, I am halfway to Colle Petito. I am seeing many English soldiers on my way here. I thought Americans occupied our territories, not English. No matter to me, as long as we're done with this crazy war, and soon, I can hug my brothers. There is a small bar open here at Madonna Della Pace. I will grab a soft drink. I brought a bottled water and sandwich with me. I ate all. Mom always says I don't eat much, so this time I did eat everything.

As soon as I am at Ninuccio's place, I will rest for an hour. After that, I'll get everything ready. I hope Monday morning we can leave early for Francavilla. Mom will be by herself, and I will worry a little. It's been a long day talking to Ninuccio at Collo Petito. He's telling me in Atri, life is normal except for all the youngest in the war. No one is back as of today. His comment about the worst will come, saying we will see many mothers crying, and many little ones without a father. He did experience war before, possibly he remembers the last one. Many dead and many missing, or so he says. "Your father and I are lucky to be able to talk about it today. Many never return home. One of your uncles was missing, never found. Others like him have disappeared, some returned slaughtered, or shattered, sick, crippled. It's best not to talk about it. War leaves hunger and sorrows to families... Everyone is now asking ourselves, where do we begin? The house needs work, farmland is a disaster, food shortages, we have little to depend on. Starting all over again, this is a crappy life. I am discouraged, tired, more willing or daring to live this life."

"No news of my brothers, where do I start again? The only thing we are hoping for is my brothers to come home soon. I look around me, I have no clear ideas where to go, or what to do first. With this little garden that we have done in the spring, it will give us enough to survive these days for the house. We hope for the best. Who knows if our landlord is alive? Possibly, he will help us to start again for the next harvest season. After picking up what we have left at the cave, thanking God, we have enough oil, tomatoes, and wine to go by for six months or a little longer. This season will be hard to pick anything at the farm. A new beginning without discouraging myself, we need to move forward."

"Over two months have gone by since we knew this war was over. We hope to see my brothers home soon. Early morning, July 1st, Sunday morning, I am done with stalls work. I ask mom if she wants to go to church. Our priest will be happy to see some people there after all this time. After the mass, I see Biondo at church. He approached asking if it were possible to stop five minutes at our house. Mom did not hesitate to say yes. I would have liked to know why of this visit. So, after we got home, he asked about Marianna, saying we have an understanding and we'd like to get married. At that point, I did interfere, saying the two of you have been seeing each other since before we were displaced by this war. So, tell me your intention or get out of here, Biondo. I said to him, listen to me, my friend. I do have confidence in you, or so I know there is family friendship. I do have confidence in you, the only problem is sometimes because of that, people forget their responsibilities. So, no escapades or seeing each other secretly with my sister. When you want to see her, come here to the house without hiding yourself. Do we understand each other right? Poor boy, he was worried someone would kick him out, but we have a good relationship from now on, so don't mess up."

"After that chat with Biondo, I was walking back to the main road with him, chatting. He's a year older than me. I saw a guy coming up about five hundred meters away from us. I said to Biondo, that is Joe, my brother. He said, you might be right. I started running toward him. I couldn't believe my own eyes, that was him. Hugging him, he looked at me saying you are a big boy, Toto. I was so happy to see him. He didn't change much, lost weight overall, nothing to worry about. He had a shoulder sack I grabbed, saying did you bring me anything? Laughing, he said, just fear, little brother. As soon as we got home, mom started crying. Lena was so happy. All of us were so happy to see him, even Josie. The only thing she looked for was Federico, but she also celebrated with us the return of Joe, the little one. Ginuccio and Nicoletta did not want to approach him as if he were a stranger in the house, afraid of a man they do not know. So, they both ran to me. After a while, I did convince the boy to give a kiss to his father. We are in the middle of summer, no news of Federico. Joe and I work hard in the countryside. Even the women are here helping us out. My sister Marianna, she's gone, went to live with Biondo. We knew soon or later it would happen, so we all agreed. God bless, I wish a long life and many children to Marianna and Biondo."

"I saw Joe so sad this day after he discovered about dad and Mimi's death, hardly talked to anyone. Joe and I went through some major concern at the farm. Or so I explained our landlord disappeared over two years now, possibly they will be back soon. We know one of them is of Jewish background, hope they are okay with his family, since Pescara has been destroyed, God knows where they ended up. Joe said not only Pescara, all Italy is destroyed, it will take a century to rebuild. So, Toto, we need to worry about our family for now, no one else. I look at him, he's happy to be home, I see bitterness in him, but he is fine. He is like our father, closed in on himself. Joe and I working at the field, cutting cloverleaf for the animal, what is left to be stored for the winter. I asked if he wanted to talk about his war journey, where he ended up, how he survived, these years. He didn't say much, most of the time in Yugoslavia, almost two years prisoners of Germans until he was free. I asked about Federico, if he knew anything, he had no clue about our brother, where he is. Then I asked how it is with Lena and the baby, he said everything is fine. I asked if he would start the first year of school this year, he said no, next year."

"Dinner time, all the attention was on him, as if I no longer existed. Mom prepared homemade pasta with chopped potatoes, a little juicy. Early morning, I asked mom to give up her room to Josie. She said yes, it's a clever idea, I will share yours until later days. I said until I get married. She laughs at me, saying soon you'll find a nice girl, then I will go to sleep with the cow. After church, I will take a walk to Zio Tommaso's place, Pietro's house, and Eleonora's, see if everyone is okay. After Zio Tom's house, I went to the main road down the shore for the first time after two years. Oh God, what a disaster here. Our sea coast

, you can only see rubble and American and British soldiers. Pietro's house is also ruined, he still has not returned home. Who knows if they stay at Nuccia's parents' place near Eleonora. I will go next Sunday, I'm tired, I'm going home. Walking up the gravel road, I went by to la Pera fountain, to see if anyone was there. I was too tired to go by the village and check on the old people today. Soon I arrived at the fountain, I saw a man sitting on the low wall, where ladies do wash all clothes, a skinny man, he is very slim, dry/macro. I said to myself, Mamma mia, unrecognizable, like a skeleton. I approached the guy, I said, My god, Federico, he was there unrecognizable, sick, who could not stand on his own feet. He said I need to stop, no more strength to walk home. I was so happy to see him. I said no problem, I will carry you home... he laughed, saying no, just carry my bag. As soon as we got home, mom didn't recognize him for a few seconds, then she started crying like she saw a ghost. He says, Ma, it's me, Federico, why are you crying? We all had tears in our eyes. No one wanted to break away from him. Everyone wanted to embrace him again and again, until it was little Nicoletta's turn! Looking up, I said thanks, God, for giving me back my brothers, the three of them. They are hugging each other, saying thank you. I need to lay down. Slowly, he goes to his room to rest without dinner or any further talking. The next morning, I wait until Federico was up. I said to myself, first I want to enjoy my brother a little, then we go to the farm working.

Late morning, having coffee with mom, I said, "See, mom, all your prayers helped to bring back your son, or to protect all of us." She said, "I do pray to God to make this world better for everyone, no more war as long as I live my life." She went through WW1, a crucial time in the twenties and thirties. Her life has been too bitter. For her, there is no more love for her life, only bitterness, sensing a normal life, suffering as a child. At this age, there is only resentment and bitterness. Federico was sleeping late when I left. I said to mom, "Make something special for him today. This is a big day for all of us, mom. The family is reunited." Without questioning, I walked away, my normal routine. In the morning, look after the stable, after that, in the farm. We have a lot of work at the farm. Thank God, now we can share all the work with my brothers and my sister-in-law. Mom will look after the housekeeping, at the same time help me with our occupants. Talking about our animals, we need to pick up our sheep in Villamagna. This weekend I will go. I never saw Zio Tom around, possibly he's there. We all grew up, so now we need to organize our share of work at the farm. Possibly that's what mom wants to talk about. Soon, we will find out from her. I am so sure she needs to talk to all of us and have some rules overall for the family.

After Marianna left, there's more on mom's shoulders to look after. Josie and Lena help mom in the kitchen. We need them more in the field, so mom needs to worry about housework.

In the middle of August, after picking up our sheep in Villamagna, I never saw Zio Tom. I wonder where he ended up. Since the last time I was there in Villamagna, I never saw them as today. I hope they are okay. I asked mom about that reunion she wants to do with all of us. She says this coming weekend we will talk about it after mass. Sunday mass, only mom and I go. After that, I stopped by Diana's house to see if she's back. They are back okay. For some reason, not much happiness to see me. I was happy they're all safe and back home. I left without saying anything. I am a big boy now, I don't need to put up with any of their nonsense. I need to look forward. There are many beautiful women in this world. Supposedly at the village, there will be many beautiful girls. I will go and say hello to Mr. Falco to see how he is doing today. As soon as I saw him, he was in tears. I asked if everything was okay, what I could do for him. He said, "No, Toto, I am good. Remo's not back as of today. Possibly that makes him sad."

Later, at dinner, after we finish eating, mom asks everyone to pay attention to her. She starts with a few positive words, saying, "The last few years, I lived the worst of my life. Today, I am happy to see my family together. After our loss of your dad and your brother, came a time I didn't want to live this life anymore. Today is a new day for everyone. We need to move forward with life and make the best of everything together. Always, I am here to advise all my children, regardless of your age, from Leonora to Toto, from the oldest to the youngest one. For me, there is no age, always, you are my babies. From now on, we will work together with one leader overall. Any major decision needs to be made, we will sit at the table and talk it over. If everyone agrees, we will go on; otherwise, we will let it go. So, Joe is the oldest, he will oversee the house affairs. Federico will support him with minor decisions, unless we need to get together and talk about it. I've been left out from any major responsibilities."

August 1st, 1945, middle of the week, little Nicoletta's birthday, she's four years old. I will go to the village. I hope to find something beautiful for her. There's a seamstress who sews at home; sometimes, she has trivial things made by hand for gifts to the little ones. These days it is difficult to find something for the little one. Otherwise, I can build something myself. Later in the afternoon, I stole some fresh eggs from mom, a dozen, tying it in a handkerchief carefully, otherwise, I'll make an omelet. So, I went to the seamstress. She is called Mariuccia, a name so rude, no meaning. So, when I was there, she said hello, Toto, "you brought me something?" I said, "Fresh eggs, but do not say anything to mom, I need something from you. Today is the birthday of little Nicoletta, do you have anything for a little girl to play with? Something like a little doll." She showed me some small dolls. I was not happy about all of them. Then I saw a doll with assorted colors, much bigger. I asked if it was possible to take the bigger one, it was about thirty cm, a nice one. She said, "Okay, you owe me one." I said, "No problem, my lady." She sews for all of us farmers and neighbors; she is old, perhaps older than mom. Hiding in a paper bag, I hurried to go home; it was already late. I had to find an excuse, so I took off my shirt. On the street, I found some good figs, beautiful black, the size of pears.

After I got home, dinner was ready. Joe wasn't there. Federico said he would be late, so I went on and ate. I was not too happy or satisfied for some reasons. Since he came back home, he always had something to do. After dinner

, I called Nicoletta; she ran into my arms. I said to her, "Where's papa?" She pointed her finger at Federico. I said, "Good girl. Now, Zio has a surprise for you." I said to mom, "Nicoletta, there's a bag on top of the fireplace for the little one. Can you get it?" So, I said, "Happy birthday, Nicoletta." Everyone was surprised by my good heart for the little girl's birthday. So, mom gave her the doll. She was in the clouds; she had never seen something like that before. Today, I saw Nicoletta playing with the doll. I said, "Who gave you that?" She said, "Nonna. Mom reborn since we are all together. Finally, she does many good things for our home." I visited Zio Tom; he's back home. I went to see him; we chatted a little. He said after that visit I did at Villamagna, they moved again, to some relative further north. It was too dangerous to stay in Villamagna. Then he said, "I have something for you." He showed me the bicycle, like new. I was happy. I didn't know how to ride; I need to learn soon. Unbelievable, he did a decent job on it. Thanking him many times, I asked if I had any money. He said not to worry about it; some other time, you will help me out at the farm. In our countryside, it's not easy to ride a bicycle; we have a lot of ups and downs. It will be good exercise after I learn how to ride this bicycle. Asking if he will help sharpen our tools, he said, "Come by Sunday morning; we will do it together." After sharing a coffee, I left so happy to take the bicycle home. Now, I need to learn how to ride properly. I am sure Federico will teach me how.

After that long week, I am using our cows in the field almost every day. Magna and Violet are good with me. I am satisfied with the work we do together. Sometimes I take Pippo; he's more usable in a tied area. I am glad they give me responsibilities to work with our cows. They love me more than anyone else. Everyone else works in the field plowing dirt. Soon we need to prune all olives and vineyards; there are a lot of branches to be cut and saved for the fireplace. Winter is coming soon, so it will be a good supply for the house. Mom always uses the thin branches to cook and leaves the bigger trunks for wintertime; they last longer.

Later in October, Joe and Federico help another farmer to fix damaged Capanelle or lines of concrete stakes, most of it close to the seashore where a lot of bombing was during the war. God bless them; they are good at those jobs. Many of them pay in cash, so mom can use a little money for family shopping. It's not easy these days to keep up with what she needs for the house. Thank God she makes a lot of homemade items to survive these days. Considering many people get government support every day to eat, we don't, thank God.

After that day, I never saw Diana anymore. Possibly I need to talk to her alone one of these days. She's not that little girl with ponytails when I first met her, before we started school together. Now we are grown-up persons, so she needs to tell me what she wants to do. Both of us need to go our own way; the sooner, the better.

Soon it's Christmas. I am so sure I will see her. I will talk to her regardless of who is there. Possibly I could invent a little serenade. I will ask Uncle Tom if he would accompany me to do it before Christmas. Who knows, I might get lucky at Christmas. I can go to their house and talk about us. Asking Zio, he said it's possible we risk getting shot by the parents. I said no way; it's something normal to bring a serenade to a young lady. So, we did a short song the way I was programmed before we were displaced by the war. Zio was there just past midnight or so. Federico came with us. Then they didn't bother with it. Not even a light went on. Without hope, we left. Finally, I understood that I was wasting useless time with her, or should I say with her family. Federico told me to let go; they are people looking up for the sun, they never settle for the moon. I did understand that was the same for Diana. I hope we remain good friends in the future. With tears in my eyes, walking home late at night without Federico noticing anything, I continued to sing, "Affaciati bella mia, I will go away without you, tomorrow there is another way, more beautiful than you."

Federico embraces me, saying, "One you lose, and two you find, brother." So, I laughed; without any more words, we walked home. We were very sorry, also because not even thanks for the serenade we did. Later, I need to do something bad. I ask Federico if he will help me out. New Year's night, about three in the morning, the two of us went to Mr. Cocco's house. We stole over ten bundles of hay. We loaded Pippo with six bundles, and two bundles each of us, Federico and I, looking at each other. I said, "We will come back for more." After we got home, I said to Federico, "I need to go back one more time." He said no, I said yes. On my way there, he came, saying, "I will not let you go by yourself, brother." We took eight more bundles of hay. I said, "You go straight home; I need to do something." He was worried. I did take some loose hay, dropping here and there, always to Diana's house, making it look like they stole from them.

The next day, I never forget Tuesday, January 1st. Mom asked me where that hay came from. I said from the sky or "Babbo Natale arrivato tardi." Santa comes late; we needed that supply. There was a big fight between the two families because of what I did. Then, regardless of what happened, the two never broke out. Possibly someone got in the way, helping to make peace between them. It was only hard feelings for a short time. After all, everything went their way. Brunetto married Diana the year after, so she married grandpa. God bless. I can only say this to her, whoever that is, be a good person, because the hard escapes our commands, and we can only obey it. The family will grow again. Josie will have another baby soon. The countryside starts producing. After the beautiful pruning in autumn, we can see that our vineyard and the olive trees are thriving by measure. There will be a good harvest this year. Our landlord will be happy; he's back from wherever he was, possibly hiding in some places, God knows where. My brother and I are building up a good understanding between all of us. They honor my wishes and treat me as a grown-up man. For them, I am the kids' brother, always. My responsibilities are to worry about our occupants, help mom, and work in the field with the cows. Federico and I are more involved with farm work. Joe is involved more in repairing other farmers' vineyards, barns, or digging wells for people. Many times he needs help. Federico and I always quickly give him a hand. Working as one family makes everyone's job easy for us and our house ladies.

After my disappointment with Diana, I never looked for anyone else. Mom always invites me to go to church with her for some reason, but I keep away from people. I'm not interested in anyone. Joe keeps asking if I want to meet his friend Zino's sister, but I'm not in the mood to meet anyone for now. She's always suggesting someone from the village. This year, after so long, we celebrated San Mary's festivity. I was there for only a few minutes, without seeing anyone. Just a good morning, good evening, and goodbye, nothing more, nothing less. My sister and sister-in-law keep suggesting ideas. "Toto, she's perfect for you. You're almost twenty; no one will marry you anymore." Inside me, I say, "But who cares?" As the saying goes, when opportunity arrives, we take it on the fly. Otherwise, I'm not in a rush to get married.

Later that year, on a cold weekend before Christmas, I paid a visit to my sister Marianna. She had given birth to a beautiful little girl. As soon as I got there, before I even stepped in, she started complaining. I asked if she was okay, and she said no, no one helps her family, and nobody cares about her. She made me feel like a piece of shit. I told her that's not true; we're here for her all the time. The only thing is, she's a city girl, not a farmer lady, so she should stop complaining. I assured her that things would change for her, and Mom and all of us would help her as she needed. After a good talk with Marianna, who is older than I am by four years and who often scolded me when I was a small boy, I stopped by to see Leonora. They had moved close to us, about a 10-minute walk away. As soon as I got to Leonora's house, it seemed my sisters had agreed. I started shouting, "You've finally come alive! We needed you in the last few days. Where were you?" I told her to hold her horses and explained that we were just a walk away. I asked why she didn't come and ask for help. I had come by just to say hello, and if she needed any help, I would help her.

Then I asked where my beautiful niece was. Leonora asked why, and I wanted to know if it was true she had a boyfriend. She said no, they had gone to the village and would be back later. Then she asked who told me that, and I said, "So it's true she has a boyfriend?" Leonora confirmed that maybe there is a boy interested, but her daughter is too young. She's only seventeen, Toto, no time for a boyfriend at this age, besides, the guy is older than her. Then she asked if I knew him, and I said yes, I met him once before. I don't remember where, but he's a handsome guy. I told her to give it some thought and that in life, those who are content are the ones who enjoy it.

Later in the fall, I told Mom I was going to San Silvestro today for mass. I wouldn't be coming to St. Mary's church. There's someone there I need to see—Zino, to see what type of person he is, or so the intention he has with my niece. She didn't like the idea of me getting involved with it, but I assured her there was nothing to worry about. She knows me; I don't like trouble. I told her I would see them for lunch later. We always have Christmas lunch later to give everyone the chance to go anywhere or attend later mass.

Going to San Silvestro with my bicycle took me fifteen minutes. I like to be there before nine for the first mass. As soon as I got there, I sat in the last row. I always like to sit in the last row for good reasons. It gives me satisfaction to see and observe people— what they do, all their moves. My favorite bench is in the last row. I didn't see Zino this morning, so maybe he'll be at the later mass. I decided to wait. After mass, I went for a coffee. On my way back to the church, there he was, together with someone else. I figured one of them must be his mother, and the other, a young lady—I wonder who she is. With a cheeky face and a little excuse, I approached him. I said, "What a surprise, Zino!" With an excuse, I asked if he had two minutes for me. With that, he introduced me to his mother and his sister, Eva.

Introducing myself as Joe's brother, Zino's family already knew Joe, which annoyed me a little. So, I said we would talk another time and got rid of it with a lie. It was an opportunity for me. Meeting a beautiful woman, a girl very simple, there is also an understanding through my niece and her brother, who can have an advantage over her. I said to myself, "Okay Toto, don't take things easy; you just met someone possibly good for you." As soon as I got back, I saw Federico at the stables cleaning up by himself. I asked if he needed help, which is my job, brother. He said, "I don't mind, you need a break sometimes." I helped to finish what was left of it, and then we both sat on a solid bench, having a cigarette together. He seemed sad, so I asked if something was wrong. He said no, but I know him too well; something was on his mind. I wished I knew what.

This year, for the first time, we had a new harvesting. After the olives, there were these berries called soap nuts. They required a lot of work, so Joe invited our niece and a couple more people to help us out. It was a surprise. Our niece brought along Eva. As soon as I saw her, I lost my breath. I was so happy to see her. I started talking to everyone, looking like a cicerone, like a joker, amusing people. For some reason, I made her laugh over nothing. So, I asked if she saw anyone, and she said yes, but my parents aren't too crazy about it. I said, "Then now you've got me to take into consideration." She started laughing again.

A little time went by since I saw her again. I knew where she goes to church in San Silvestro, so on Christmas day, I went by just to say hello. After that, we were friends, two young people getting along. She came by sometimes on special occasions, and we got to know each other more than once. Occasionally, I saw Eva. Finally, we started getting along quite well. One of these days, I will ask her to marry me.

Today, while working in the field with my brothers, I asked Joe what he thinks about Eva. Federico said, "Marry her." I said, "Not easy; I have no money, not even a place to sleep. Her family is fine economically. What can I offer her—misery?" Joe told me, "In this world, you will only get what you seek, so try to find it." I said to him, "In a few days, it is St. Joseph, March 19th. Let us go to the festivities. She might be there." Joe jokingly said, "So, we will steal her and take her home." Inside, I thought it was a clever idea. This year, I will be twenty, and she nineteen. So, I said, "This will work before someone else steals her from me."

I'll never forget the day of St. Joseph, March 19th, 1947. Joe said we should go to the church at Francavilla for the festivity. It was later in the afternoon. Joe invited Eva to come home with us, and she said okay. Having dinner with us was getting late, and she said she needed to go as it was getting late. But my mom and my sister-in-law said no; she should stay here tonight. My mom said, "You can sleep with me; tomorrow you can go home." She only lived twenty minutes away from us. I said to Mom, "I can walk her home if she wants to go." Mama told me to shut up. Joe and Mom had all programmed to keep Eva here at the house. Otherwise, why not let her go home? She was even more innocent than me and said okay, she'd stay.

Mom had already planned everything with Joe to keep Eva in the house. She extorted her. If she refused not to marry me, it would be difficult for someone else to marry her. I never thought of that. I like Eva; she's a beautiful woman. We are young; we could wait a couple more years before getting married. Getting married so young is like following my siblings' road.

In early spring 1947, a couple of days went by, and Eva was sleeping with Mom and little Nicoletta. I never asked for anything. I said to myself, "Possibly, she will change her mind later." Over the weekend, I saw Eva helping Mom at the house and the stables with our occupants. We have not talked about us so far. I hope I find the right words to make her comfortable here with us. We are a big family, not an easy place to make herself at home. Our home environment is great, but there are three children, my mother, then my brothers and sisters-in-law living together. It will not be a walk in the green to get used to living here. Joe did the hard part with Eva's family, even with a few lies, blaming the two of us. The fault doesn't fall entirely on the Nocci family.

I am so sure their family doesn't make a big story about all this because my niece is involved with Zino. I hope soon we are able to meet the family about this situation overall. Mom is great with Eva; she makes her feel so comfortable to stay here like a little girl. Every day that passes seems so long to me knowing that she's at home with Mom. Eva and I are so young; she's nineteen, I am twenty. This morning, my brother Joe says, "Toto, when are you going to see Father Rocco to get married so you can sleep together with Eva? Otherwise, you know very well our rules. Nocci people wait for the woman to become our wife first before going to bed with her." I said to Joe, "All of you did respect these rules? If you did, you are a bag full of shit. I don't remember any of you being like that. So, guys, stop breaking my balls every day." Josie is more polite than everyone else, telling Federico and Joe to leave me alone. It's not their business when I will commit myself to Eva.

In mid-April, we met with Eva's family. Soon, we will get married in our church. We asked our compare Mario and his wife to be the best man and maid of honor. We planned to celebrate everything in one day at my twenty-first birthday.

After Eva and I got married, we all work together on the farm with my siblings as one big family. Today is an enjoyable day; Eva is expecting a baby, she says possibly sometime in March next year.

Everyone in the family has given her good wishes, and I will pray for her. At the same time, we all are suffering. Many of us in the countryside are facing a shortage of food and other supplies. The last time I saw something new was at my birthday when Mom bought me a pair of dark grey trousers, a white shirt, and a pair of shoes, which I only wear on Sundays. It had been years since I had seen something new. I always wear my brothers' old clothes or other things. We are a big family, and for various reasons, we always run short here. I am not happy about all this; we work like donkeys every day in the countryside plowing dirt. We all work like mules on the farm, but in the end, there is never satisfaction. As a proverb says, "All you need is health and a pair of shoes that you can travel all over the country." I don't believe in all this; I want more for my family and my kids as much as possible.

Later that year, before the Christmas holiday coming up, Eva and I went back to her parents' house a couple of times. Since she's pregnant, her mom looks after all her needs. Possibly, they do that to make her feel at home and ensure she's okay. Eva has two brothers and two sisters; both sisters are married, and the boys are single. Zino is the one who connects us; without him, today we would not be together. I am sure Eva's mom will do the impossible to see Eva happy. They seem to get along very well, and Eva does not hesitate to go and ask her parents when she needs anything, including for the house.

Since Eva and I got married, Mom always cuddles her like a little girl. She will be the last daughter-in-law of the family. Not for anything, I don't want others to become jealous because of Eva. I said to Mom, "Nicoletta, easy, don't be so nice to her; otherwise, she will get used to it. Soon, there will be three children you need to worry about, possibly in early spring." Who knows if it will be a boy or a girl. We'll see. Lady Bruna visited Eva, saying it will be a boy, and he will come later in March sometime. I am counting the days. I asked Eva if she's okay if it's a boy; we'll call him Mimi. If it's a girl, she will pick a name. So, I asked if it's a girl, what name she would give? She said, "Your mom has Little Nicoletta; my mom will have Nunziata." I said, "Annunziata, like your mom's name."

On Christmas Eve, after I completed my work at the stable, I brought in some extra wood for the fireplace. It will last Christmas day. After dinner, Eva and Mom went to church, and everyone else disappeared to visit family for Christmas. I stayed home all by myself, thanking God lately for no headaches. I filled a glass with wine, lit a cigarette, and went for a short walk. It was almost dark. Friz followed me, barking. I said to him, "Lately, you bark too much; you're catching up for when you were a little puppy. You're a great dog, looking after our animals at the sheds, most importantly, protecting Mom's chickens. No foxes come around since we have him. He is a good guarding dog. Since he's been around, we've had fewer travelers coming by, only on Sundays sometimes. This winter will be a long one. Since mid-November, it has been raining and cold. Luckily, we finished all seeding prior to the rainy season. With my brother here now, everything is much easier to get done. Past midnight, the ladies were not back; I am going to sleep. Tonight, Friz, you stay out and look after the house; watch Mom's chickens, okay?

On Christmas day, after mass, I stopped at Leonora's house for a coffee. She's like a second mom to me. Since I was small, she always looked after me before she got married to Franz. Having coffee with Leonora, she asked about Eva and her pregnancy. I said she is getting a big belly but not complaining so far. Then she asked if we picked a name. I said yes, if it's a boy, it will be named after our brother Mimi; if it's a girl, her mom's name, Nunziata. She liked it. I said, "Come on, on New Year's Day, stay with us for a change; we are having lunch together with Federico and Pietro's family." On New Year's Eve, everyone greeted Eva for the baby coming soon, possibly in late March. I said to all, about me. Pietro said, "Let's go for a walk, Fratellino, little brother." We walked a quiet bit, talking about plus or minus family problems. Then he said, "You know, having a family is a particularly important big responsibility. Soon, you guys will need a bigger place, so, for now, you need to take care of them. Later, you worry about anything else. Now, you pay attention. Listen to me, little brother. First, you must drink less. Then, the habit of smoking is not a good thing, but we all have it in the Nocci families." Pietro is a good man, always looking after his family. He got married at twenty, possibly early, without anyone's help. He has four children to worry about today without asking anyone for help. He also went to the military two times, first for regular duty and a second time during the war. He never complains or asks for support from anyone. Pietro is a man of God, respectful, and honorable.

Winter 1948. We are all waiting for Eva to give birth to our baby. Finally, on March 18th, we had a beautiful baby boy. I was so happy. I said, "Hey Mimi, welcome. God bless you, son." Now the family is back to full strength. Joe named his son Luigi, and you, my little one, my brother Mimi. Eva was well, and we were so happy planning when we would baptize Mimi. I said to her, "I will talk to Father Rocco to give us a date."

Early April. This morning, Mom and Eva needed to go back to the doctor again for the baby. He's not well. It's only been a couple of weeks since he was born. I ask Mom why he's so quiet. Our family doctor came again, and after visiting him, he said we need to go to the hospital; there's nothing I can do for him here. So, we brought Mimi to the hospital in Chieti. I was not happy. It was over four hours before they visited him. After that, finally, the doctor came and gave him some drops. We hope this will work. They sent us home the same day. This morning, he seems to be better. I went farming with my brothers. Later, when I got back, I asked Eva how Mimi was doing. She said he's a little better for now. Later that night, Eva breastfeeds the baby, but he doesn't drink enough. The poor little one is not well. She is desperate. The baby needs care, and it's possible we need to see another doctor in Pescara. We need money. Going to Pescara to see a specialist for babies is costly.

Later in April, I woke up early; I couldn't sleep. It was about four in the morning. I had another strange dream overnight. The baby is sleeping; he's so quiet. He never cries at nighttime. He's a good baby. At dinner time, I asked my siblings if we need a little support to see the specialist again for Mimi. I know we have no money these days. Perhaps I can ask our landlord for it. They said good luck; he is more desperate for money these days than us. Eva says not to worry; if I need money, she will ask Mom. A couple of days went by. Eva needs to ask her mom if she will help us. The doctor gives us bad news, "Il piccolo stava morendo, il cuore non ce la fa più." The baby is sick; his heart cannot hold on for long. It's such sad news. Eva and I were desperate, didn't know what to do. We went back home, kept him warm, and fed him a little at a time. It was the middle of the week, Wednesday night, I couldn't sleep. I got up, walked outside. It was a beautiful spring day, almost dawn. Soon everyone would wake up. I lit up the fireplace so when the children got up, the room would be warm for them. I took care of our inhabitants at the stalls. Joe left early; he's working with other farm people, fixing Capanelle wire. Federico and I worked more in the field every day, like donkeys. Mom came to the field, saying, "Toto, come home. The child is sick; you must take him back to the hospital in Chieti." I rushed home; Eva was crying, or so Josie said. We went back to the Chieti hospital. A few hours later, the doctor gave us the sad news. I knew the baby was gone. She hugged me so hard. We knew it was over. The doctor we saw in Pescara said he would not make it; his heart was too weak.

As a famous poet said, it is better to be born and live one day: than never born.

My little Mimi died on April 29, 1948.

My brother Mimi died April. 29, 1940's.

I cried for hours. This reminds me of when I said to Mom, "Life goes on; crying will not bring Mimi back to us." I asked God many times why all this penance, an illness that persecutes us like death. God lets us live a quiet life, like so many others in this world. Eva and I said, "Our Lord, you needed our little angel; here we are. Bless our little son who will watch us from up there in heaven."

Later, in September 1948, we are working at the countryside on a muggy day. Eva says, "Hey, Toto." I said, "Are you okay?" Normally, after the baby's death, we were so worried, we never talked about anything. She gives me a smile. I said to her, "I am jealous of your smile, especially when she smiles at others." We were carrying boxes to the wagon. I said, "What do you want to tell me?" She stops for a few minutes, saying, "I have a feeling I am pregnant again." She has given oxygen back to my dead heart. I didn't know what to say, so I said, "No more boxes for you. I will worry about it from now on. No heavy work, Eva. Toto will work extra hours to make up for your share." She laughs, saying, "Easy, not sure yet." I was singing again like a free bird in the sky. Time went by as usual, and chilly winter came. I was so impatient to wait for the baby. Eva, with her big tummy, started getting some pain. I said, "Is it time?" She says, "No, soon. It's Easter; I hope it's before that; it's killing me. My back hurts so much." A couple of days later, I said to Eva, "I am going on Thursday for Christ's Passion. You will be okay." She said, "No problem; we will look for you if we need you." With that actual group, we were singing and playing Christ's Passion. Early Friday morning, we were doing the last couple of houses when we saw a family friend, Attilio. He said, "Your wife has a baby boy." I was so happy about it. I changed the song from Christ to Eva singing "Affaciati alla finestra bella mia, che adesso arrivo io," song. Zio says, "You crazy boy." I said, "No, we go home now." Eva was waiting for me. I said to Zio, "Enough for this Christ's Passion. Next year, we do it again."

On Easter day, we were all at the table having lunch. Mom prepared a cup of soup for Eva, saying, "This will be good for you." I said to Mom, "Don't spoil her, or you'll need to do that every day." Eva said to Mom, "What shall we call this little one?" She said, "How about Antonio, like his great-grandfather?" Eva said, "We'll see." On Baptism Day, we decided. Eva invited my nephew, Leonora's son, to be the godfather to the baby. Without asking, she said he will be called after his little brother Mimi. I was shocked but happy about it. I never thought she would do that. Federico and I talked about space now at the house and the crucial time we are having at the farm, what we are going through lately. He agrees with me; it's time for all of us to go on our own soon. He said, "Don't worry for now; we will talk later this year." Then two years went by, and we never talked about separating from each other. We are living like anchovies in a box.

Later, in spring 1951, Eva gave me wonderful news with a big smile and said, "You're going to be a dad again; I'm pregnant." It was the month of May. I wanted to scream for joy. She said to shut up; she doesn't want anyone to know for the moment. I said, "Why not? It's beautiful, Eva." I was happy. Later, I wanted to tell Mom about it. She said no, for now, let her decide when to let everyone know. Later, in August, Eva was showing a nice little tummy. Mom said, "When is the baby coming, Eva?" I said, "What baby?" She guessed, "You can lie, not hide." Eva said, "Can you see, Mom?" "Yes, he looks like he will be a girl." We all laughed about it. I said, "Only God knows." On December 13th, 1951, Eva and I had a beautiful girl. We called her like Eva's mom, Nunziata. A girl and a boy, now we have a king and a queen. Annunziata was born on the day of Saint Lucia, but it is more than right that she bears the name of my mother-in-law. I asked her why she calls her Anna. She said, "I made a vow to Santanna." I said, "Then why don't you call her Annalucia, the day she was born?" Then she didn't insist on me. She would have liked Annalucia, but the decision was made by her on the child's name. Living together as one family, it's impossible. The family has grown, and space is not enough. We are all starving under one roof. Separation was in the air since the family has grown up. It's best for everyone to be on our own. After that little chat between us brothers, no one said a word. The decision was made for a new path to be taken for the goods of all.

Chapter 8
Last climb of my life

Later in the summer of 1953, I am worried about Eva and my two children. For the first time, I understood that no one cared about the other. For a long time, there has been a rumor in our relationship, between me and my siblings. What has happened in the last three or four years is not fair. The one who is suffering the most is Mom and Eva. Federico and I work like two mules at the farm, but in the end, there is never a penny to spend on ourselves. All this is because each of us has a family, and they are not free to take care of their own personal intentions. The time has come to separate ourselves; otherwise, some quarrel will happen sooner or later. Eva more than once complained about personal things that I don't know what she is referring to. All this bothers me; my head does not work well. So the best thing is to go our own way. Eva and I are the youngest in the family; now we have two children. It is more than fair if we thought for our family. Even Federico with four girls, only Joe with a boy. The house is small for all of us. It is more than right that each one goes on his own. In the last few months, everything has happened, so maybe I need space. It's time for our separation, also because it's as if we do not exist anymore.

Winter 1954: All my siblings find a place to start a new life. Eva and I have been looking and asking around many people if they need a farmer for a brief time. No one out there will help us out. So, one day I saw Vallarino, the guy from the animal slaughterhouse. He bought Pippo from us a little while ago. He's a good man, runs a butcher's shop in Pescara, or so he buys from many farmers. I asked if he knew a place for my family to live for a short time. Vallarino is the only person who can help us out right now. He says, "I will ask around, unless you want to go far from here." Saying, "I have something for a temporary start." I asked him where. He says, "At Sanbuceto, northwest of the airport of Pescara." I asked how long we can have the place. He said, "Maximum two years, Toto." I didn't give him the okay without talking to Eva. I bought myself a little time, saying, "Let me talk to my family first. Possibly in a couple of weeks, we will let you know."

After dinner, I consulted Eva about moving to Sanbuceto. She didn't like the idea. She's pregnant with two small kids and a baby soon. It will be hard for everyone because it is a little too far away from our families. I said, "For now, the only option we have, so we will keep looking." Eva comes from a healthy family; it is hard for her to leave this poor life. Later that year, we did find a place near Villanesi. It belonged to Miss Marinelli. She said we can use it as long as we can fit our family there. The house was very old, one-bedroom, large kitchen, and a place for storage. Very depressing condition. So, we settled there for a brief time. Eva had the third child; I was worried. It wasn't enough for all of us. With Mom and three kids, we needed more space. I decided we go to Sanbuceto. It was later that year we made that decision to go to Sanbuceto. We need to start all over again. We didn't have much. Joe and Federico said, "Take the cow with you there." The only thing we had to start, so we take some flour, little oil, and some jars of tomatoes. We did have a small parcel of land; we kept it as it is, the land, house, no improvements, considering we need to give back in a couple of years. The owner will be back here next summer. Vallarino promised us we are good until then. After that, God knows where we are going. I need a new job. I said to Eva, "I will look for a part-time job; we need extra income to survive. You cannot run to your parents all the time for help." Vallarino helped us out many times. Sometimes I go and work a couple of hours at the butcher shop helping with cleaning or other labor work. Many times he gives me some meat to take home besides money, including for my siblings. The last few years have been too rough on our life. We survived selling anything we have, including some of Eva's personal items, such as bedspreads and linens she had from her parents when we got married. I am ashamed of myself; I cannot find the proper job to feed my family, like a normal father or husband. I ask God many times for help or to give us a better life. Sunday afternoon, after finishing washing where they kill animals, full of shit and blood, I asked Vallarino if I could have or do more hours there so I could earn more money. He said no, but if you want to work like a laborer with masonry guys, there's something in Francavilla. I said, "Anything." So I agreed to work with the bricklayers as a laborer. Later that year, my son started school, first year. We need to settle at one place so my kids can go to the same school without breaking the year apart. Eva was worried. Working in Francavilla, going so far with bicycles is dangerous. You know the road is getting bad every day. She said, "Why don't we go back to Villanesi zone, if we find something there?" Then she said, "Possibly we can use Mom's place for a brief time until we find a permanent house." I said, "We'll see, Eva; there is Dad's relative's old house at Villanesi north side;

possibly it will be okay for a brief time." The only thing, Mimi just started school here. We need to wait until next year. She was right; the roads are dangerous. I am on the road every day; it takes me an hour in the morning and an hour at night. Possibly we need to move next year, so better move now. We left Sanbuceto near Christmas time; Mimi needs to change school in his first year, moving into a house in Villanesi. Less than two years, we moved three times. Why doesn't Christ give me a place to settle with my family once and for all? We had a bad winter; later February 1956, so much snow. Hardly can walk on the roads. Eva was expecting again; she will have the baby in the fall. So we need to find a permanent place for our family.

We are having a tough time. The Lord is still punishing me. Eva lost her dad, my father-in-law, in a fatal car accident. After that was my brother-in-law, Franz, in another car accident on the same road, in the same area. So much bad luck. Since WW2, there is no explanation why all this. I said to Mom, "Tell me our family history. We live a miserable life; I don't like it at all. It seems something has persecuted us for years." She said, "Figlio mio," she means my son, "It is not history that makes the family; it is the family that makes history. You'll see that one day; you'll agree with me." Later in the summer of 1956, we moved to Eva's mom's house; they had a main floor we could use for a brief time. So, later, we did find a house suitable for us, a walkway from the shore. Perfect for my family, a small little community to live on in the suburban area of Francavilla, a walkway from anything including school, near Mr. P's bar, perfect for my boy and my beautiful girls. After we moved, Eva had another baby; she's incredibly quiet, like Mimi, my first boy before he died. Mom said she looks like me much more than the others. No matter, as long as they are healthy. We are a big family; this house soon will not be good enough anymore. Or so every time we have bad weather, Altamarea, the house floods. Soon we need to go. Mimi and Nunziata, they'll need to do first communion and confirmation; after that, we'll see.

A couple more years went by, and Eva was expecting again. I got involved with politics; it was my dream. Eva doesn't like what I do. Since I've been involved on a part-time basis, many times I ask my candidate, since I am here, we never talk about the birth of the Italian Republic reform, from June 1946, the new republic state we will have a new constitution, if I don't go astray all this was the task by the DC, followed by the PSI and by the PCI, nothing was done only words and promises. After so much disappointing results, all of it end in the late '40s, when women could also vote. Unfortunately, we were all waiting for him to dictate the fate of Italy, all this resulted in a competition at the national level between the two main parties DC and PC, two different parties, the PC was aligned on the labor force, while the DC more to economy, financial systems. The point to accepting and be part of the Atlantic sphere. Well, all that did open a conflict between parties, those days I did get involved, was the right time, been part of the PC possible I choice the wrong party. then, I got to know many peoples, I come across a debut of the Democratic Social Party or so. They did in the last election, unfortunately, we both lost. Early '60s we moved again, Eva and I had another baby girl, thanking God now we have five girls and one boy. So, this place will be great for us, La Vir-Zella, a bigger house in the same neighborhoods, more land for less money. Eva can plant much more of assorted Vegetables, here. We can also sell to the market or to the wholesale. This place has a separate small storage room, furnished with a fireplace and wood-oven to cook bread, perfect for our family. Mom can enjoy making home bread and pizza for us; most importantly, my kids can walk to school. Zio Tom came to visit us, invites me to work out some land. It is a terrific opportunity to gain some financial support from it, the land needs a lot of work, full of weeds and thorns, needed my hand to put it in good condition, without fear I said yes. Continuing the part-time job at brick manufacturing, crazy shift four am to ten, asking my son to help out in the morning couple of hours until school time, will save me time for the farm work. after school or so he can help at farm Zio Tom found for us. Asking my brothers to help me before the winter, not too much availability on their part, so a friend Gino F. said, I know you're good with cows, take mine, so you can plow with a couple of days and then everything is easier. This land will give us a boost to our struggling life, I said to Eva we can seed over two thousand of tomato plan in spring or so other vegetables, we need everyone to help out, mom will watch the kids, you and will work at the field. I manage to plow all of it before the raining season, hope to find some people in the spring to plant all, it will not be an easy job, so many seedlings to put on to the ground, God sends them to us. Lately it's not easy to stay in touch with all my siblings all their families, but when it comes to helping them, I'm always ready, but vice versa when I need no one is available. Then, my wife she's right, think for yourself, not for others, I do not agree sometimes people need help, so we must do our best to do so. We didn't see my siblings for a long time, we need to get together one of these days, since my brother-in-law's death, Leonora the only one I stop by sometimes. She suffered a lot, all her kids are grown up, or so a couple already married, she reminds me so much of mom at a younger age, suffering without a husband, and too many worries in life, or so all others occasionally we do see each other, Vice versa, Marianna she's a tough one, always pretending and keeping her family in the leach without losing control of it. Christmas holiday, we are having lunch, Mimi says, I see you and mom suffering this day, I was at Signora Tina, at the grocery place, she tells me, you need to see her soon, I know what all about dad is, we need money. if you guys want I can quit school and go work full time, my cousin Ina she will take me there, for a brief time, after we get back to our feet I go back to school and finish grade eight. Without me saying anything to him, early January Mimi went to work, before his thirteenth birthday, hope next year can go back, later summer, our harvest went well, including veggies sales, I said to Eva this harvest helps us out to pay some dead, or so we have additional money for us to spend for the kids and ourselves. Late in the week one of my nephews came, ask for help, they were dying of hunger, I was so innocently, they new I had the money. Without asking Eva, or Mom, so I give it all to him, then I realized, he had stolen my children's bread, after a brief time Eva noticed it, scolding me what I had done. I was confused, I left, going to the countryside retrieve the last remaining vegetables at field, I did spend a few days there without going home, sleeping at field shack. After a couple of days at the country site, I said to myself now I can go back, Eva will forgive me. Time when by, the money was gone we never recuperate any of that money, I did work hard to make up the damage I did, unfortunately, my head never does the right things giving many problems to my family, Nunziata start working to help home, she was only thirteen, working in a factory near our house, Mimi brings home good money, I am the one can produce, if I do, I will spend before I earned. Later summer I never forget, I got an excellent job, full time at Vallarino place, starting early morning, to noon. So convenient in the afternoon I can work to the farm, hope I can make happy Eva this time, later the year mom was sick, she's not well, hope she will be okay. January 19, 1965, a sad day for all Nocci family, my mom Nicoletta passed away, God bless her, now she can join my dad on the other side of this world, losing her it's like losing part of myself, many people at mom funeral, after the ceremony all my siblings come to my house thanking me for what I have done for mom. Pietro has been so close to me lately, I've been having rough days when I do need anything, I do see him, no one else. Now mom is gone, my girls can have the extra space my mom was using, all my kids are growing up, lately Mimi doing mini jobs on his own, earning extra money to support the family, most of it he gives to his mom, possibly in the future he wants by a small partial of land to build a house for everyone. God forgive me, with the money I gave

away at the time we could own or build a house. I do know I'm doing wrong things, but I'm doing it, with good faith, without malice. For a long time, I can't control myself anymore, I don't want to do things, always the wrong ones unfortunately. He is good with his work, very independent, and even created a deal with our landlord, who will keep it for free has long as we live in this house. Many times I come back home drunk, the last few years I am a disaster, or so I created troubles, leaving Eva and the kids alone for days, without any fear, this morning, after breakfast my son said that he wanted to talk to me, not yet maybe he wants to buy a car who knows, lately he does not respect me, but inside he suffers a lot, he loves me so much, that sometimes it is difficult to show it. Since my mom death my life went from bad to worst, I don't know why possibly the alcohol not helping much, I need to stop drinking. Soon it's Christmas I will do A little foil to the Madonna that I stop drinking like a camel.

Christmas week, early morning, I stopped to see Vallarino, the butcher man, asking for a full lamb for the Christmas holiday. He wasn't very happy to see me, so he said, "You're still alive," with a firm answer or said that to the needs of a worker. He said no, but show up sometime. Then I asked if he had a little lamb for my family. He said yes, but I'm coming to take the lamb to your family.

After Christmas holidays, early morning, my son approached me, saying, "Dad, can we talk a little? I want you to listen to me without interrupting me. My sister Nunziata and I, we are going to leave home soon as you know. For years, Zio Zino wants to have you and mom there in Canada. I know that you and mom never considered moving to America. I understand very well the reasons, but I am not you. So, the two of us will start our visa process as soon as possible. If all works out, by the spring, we are gone."

Spring 1968, this morning my son approached me, saying we will be going in a few days. "I don't want to repeat the same things, Dad, but you need to correct yourself with many things. Pa, unless you cure your bad habits, you and I are done. After I'm gone, don't look for me or ask for help. All these years, you've been a ruin for all of us. I don't know how mom has put up with you until today, closing so many holes everywhere for you. Sometimes I'm ashamed just talking to people. Please look after yourself. Now you have four more children to worry about without me and Nunziata. Dad, there are a few things I'd like to discuss with you and mom, a few things before we go."

There is so much bitterness in his words, because so much sadness in his eyes. For him, anything I do is wrong.

Easter week, my two older kids left on Passover day. All my family came by to say goodbye to them. Everybody's saying it will be good for them; Canada is a prosperous country. They will do well there. Hope they will survive without us and the rest of the family. I did my best. I ordered a taxi for them to go to Rome. There will be a flight direct to Toronto, Canada, without stopping. All arranged by my brother-in-law Zino. They will go and live with them for now. There is also Eva's sister, Giovi, there, so I hope my kids will feel at home with them. Later in the evening on April 11, we were having dinner. I said to my son, "Are you ready for this new venture?" He looked at me and said, "I am." After dinner, all the girls went to bed, leaving only me, Eva, and him. He said a few words. "Mom, Dad, what has been between us the last few years does not matter. I hope that in the future, Dad will become responsible for his personal acts without harming the family. I will do my best from Canada to stay in touch with you from the first day of my journey staying there. Then we'll see in the future what will happen, if I come back home or I'll settle there forever. So, mom, dad, I am worried about you guys. I hope all will work out. Don't forget you have your family here, including many siblings. Ask for help if you need to, as we did help them in the past, Papa."

My daughter Gaby, using Mimi's motorbike, had an accident, destroying the moto, and hurting herself a little. Thank God she's okay. We all worried about her. We never let my kids in Canada know about it. I didn't want them to worry about her for now. Eva and I don't talk much. I do know they are okay in Toronto living with my brother-in-law. So, they will keep an eye on them, less to worry for us here. I know they are writing almost every month to their mom. Eva doesn't talk about it, possibly she doesn't want me to know what's all about. Possibly it's nothing. I hope all good news from them in Canada.

A whole life, I've been caring about my family, believing that I did or doing the right things for everyone, but for some reasons to another, it seemed to be doing everything wrong. I don't know what's wrong with me. Of course, there's something wrong with my actions. Maybe it's my brain that doesn't work well with all my thoughts, maybe I was whipped by my kids' stuff, or the smoke, or the wine. I don't know who to blame anymore. I'm going to see my old doctor. I need help. Dr. Cicca will help me out.

Later fall 1968, After seeing Doctor Cicca, he gives me a piece of advice, telling me to be admitted to a clinic where I can cure myself. At that point, I did talk about it with Eva. She said yes, hoping that it will work. I said, "I hope with a brief time I will come out free of this disease. I am looking forward going back home helping my family; it is my priority." All seems to go well. A new life for me or so seems to gain weight. I do eat more now, no alcoholic anymore, just water. Almost a year went by, later year 1989, Eva said the kids in Canada soon will get married, Mimi at the end of December, and Nunziata in the next spring '70s. I said that is good news. Then I asked when they come back to Italy. She said, "I don't know. Mimi will come back at Christmas. Let's see the next letter."

We were all curious to see them again, my children coming back one day, seems an eternity since they left. After that last news no more letters until early December. Mimi sent a Christmas bonus to Eva, saying, "Mom, Dad, possibly we will surprise you guys in Xmas for a short visit. I'm getting married on the twentieth of December. After that, Rosetta and I will come home for a short time, spending Christmas holiday with you guys. So, hope all will work out. We will be there between the twenty-second or third December."

I was counting the days, since we got such great news from Mimi and Nunziata. Finally, we can all hug them again after so long; we all anxious to see them home. Eva says that now they have a little accommodation of their own, as soon as they get married, I'm sure they will be satisfied with themselves, and what they are getting out of life.

Later December, two days to Christmas day, no sign from my children from Canada. Who knows they changed their minds, they will not come. Late evening, after dinner, they didn't arrive. Past eleven, who knows, hopefully tomorrow. It was almost midnight, someone knocked on the front door. I said, "Eva, who will be at this time of night?" Soon, I opened the door. It's my boy, who I was giving up waiting, or so his beautiful wife Rosetta. I was looking for Nunziata; she didn't come. Eva and I continued to chat without them saying anything. It was just the two of us. Then he said, "Dad, mom, let us say something too."

Eva didn't stop asking, so after he said, "Mom is very tired, so after hugging the little sisters, they went to bed. Eva gave up our room for a few days that they will stay here with us." In the morning, we were all in the kitchen, discussing their stay in Canada. So many questions, or I noticed that Mimi didn't like to talk about his new country. With Rosetta, we come to a good understanding. For a young lady turning seventeen, same day they arrived, noi diciamo na bardasciella, into our dialect language, a little girl. We spent Christmas holidays together. Or they visited Rosetta's native town in Puglia. All my family came to greet my boys, even Eva's family, all present. Their presence of Mimi and Rosetta here in Francavilla, our house was always full of people every day, to get to know Rosetta and see Mimi again. Last days of their stay here in Francavilla, who knows when I'll see him again. One day we'll go there in Canada to visit them, so we could get to know America. Rosetta, she is a little doll, while Mimi, he is a resolute person. I note a lot of change in him, a handsome man very much like my family, or so a little of Eva's side. May our

Lord bless them and give him so much luck, not like me who has had a bumpy road of hills to climb.

I asked Eva to make something special on the last night we're together before they leave, like a nice baked chicken or a mixed salad, which Mimi likes. It would be perfect with chicken. We spent the evening together; it flew by. Mimi and Rosetta will go away tomorrow. Who knows when we will see him again, hopefully soon. Almost midnight, everyone went to sleep, except for Eva and Mimi; they had too much to say. I went to bed, leaving them alone. Eva came to sleep almost at one. I pretended I was sleeping. I'm sure all this time we've been talking about our future. Who knows, hopefully one day he'll come home to help his mother. We only have him, the only boy. God took the other one; better not to think about it. Tomorrow is another day.

Mimi and Rosetta left; I am depressed. Over the holidays, I had a sip of wine and a couple of cigarettes. After that, again and again. Later in January 1970, on a cold Sunday morning, I stopped at the cemetery to see my mom's grave. It has been five years since she passed away. On my way back, I stopped by St. Cecilia village, where all the peasants who were killed during the war reside. They are my fellow villagers, and some even long-term relatives, killed in 1943, before New Year's Eve. Now they have a small monument just for them. May God punish the guilty, whoever they may be, in this world or the next. This day, I am back to square one. I start smoking and drinking again. Eva was desperate. Sometimes I didn't come home on time for dinner. So, my family began to scold me. All my siblings, my own family, they extorted me for what I do, threatening that I would be reinstated in an asylum again. I was worried; I didn't want to end up in such a place. So, I promised everyone to stay home without creating problems for anyone, no drinking or smoking anymore.

In February, Eva received a notice of eviction if we didn't bring our rent up to date. She was desperate. I asked for some help from my siblings. I had been bitten to death because of what I did. No one helped out; possibly Eva's brother did or my son from Canada. We did resolve that issue, but we have many more to worry about. I don't know where or how I can resolve this tragedy I created. Eva was communicating with her son in Canada; early March, we received the news that Mimi was trying to get visas for all of us to go there to them in Canada. She wants to go as soon as possible; she couldn't take it anymore with me. He wanted to leave as soon as possible, but there were some small problems of conduct on me, concerning my service with the CP party. In one way or another, Mimi did resolve it without any problems. In my opinion, it was the hand of our marshal of the carabinieri in Francavilla, obtaining a good clean record for myself. No matter, I never did anything wrong all my life, just helping others.

Later in May, we moved to Toronto, Canada, sharing a house with my son until we find a place to live on our own. It's a new country for Toto. Unfortunately, I can't understand a word of English, but there are so many people who speak Italian I will learn a little. Living here with my son is not possible; there are two families plus his in-laws all together. It reminds me of when we were with my brothers, a crowd of people. Summer went by, all my younger girls start school in September, thanking God. Now we settle here; Eva finds a good job, working in factories with great pay. I am not in my perfect condition, but I will manage. I am adopting in all areas of work: construction, restaurant, farming, anything that comes at hand.

My son buys a new house near the Italian garden, a new neighborhood. They just developed that area, northwest of the city. They buy a raised bungalow, finishing the basement for us so we can stretch for a couple of years. Later in the early seventies, my life becomes a little critical without gaining much on the financial level. It's very difficult to get a good job. Eva, little by little, she puts some money together, so she finally buys a house near our son. Everything went great, easier. Gaby got married to a friend of Mimi's; the others are at school, two in elementary school and one in high school. My wife and kids manage to have our own place without my help. I didn't do that while helping out my younger family. Changing jobs here and there, we are struggling thanks to me. I did the best I could, making many errors in my life. Sometimes I did come across a decent job, without knowing how to keep it. I am okay in the morning; my major problems are later in the day, after I start drinking, without having a limit of it.

My drinking and smoking habits never stop, creating endless problems for my family. Sometimes I wonder where all my childhood dreams ended up. I imagined a world of my own. How did I arrive at these conditions of life, without yesterday or tomorrow? Sometimes I wonder how to correct myself. Unfortunately, I can't stay away from the drink. Working in some restaurants is even worse; everyone offers me a drink, and I don't say no. I drink one, two, ten — who knows? At the end of the day, how many glasses? I keep drinking without realizing what I am doing. The biggest problem is when I go home; I make a disaster or a mess in the family. My life no longer has value. So, I would like to ask for help sometimes, but I don't know how or who could help me without being hospitalized. My whole family loves me, but I don't listen to them, to their requests for my life. All this seems impossible, like asking a child not to touch the biscuit. I want to change, to give a few years of contributing to my young girls or a better life to Eva, I just don't know how. Many times, when I get home drunk, I ask to be forgiven. Then they are right, I've been forgiven too many times. There's no more space for forgiveness, only I change or the door is open.

Later in the seventies, Eva had enough of me. She said she would sell the house and go living in rental. We can't keep up with the mortgage and other expenses; soon we will be without a house, back to square one. We need to rent a place; she's right, my contributions are so poor she cannot keep up with it. Today Eva told me, what you earn is not enough to sustain yourself, not even for the alcohol you consume. Therefore, find someone to support you because I can't take it anymore. Not words, she for all the reasons, in the world, our son can help us, start over with the possibility of rebuilding a new life together. But it's not that I bother anyone, just this damn habit of drinking that ruins everything. I will talk to Mimi and Rosetta; possibly they might have a solution. One Sunday morning, I stopped at Mimi's house in Agincourt. My son wasn't home. My daughter-in-law first thing asked if I had breakfast; I said yes, a boiled egg. Then she said she would make me a coffee. I asked if it was okay to have a glass of wine; she said, "Papa, not at this time in the morning." She said no, stating that it's too early in the morning, and that I need to learn in Canada, no alcohol can be served before lunch. I think you're exaggerating. Jokingly, I said, "Where I work at George's, the Greek guy, he owns a restaurant in Willowdale, they give me a drink anytime." She got upset, saying, "I will come and see him one of these days. If they don't stop that, I will report them." I said, "Shit, now I am in trouble with my boss if she comes there." Mimi was not home because they are building a house for themselves in the west end, closer to where we used to live before. For themselves soon, they will move there, a much bigger house that can fit two families easily. I should talk to them today; otherwise, I need to come back another time, possibly when he is here.

In 1978, we moved with my son; she's more relaxed. Mimi built a new house here in Toronto; being a builder, he can move anytime he wants. He gave me the chance to work with his group; no way I can resist him. Heavy work, or so he is too bossy. Working with him is like being in the military; I am like a donkey, work, work. I had one Pippo; in the end, the poor guy ended up in the slaughterhouse. Mimi is never happy; he screams at anyone. Sometimes I feel to smack him one, especially when he's not satisfied with the work we do, including his brother-in-law; he is presumptuous. I am wasted working at the construction site; I go to a couple of restaurants to clean up bathrooms and floors. They pay me well, or so I eat for free, and drink for free. Eva wants me to work with my son; that way, anytime I am out, she knows where I am. Unfortunately, he is very cruel, part of his job. Having more than one project in progress is not easy; he wants everyone to respect the rules, both in terms of safety and quality, expecting the best from everyone with no excuses. Working for him is like being under fascism; not easy to follow its rules or its way.

In the late eighties, my way of life became unbearable. My whole family did not like the way I do things or my behavior living, so I decided to leave the house, looking for a place to stay by myself, where I do not account for my actions. I am a smart man; I can get myself a great life living the way I wanted. Knowing a few things and some political people, they will help me out. First of all, I am entitled to an Italian pension as of yesterday. I do have a disabled pension to support myself, or so I can apply for Canadian working pension; so overall, I will get three pensions on my own. Almost a year since I left home, I do go by sometimes to see my grandchildren. All my kids are married; they are well off, and Eva lives with her son. I drink and eat anytime I want; I had my first Canadian pension cheque; soon I will receive disability support, and I hope soon the Italian pension. I live like a king. In the early nineties, finally, I have my Italian pension with arrears. I will go and visit my son; I would like to share a little with him. It's my broken heart; we have quarreled many times, but it's a great good. My girls are much better than him; they all love me. I've been so wrong with them that sometimes I don't know how to repair my mistakes. I said to my mother many years ago, "Life goes on for better or for worse." Now I am here and crying about things I did; only God knows sometimes how bad I feel for the mistakes I made all my life. Christ, forgive me. All my life uphill, without a break, giving so much without receiving anything in return. Thank our Lord who gave me Eva and six beautiful children; I know it's a lot, but my life has always given, running or reinforcing something. I survive poverty, always adapting to others. Many times I ask for mercy of action; no one says don't worry; soon or later, all will be over. Sometimes I wonder why live if there is no purpose in life, as if to say living another day or a hundred years, this life of mine will never change. Then what does matter in this world? For me, there are two types of people: first, those who don't care about you at all, while the other, like it if you're in trouble. No one cares, as a poet once said, "

You must love yourself." I do, with my political contacts. I know this guy is good, always. This guy is good, always helping those in need. I will see the manager for Villa Columbus Centre; they promised me an apartment for old people. So far, nothing; I have been waiting for months. If I don't work this month, I'll make a mess. I will talk it over with the administrator; a little pressure will be good; otherwise, Sunday when I see my son, I will tell him all about it; possibly he will help me out. Early Sunday morning, my grandson came by to pick me up. A good-looking boy, all Nocci. I asked if he still goes to school; he said yes. I asked what he's studying or learning; he said to play cards. I wanted to slap him, in my own way. Then I said to myself, this is not a joke. He doesn't come anymore to pick me up when I do need it. He's twenty years old, already owns a car, pays for his own school, and has been doing karate for years, a third-degree black belt. Many times I tell him to stay out of trouble; otherwise, his dad will punish him. His name is the same as mine, Toto Nocci. We have said in the old days, "When the little pig is born, the big pig can go to the slaughterhouse." I am not ready for that.

As soon as we got to Mimi's house, he was playing soccer with his younger son Anthony, saying, "Hey Toto, who brought you here?" I said, "Who loves me the most!" He said, "Of course, his name is like yours." We chatted for a little while, him asking how my leg was as I had been complaining about it lately. I said, "I will survive for now." I told him about my rear pension from Italy; I wanted to share it with him. He asked me how much; I had an envelope. I said, "Here, buy something for yourself and Rosetta." He said, "Thank you; I will." Then he asked if I did the same for the girls; he knew I didn't. Without saying anything, he told me, "I will share with my sisters." I was upset; I said, "Give me back the money." He said, "Too late now, papa." But he offered me some cheap bottle wine people gave to him, saying I could have it as long as I promised not to drink it all at once. After that, before I left, I asked if he could help me out with an apartment at the old age home, the Colombo Centre place. Then I told him I had been waiting for a year, and no one gave any hope when I could have the place. "God knows when it will happen," I said. He said, "Leave it all to me; I'll see what I can do, provided you don't create problems for us. I know too many people there, okay?" Two weeks later, I got the room at Villa Colombo, a small bachelor, perfect for what I needed. They had all I needed here: a little parkette where we could go and smoke, a restaurant, a bar, anything I wanted. Many times I ended up in the hospital; I couldn't walk anymore. Regardless, I would walk to the LCBO by myself to buy liquor or beer. Many times my granddaughters came to visit me.

When they couldn't find me, they would get angry, saying, "Where the heck did you go, grandpa?" I said to one of them, "The reason I am alone here is that I don't need to tell anyone what I do every day." A few days ago, I was walking along the sidewalk, and someone was honking at me. I had just come out from the hospital; I was carrying a case of beer in my hands. I said, "Who is it that rumbles the boxes?" It was my daughter-in-law Rosetta and Eva who came to the hospital to see me. They were angry. I said, "You don't want me to be dismissed; I'm not sick. Stay there; you will get sick."

Since that day, Eva and Rosetta come more often to help me out, to clean up my apartment a little. I asked for some money; I was broke. Both said no. "Here, you have all-inclusive; you don't need money, so wait for your next pension now," they said. "That way you will have some for the end of the month when you have," Eva said. "By the way, don't call Mimi for it." Today it's only the middle of the month; two weeks without money is no good. My right leg is punishing me badly; I can't walk. I use the cane to move around. I did talk many times to my family about it. My doctor said nothing can be done. I can walk around as long as it's a short walk, no stairs climbing, otherwise, there will be troubles. Today when I saw Eva, my heart wept with the pain, which I caused her and my family, all because of alcohol, also because sometimes I can't understand what I'm doing. Regardless, they manage to take pity on me, even today. They come to help clean up; that shows the love they have for me, bearing with me for my needs.

The last couple of years have been much harder, so much pain, no work. My body can't take it anymore. At only sixty-eight years old, my life has taken the road that will lead me to the end of my life. I asked our doctors for help, and as when I was a boy, I sought help from our priest, Father Rocco. He could only pray for all of us. Good days, even if we suffered from cold and hunger, yesterday seemed more beautiful than today. Later winter, I am locked in this small bachelor, unable to go out. Here, the winter is cold; it's not like Italy where in March we picked fresh almonds or flowers in the stream. In Canada, we have a freezing winter; no walks in the neighborhood. My day is from my room to the kitchenette area or recreational room where all old people spend most of their time. I do go to a restaurant next door, a few meters from here. Since a year ago, I was working a few hours a week there, washing dishes, cleaning bathrooms, and floors. Not anymore; I am retired from all that, or I don't have the strength to do so. Only what I need to do is keep my apartment clean.

March 21st, 1993, a spring day. I was on my way to the cafeteria for my normal breakfast. My son walks in; I was surprised. Normally no one comes early in the morning to see me, only at night sometimes. He says, "Come; we go for breakfast together nearby." He takes me to a mancia cake place. So, he orders French toast just because he likes it. I said, "I don't like it." He gives me a dirty look, reminding me of Mom. I said, "Order me a pancake and scrambled eggs." After breakfast, I ask if we can consult another specialist for my right leg; it looks like it will get worse. I am sure there is something that can be done; soon I won't walk anymore. He promises we will consult someone else. After that, we did see two other doctors for it, only they do more analysis, never a good result. Over a year went by; my leg is punishing me. Hardly I can walk. I tell my son after the Christmas holidays; I want to go back to that specialist at Finch hospital.

Later January 1995, he did set a date to see a specialist at Finch hospital again. He said, "Be ready; I will pick you up on Monday morning at seven. I will pick you up, and we go." I was happy about it; possibly, this guy might help me out. We spent the whole day there, so many investigations that they have done, without giving me an answer. I ask when they let me know. Eva was there, too. On my way back to the old man's house, Eva said, "You must be patient; in a few days, we will know something." After Mimi left, slowly, I walked to the dinette for my regular dinner. A gentleman approached me, saying, "You are Mr. Nocci's father." I asked what he was looking for, saying, "I am a soccer coach; I know Mimi very well. He did national coaching in the eighties." After introducing himself, he says, "My dad is here at Columbus Centre; the two of you should get together and play cards sometime." After that, he took off without any introduction. I have enough friends already; no need for more. Or I have my daughter and grandchildren; my life is busy enough; no space for other people.

Middle April, finally, we had another visit to the specialist for my leg. This time it was at Finch Health Centre, it had been over two weeks since all my examinations. This time we didn't go to the hospital; Rosetta and Eva came, and we went to the building next door, the specialist's personal office. So, he said, "Toto, after all the examinations, we have completed our report. Here's my recommendation: no operation. Your heart will not handle such an operation. In the future, I want you to follow my direction, protect yourself from climbs, no stairs, or unnecessary efforts. Otherwise, you will get worse, and you may end up in a wheelchair. If you want, we will talk about it again in a few months, with the hope that your heart will improve. That means no smoking and no alcohol. So, it's your call to get better or worse. I will see you in three months." After that, the diluents note by the specialist left me destroyed. Eva and Rosetta did give me some comfort overall. Mimi didn't come, saying, "Now it's up to you, Mr. Nocci, to eliminate alcohol and cigarettes if you want to get better." It was easy for them to say after a lifetime. Now I am quitting smoking; who gives a crap as long as I live? My dad always says, "Meglio un giorno da leone che cento da coglione." I meant to say, "Better a day as a lion than a hundred days as a jerk." I remember so well; Dad used to say, "Only God will take me; no one else will be able to. There is no devil or man who can kill me." He did survive illness for twenty-two years; I will do the same.

It's May; my son has promised me that he will come and pick me up for the next long weekend. I hope he shows up. If he doesn't come, he won't get anything from me in the future. Children are all the same; they just want to take from you, never give. I don't need anyone. The last time I asked for support from them was to help me in my life. I always managed on my own since they kicked me out, or I should say I moved out. I managed all by myself without anyone's help. Possibly, I deserved all this. Regardless, I am their father, not an animal like Friz to keep outside in the cold. Many times I slept at the workplace in the past. The Lord is in heaven, and on earth, he can see very well whatever I have done, thinks right or wrong in my life. In the end, I won't care how people judge me, who I am, or what I do. I will judge myself for what I have done through my life, good or bad. Now everyone is judging me. When I was in the snow and gathered vegetables in the ice, I was a hero. Or when I went to steal wood for the fireplace, I was a great man. Or stole hay from others for our cows, I was a giant. Now I am a piece of crap for everyone. But I'm sure of one thing: in life, they can take you out of the things you love or from a will that you have left behind or deny you the freedom to do things in your own way. One thing is certain: they can never, ever remove your name from the register of when you were born to the day you die. My life has always been a hurricane; ever since my dad died, I don't know where my path has changed direction, but I have always given without taking. It is the destiny of every person, already written in God's register.

Sunday, May 23rd, 1995, a long weekend in May. Mimi just picked me up; I will spend a couple of days at his place. I love the house they have, always in Woodbridge, an Italian neighborhoods area. A big house, with three kids and Eva in the house; he does need a big house. That reminds me of our big family back in the forties, together with my siblings. Later that week, I felt sick; my head was spinning and falling to the ground. Luckily, someone rescued me, calling the management at Villa Colombo because of my condition. They called an ambulance to take me to the hospital. The closest one was Humber. I spent the night here; later in the morning, my family came by. My English is terrible; Eva and Rosetta will talk to the doctor, seems everyone worries about me.

Since I am here, many blood tests, or so they put me in this tube, so noisy, the noise drove me crazy. This big guy shows up, possibly younger than me, not by much, saying just like that, "Toto, you have cancer." I said to myself, "This guy is crazy; he doesn't know what he's talking about." I said, "Excuse me, this is a joke, right?" He went on saying, "I will consult your family. My name is Dr. Berger; I will look after you. We need more exams to see how deep it is." I asked when I can go home; he said out of the question; you will be here for a little while. I said, "What? I went for some physical examinations not too long ago because of my leg; they did all types of examinations to my blood, urine, x-ray, and more. No one says anything about cancer."

All my family came by, including my grandchildren. There are too many; sometimes I don't remember all. On many occasions, they come to visit me here. It has been a couple of weeks since I am here; so far, they never tell me what it is. Early July, they gave me medications. I don't know what it's for, or so I ask why so much pain. One of the nurses speaks good Italian; her name is Connie. I said to her, "What the heck name your parents gave you? To me, it seems like an ice-cream name." So she said, "Concetta." I asked why these needles, what is for, I need to know, can someone explain to me better why I get so much pain in my head and my body. She told me to have my doctor and family explain better to me; I'm not authorized to tell you anything about it. I don't believe this. Later that night, Eva came, so I asked what is going on, why all this medication. She said, "Your kids can tell you, or so. They need to do some more tests or so. Soon they will start chemo." I said, "What, chemo? Chemotherapy is a drug treatment for cancer, Toto. I am sorry; we didn't want to tell you so soon. Unfortunately, your specialist says it's necessary; without the chemo, your life will be cut short. This will keep you alive." So, what type of cancer am I dealing with, Eva? Mimi said, "Dad, it's not an easy one. I am not an expert in this. The only thing I know is it's bone cancer or so in your lungs. Not an easy one to cure."

For a few minutes, I stopped; I am dying; no one told me that. I said, "Okay." I looked to Eva; I asked, "Please, I don't want to stay here; I want to go home. Take me back to Italy; I don't want to stay here anymore; do you understand me? I do want to go back to Italia; die in my native land in my town, where my mom and dad are buried, my whole family resides there." Mimi got upset, saying, "We are your family; since you married mom, you did create your own family. If you forgot all about it, we didn't. You and mom did build this family; you have six kids, not counting your grandchildren. Your family is here, not in Italy, DAD. Stop complaining; love us for what we are, as much as we love you for what you are. For the last time, I am asking you to stop pretending you don't have a family because since you left, we are here for you every day. For some reasons, you don't remember or you don't want to remember, but it's been years since you forgot that you have a family of your own that you and mom created. So stop talking without meaning. YOU DO HAVE A FAMILY. I do want to remind you; we did survive without your contribution or your support. Papa, for years you did forget all about us. I don't want to hear about Italy or anything else. As long as you and I are alive. So please stop asking or pretending from us; none of us draggle you to this condition. Has today when I do come to see you, I don't want to hear no more stories or complaints. For the last time, I am asking you to be a Nocci, no one else."

Everyone left after Mimi's quarrels, possibly he's right. I will consult my doctor in the morning; he will tell me if I am okay to go home or need to stay here. Mimi doesn't talk much; when he does, it hurts when he says something, like today. He meant all of it. Here in the hospital, they say that the doctor I have is one of the best for this disease. I am sure he will help me to recover. I believe that it is not a matter of life and death; it will be something that will heal in time. Then I will ask in the morning. A few days later, I am seeking information about when I can go home; no one tells me the truth here. I call Mimi; he doesn't want to talk, saying he will stop by sometime. It looks like I am no one for nobody. I will go home soon; staying here, I will die for sure. Eva comes by almost every day, bringing something to eat, much better than what they give me here. We are Italians; a bit spoiled about tipping, not because I want to criticize anyone, but Italian cuisine is not to be touched. I can't believe myself; with all this pain, I can't move anymore also because I've been chained with tubes everywhere. Damn them and when they brought me here. It's riskier in here than when I went to Atri during the war. All my life, I've done it all by myself without anyone's help or asking anyone's. Today, this nurse gives me a new medication, which warms me up a little. I asked what type of medicine it is; the nurse said a special one, something that lessens the pain. So, it's called Morphine, Mr. Toto. Then I ask or so what time the visits are in the evening; she said, "I don't know, from six to nine, I believe." Lucky me, this one she does speak Italian, the only one I can communicate with. All the others don't understand me. I asked several times for a glass of wine or a beer; they say no, you shouldn't have alcohol in here, juice, and water.

This place reminds me of when my brothers were prisoners. They told me that there, they only had water and soup of potato skin, like animals. I need to go home; I've been calling my son and my daughters many times, but no one says okay. They keep saying I need to stay here for a while, like a little puppy in a cage. I do have political contacts here in Canada and also in Italy; possibly, they will help me out to go back home to Italy. It's been over two months since they brought me here. I've been taking tons of pills and syringes every day. Later in August, slowly, I help myself to the window. I'm looking outside through the window of my jail. I can see the beautiful day. However, it's not as beautiful as that blue sea that I caressed in the morning when I went out of the house when I was a boy. Our Adriatic Sea was beautiful, where perhaps even today dolphins play. And yes, our sea was big; dolphins were not lacking. Even Pescara had the memory of the dolphin. I remember well, from 1936 when our team was born.

Later at night, my son always comes after seven, never in the morning. Since he has been in sales, he sleeps in the morning, like my sister Marianna, a sleeping-head person. No one takes after me and Mamma Nicoletta, early birds. Dad had a saying, "Who sleeps does not catch fish." He was right; better be first to get the best seat in the house. I'm talking to myself again. Mimi is here; he said, "You talk with someone?" I said to myself, "It's about time you showed up." He asks me if I did my daily prayer or if I got the nurse upset. I asked him if he came to see me or if he's giving me a hard time about what I do all day long. After we chat for a little, then, I told him he is the best of the best. The Nocci family needs someone to carry on the tradition the way I did. We do have a history; I hope he will keep our tradition going. God bless him with three kids; two children, my family will go on.

September 7th, 1995, I am so nervous. I am screaming like an animal, obtaining something from the nurses is so hard. I will call Eva to bring me lunch today. This is bad; no one listens to me, like I am an animal. If Rosetta and Eva come today, they need to take me home. I hope they will bring me some lunch; after that, I want to go home. It has been a difficult day. Eva and Rosetta never came to bring my lunch. I am a nervous wreck today. Later in the evening, finally, they show up. Rosetta and Eva come with only some fruit; no lunch or dinner. I am putting up with the food they give me here. Rosetta gives me a hard time, saying I am creating trouble for the nurses. After they left, saying they will be back tomorrow night for dinner, I hope to see Mimi or so.

Lucky me, the Italian nurse is here tonight, telling me I've been bad the last few days. These people don't care; I am in pain all day long. Everyone without a heart. I learned one thing in Canada: a few words all my life, "Shut up and hurry up," or so, "Work and shut up," nothing else. I know they called my son today, complaining about me. Rosetta told me about it. When he's upset, he won't show up, possibly because he doesn't want to see me or because he doesn't feel like screaming at me. Either way, he is worse than an animal when he gets upset. Same character as my dad Luigi when he was alive. I should name him Luigi, not Mimi like my brother.

Later at night, I can't sleep. I called the nurses too many times. Then I said to myself, "Why has life been so mean to me, and I'm a human like everyone else?" I better go to sleep; in the morning, I will call Mimi. He's carrying my brother's name; I hope he knows that. Well, we'll make peace, once and for all.

4:00 am, Mimi's house. The phone is ringing. Rosetta answers, saying it's Humber hospital. I said at this time. She said, "Dad is gone."

Loving Nocci Brothers , Missing Mimi, and Joe

Toto Nocci born May 3rd, 1927

Died September 8th, 1995,

Pietro and Federico photo

Nocci Family: Leonora 1909, Pietro 1911, Joe, 1915, Mimi 1918, Federico 1921, Marianna 1923, Toto 1927.

December 30, 1943,

The Massacre of twenty peasants.

A view that everyone envies.

www.ingramcontent.com/pod-product-compliance
Lightning Source LLC
Chambersburg PA
CBHW051258120626
46547CB00015B/2002